SCIENCE AND THEOLOGY

SCIENCE AND THEOLOGY

Questions at the Interface

Edited by
Murray Rae
Hilary Regan
John Stenhouse

Assisted by
Antony Wood & Jefley Aitken

William B. Eerdmans Publishing Company
Grand Rapids, Michigan

This edition published through special arrangement with T&T Clark by
Wm. B. Eerdmans Publishing Co.
255 Jefferson Ave. S.E., Grand Rapids, Michigan 49503

Printed in Great Britain

Library of Congress Cataloging-in-Publication data

Science and theology : questions at the interface / edited by Murray
    Rae, Hilary Regan, John Stenhouse : assisted by Antony Wood
    & Jefley Aitken.
        p.   cm.
    Proceedings of a conference held at the University of Otago,
    Dunedin, N.Z., Aug. 1993.
    Includes bibliographical references and indexes.
    ISBN 0-8028-0816-6
    1. Natural theology—Congresses.   I. Rae, Murray.   II. Regan,
    Hilary D.   III. Stenhouse, John.
    BL182.S35   1994   94-12331
    261.5'5—dc20   CIP

Table of contents

Preface

For a week in August 1993 some hundred scientists, theologians, philosophers, historians, and ministers of religion gathered in Dunedin, New Zealand, to discuss the interface between science and theology. This was the second international theological symposium held in Dunedin, and was organised by the Otago Theological Foundation in association with University Extension of the University of Otago. In 1991 there had been a symposium on "Christ and Context: The Confrontation between Gospel and Culture". Following that symposium the Otago Theological Foundation was established to provide a forum for theological engagement from a Trinitarian perspective, through organising public lectures and the holding of theological symposia. Papers presented at the 1991 symposium were subsequently published[1] and the success of the volume *Christ and Context* has encouraged the symposium organisers now to produce *Science and Theology* with contributions from the lead speakers at the 1993 symposium.

It was fitting that the University of Otago, in association with the Otago Theological Foundation, should again be involved in hosting a prestigious international theological event. The university was founded 125 years ago by the administration of the Otago province with support from the Presbyterian Church, reflecting the involvement of that church in the settlement of Otago in 1848. Although the university eventually severed its ties with the Presbyterian Church, the relationship between religious and secular learning continued to be the subject of lively debate within its walls, and it is no surprise that the University of Otago pioneered theological teaching within the national university system. In 1946 a university degree was offered to theological students who had completed courses at one of several local denominational colleges. In 1971 a faculty of theology

---

1. Hilary D. Regan and Alan J. Torrance with Antony Wood, editors, *Christ and Context: The Confrontation between Gospel and Culture* (Edinburgh: T&T Clark, 1993).

was established within the university, drawing upon the resources of the Presbyterian Knox Theological Hall and the Roman Catholic Holy Cross Seminary. Previously, in 1967, a department of religious studies had been established within the Arts faculty of the university, making the University of Otago one of the few institutions in the world to have both a separate faculty of theology and a department of religious studies.

Given the strength and traditions of the university also in the main branches of science, dating from the institution's earliest years, the Dunedin-based Otago Theological Foundation was able to draw upon considerable local resources to organise with the University of Otago a symposium on the areas of human knowledge where science and theology meet.

The Foundation is grateful to Lorraine Isaacs and staff of the University Extension for their enthusiastic support for the symposium and for this subsequent publication. Wilma Railton was the symposium administrative secretary until forced to withdraw through ill health, and her successor was Christine Johnstone; Jefley Aitken brought this work through to the final stages of publication. The symposium planning committee comprised Hilary Regan, Murray Rae, Neil Howard, Greg Dawes, John Stenhouse, Neil Vaney and Jenny Beck. Typographical advice was given generously by Ramesh Thakur.

As with the 1991 international theological symposium, the organisers in 1993 were fortunate in being able to draw upon a range of generous benefactors, making possible the attendance of the distinguished speakers who lead the symposium and whose papers constitute the meat of this volume of essays.

The symposium brought together insights from the history of science, from cosmology and biology, from epistemology and theology, challenging participants to reach out from their own specialisations to engage in multidisciplinary dialogue. The Otago Theological Foundation is grateful to all concerned that it is now able to put that challenge before a wider audience.

Antony Wood
Chairman
Publications sub-committee

Introduction

Stephen May

One of the purposes of an introduction to a book such as this, is to say two things: first, that the topic it deals with is very important; and secondly, that the way in which the book addresses this topic is particularly helpful. This way browsers and potential buyers might be persuaded to part with their hard-earned cash.

This is easy to do, for the Theological Symposium from which these papers are drawn was remarkable for one on this topic, held not only in the southern hemisphere but anywhere in the world. Moreover, the growth of the science and theology debate could be argued to be one of the most constructive aspects of modern theology — one in which theology is reclaiming ground in some ways long abandoned to the secular world. The fact of a conference such as this signals a rediscovery of confidence in the Christian community which now realises that again it has something to say to the world, and moreover that the world has something to say to it from which it can profitably learn. A dialogue is possible. Accordingly, the conference papers reproduced here address the issue: questions at the interface.

The conference took place in a university environment. Accordingly, Christian worship, still significant for many, was usually held not in the main lecture hall but in the chapel. This was not to signal that our devotion was irrelevant to the issue at hand (indeed we dedicated ourselves to the task in prayer and worship both at the beginning and the end of the symposium), but that here there was serious academic thinking at work, a debate in the *public* arena, one not limited to Christians alone. The relationship between worship and the academic exercise is worth mentioning at the outset:

Christians have historically seen their attitude to both science and theology as springing from the same source — wonder.

Two responses to the relation of science and theology are characteristic of the modern western world. They may be identified as typically modern and post-modern, and may be conveniently illustrated by two recent conversations.

Shortly after the symposium, on a glorious night when the stars shone brilliantly and a telescope was produced to study the moon, I was asked by a stranger to explain where I had been recently. An attempt to describe the symposium was met by the immediate response: "science and theology, aren't they a contradiction in terms?" They were seen as mutually exclusive. An interesting conversation ensued. This remark represents the instinctive view not just of many people in New Zealand but throughout a world dominated by modern western culture. It is part of what Christian theology is fighting and a very common misapprehension.

On the other hand, science is also in disrepute. When I flew down to the symposium at Dunedin, I was sitting next to a stranger. Open on my lap was Nancey Murphy's paper with its title prominent, "What has theology to learn from scientific methodology?" I had exchanged no previous words with my neighbour when he leaned across and said, "I think it should be the other way round." It emerged that he was disillusioned with science and was interested in spirituality. Although an airline pilot, normally flying between Hong Kong and the South Pacific, he was seeking something more than the merely material.

The context of the theology and science debate is influenced by many things as these two incidents illustrate. On the one hand we have the rationalistic scientism of modernist thought — exemplified by the first response. According to this, science is the model of all true human understanding. It has given us great advances, both in comprehending the nature of the universe and in controlling it. Through technology we enjoy an unprecedented standard of living. According to this model, theology is concerned with the private and personal realm of faith — rather than the public realm of scientific knowledge and fact. Religion is outmoded, a relic of lingering and immature superstition, an obstacle to humanity's task of understanding and expanding into the universe, a universe we now know to be immense. According to this model, science is knowledge, theology is superstition. The slogan engraved above the Rationalist Society building in Auckland sums it up: "Science, not superstition". A cafe there is wittily entitled "Rations". Nearby are the premises of the Marist Fathers, a Roman Catholic teaching order. One inhabitant of this place suggested to me that those entering his own portals might imagine another title above *its* door: "Superstition, not science". It is partly because of this continuing perception in much popular culture that this conference was called — and is so important.

The response of my other interlocutor on the plane bears witness to another, and simultaneous, tendency in western culture. This is a growing suspicion of, and disillusionment with, science. We have learned to control the world and do so much with it, yet has it really brought us happiness? Do we really have a grasp of what is important in life? In some ways technology seems to have backfired on us, threatening far worse possibilities of disaster than were conceivable before. Three issues are particularly relevant for New Zealand at present: the ozone hole; the greenhouse effect, whose consequences might include a rise in the level of the oceans with flooding Pacific atolls; and French nuclear testing at Mururoa. Not surprisingly, there has been a great increase in *green* thought, an assertion of the importance of the natural — almost to the point of deifying it. Such an approach typically emphasises humanity's links with the world — a world from which humanity has been strictly differentiated in the modernist paradigm (Descartes *et al.*). These ideas affect theology as well as popular culture. Matthew Fox's creation-centred spirituality is only one example that immediately comes to mind.[1]

What is theology to say in this new situation? In many places it has been argued that theology has lost a doctrine of creation. Its emphasis on redemption has sacrificed a large part of traditional Christian theology. It has abandoned to the realm of science all talk about the natural world. By contrast, can one suggest — as has been fashionable in certain quarters — that theology and science actually talk about the same things but in different ways; that they ask different questions — how or what as opposed to why. But is it

---

1.   For example, *Original Blessing* (Santa Fe: Bear, 1983).

true that theology asks the question of purpose and intent, thus leaving open a space for God, whilst science speaks only of what is? It has been argued, for example by Mary Midgley in her book *Science and Salvation*,[2] that the enormous successes of science have been achieved by its self-restriction: it has spoken with expertise of its own particular area. However, the new apologists for science are abandoning this humility. They are claiming, not just that science describes its own area remarkably well, but that its own area is the only area worth talking about at all (or even that *can* be talked about). Shades of logical positivism. Accordingly, we see public debates such as that between the Anglican Archbishop of York, John Habgood and Richard Dawkins, the aggressively atheist biologist. In this volume there are numerous references to the claim of the well-known American rationalist astronomer Carl Sagan that the universe "is the only thing that is, or ever was, or ever shall be".[3] This claim of Sagan obviously raises the question, "How does he know?" The remark is the expression of scientistic rationalism, the attitude that science is the solution to all our problems. If some problems do seem insoluble at the moment — or even if they appear to have been brought about *by* science — the worst thing for us to do is to lose our nerve: science will bring greater solutions in the future! This vision is advocated in non-fictional and fictional ways: for example, the television show *Star Trek — The Next Generation* clearly envisages such a positive and optimistic future.[4] Here science seems to become a god, something to be worshipped and adored.

Disillusionment with science — perhaps springing from exaggerated notions of its capacities which have now been disappointed — has a particular expression in New Zealand. New Zealand prides itself on being a country which has stood up against the rest of the world on the nuclear issue, and suffered accordingly.

---

2. *Science and Salvation: a Modern Myth and its Meaning* (London: Routledge, 1992). There was an interesting discussion in the *New Scientist* in 1992 concerning this view; compare with Mary Midgley, "Can science save its soul?" (1 August 1992) pp. 24-27; P. Atkins, "Will science ever fail?" (8 August 1992) pp. 32-35; Letters (29 August 1992) pp. 52-53.
3. *Cosmos* (New York: Random House, 1984) p. 4.
4. Compare with the interview with Gene Roddenberry, *Star Trek's* creator in *Starlog* 100 (November 1985) pp. 18-20.

Not only was the Greenpeace vessel, *Rainbow Warrior,* blown up in Auckland harbour in 1985 killing a photographer, but overwhelming economic and political pressures were brought to bear on New Zealand for its principled stand. It is hardly surprising that there has been more of an anti-science move in this country than in many others. New Zealanders are understandably proud of the beauty of their country, and anxious about the threats of pollution. Some of these are, of course, already at work, though fortunately not to the same extent as in many other countries.

From the side of theology, the theology and science debate has been grievously affected by the history of western theology over the last two centuries or so. It has been persuasively argued by writers such as Stanley Jaki that modern science itself developed in the crucible of Christianity — and that not by accident.[5] Historically, however, the two have become identified in popular culture as antagonists. The story of Galileo is particularly apposite here. The myth of the martyrs of science has become so often repeated as to be virtually unchallengeable even when its prime data are highly suspect: as is the case both with Galileo[6] and with the infamous Wilberforce/Huxley debate over Darwin's *Origin of Species.*[7] The warfare model of the relationship between theology and science is still very prevalent in many people's minds.

Lesslie Newbigin has described the historical development of the debate in terms of a surrender by theology, a retreat from the field of engagement.[8] He argues that theology has increasingly evacuated the area of the public sphere, leaving creation to science alone, and has opted for the safer area of ethics, morality, and personal or private belief. This distinction between the private and

---

5. Most fully in *Science and Creation: From Eternal Cycles to an Oscillating Universe,* revised edition (Edinburgh: Scottish Academic Press, 1986); more briefly in *The Saviour of Science* (Edinburgh: Scottish Academic Press, 1990).
6. See Owen Gingerich, "The Galileo Affair" in *Scientific American* 247, 2:132-143 (August 1982) reprinted in *The Great Copernicus Chase and other Adventures in Astronomical History* (Cambridge University Press, 1992) pp. 105-122.
7. See Edward B. Davis, "Blessed are the peacemakers: Rewriting the history of Christianity and Science" in *Perspectives on Science and Christian Faith* 40, 1 (March 1988) pp. 47-52.
8. *The Gospel in a Pluralist Society* (Grand Rapids: Eerdmans, 1989) p. 2.

the public is questioned by Newbigin and, in this volume, by John Polkinghorne. It reflects the acceptance by theology of its own marginalisation, its craven response to the challenges of the Enlightenment and also to that of any extra-scriptural knowledge. Yet traditional Christianity has claimed that the redeeming God *is* the creating God. One context at least for discussion between theology and science is the Christian doctrine of creation.

In this respect, Christians keen to reaffirm a dialogue between theology and science and the importance of creation have sometimes strongly affirmed the necessity of natural theology. Stanley Jaki is a prominent example.[9] This is regarded as crucial, not so much in itself, as in its implications for any possible dialogue and for the relevance of the Christian faith. Opponents of natural theology (for whatever reason) may thus be seen as hostile to the debate altogether. For some there are dangers too in presenting creation and redemption as almost mutually opposed alternatives. Several papers in this book look at variations on this particular issue. Nevertheless, some are still inclined to think that Christians addressing this issue tend to be apologetic or defensive about their own faith.

Indeed, some think that a main problem in this debate has been the temptation on the part of theology to accommodate itself to what it sees as the norms of science. There is a major debate here and some of it can be detected through the papers presented in this volume (notably those of Nancey Murphy and John Puddefoot). Is there a common ground for discussion between theology and science? If so, on what does it rest? Is it possible to establish criteria for the judgment of truth?

Some would argue that science itself is helpful here. It is generally agreed that the last century or so has seen astonishing changes in scientific method and content, changes to which the public at large is still acclimatising. The so-called classical physics of Newton, based on an absolute frame of reference drawn from invariant structures of space and time, has been displaced by Einsteinian relativity. In a similar way, quantum mechanics at the subatomic level has thrown into doubt all sorts of classical

---

9.   *The Road of Science and the Ways to God* (Edinburgh: Scottish Academic Press, 1978).

assumptions. This is not the place to enlarge upon these themes at length, but enough to say that a casualty of these new insights has been the idea of dispassionate, objective observation. No longer can we cheerfully talk about "objectivity" and "subjectivity" in quite the way to which we have been accustomed. This is not to say that a grasp of truth is impossible, but that the knower has to be taken into account in any consideration of the known. A useful discussion of this issue is offered by Carver T. Yu in this volume.

This alteration in the debate, from both sides, is perhaps best shown by using an example from Harold Turner who draws attention to the titles of two books regarded by some as particularly helpful in the methodological debate, T. F. Torrance's *Theological Science*[10] and Michael Polanyi's *Personal Knowledge*.[11] These deal respectively with theology and science. The very titles, argues Turner, are striking. Our dualist culture holds to a division between indisputable scientific facts on the one hand, and private individual beliefs on the other. According to this, the titles *should* read *Personal Theology* and *Scientific Knowledge*. But they do not, and this indicates the extent to which things have changed. These titles, coming from opposite ends of the spectrum, challenge the split to which we are accustomed. If theology can be said to be science, that is, "knowledge" (suggesting objectivity), science can be said to be personal (subjective). A new model of the relationship between objectivity and subjectivity is required, based on our awareness of the involvement of the knowing subject in the knowing relationship. No longer are we dealing with two different kinds of epistemology, each appropriate to their particular topic, but at two different topics — theology and science — with the *same* methodology. According to this view, it is only as we take into account that we are knowing subjects who engage with our object of knowledge with commitment and passion, that we can truly know it, and thus gain true objectivity. Thus, rather than objectivity and subjectivity being opponents, they depend on one another. The attempt to gain objectivity by a cold, dispassionate approach is shown to be bogus — and deeply dangerous, for it conceals the danger of real,

---

10. T. F. Torrance, *Theological Science* (London: Oxford University Press, 1969).
11. Michael Polanyi, *Personal Knowledge* (London: RKP, 1958).

undeclared bias. One might describe this as objectiv*ism,* and the belief that since things cannot be known in this way, they cannot be known at all, as subjectiv*ism.* Further discussion of the issue is provided in this volume in Grant Gillett's response to Murphy's paper.[12]

Many know the work of Karl Popper and his famous idea of falsifiability but Puddefoot and Murphy in this volume find other models that they consider more helpful. The assessment of which models may be appropriate is a continuing concern of the debate. Different models of that *rapprochement* may be found here. The interesting thing, however, is that as theology has begun to recover its nerve and show interest once more in science, it has found allies in science itself — and science coming to meet it.

Structure

The papers included here cover a number of subjects which may be divided into three parts.

1. The first two papers, by Owen Gingerich and Norma Emerton, are devoted to the issue of natural theology. Questions addressed include: how convincing are the arguments for the existence of God, particularly in the light of scientific knowledge? Do these arguments hold water empirically or logically? Do they provide proof or a persuasive and coherent vision of the cosmos? Are they the prologue to faith or its consequence? If natural theology has a proper place in theology, where does it lie? Of significance too is the historical context of natural theology and the debates about the cogency of the arguments for the existence of God. Why were they rejected? Thus the discussion is not merely evidential and logical, but historical and cultural as well.

2. The next papers, by Nancey Murphy and John Puddefoot, examine methodological matters more carefully. Murphy proposes the work of Imre Lakatos as a helpful way of making progress in the debate, whilst Puddefoot looks more to Michael Polanyi. Among

---

12. See also T. F. Torrance, *Theological Science* (London: Oxford University Press, 1969) pp. 4-6 on Kierkegaard's famous saying, "subjectivity is truth".

issues raised here are those of respect and integrity between disciplines. Whilst specific scientific questions are not ignored, this is more of a meta-debate, a discussion over epistemology, over what may be known in each discipline and how it may be known. Are there points of contact and where do they lie? When there is movement from one way of thinking to another, how does it occur — from particular uncomfortable scientific evidence, from a new way of looking at things (a paradigm, as we have learned from Thomas Kuhn to call it), or by some other means? How is God's will for the universe and its deep structure to be discerned?

3. The last papers, by Carver T. Yu and John Polkinghorne, look specifically at theology in the light of scientific discovery. What does relativity mean for theology: does it imply relativism? There is an interesting debate here between Yu and one of his respondents, Lloyd Geering. They consider too the challenge of quantum mechanics, of which it has been said: if you are not profoundly disturbed by it, you have not yet understood it. Does the new science of chaotic mathematics offer possibilities for understanding God's providential activity? Do the very limits of science open possibilities for faith, as it depicts a world crying out for explanation from beyond itself?

Like Gingerich, Polkinghorne is a physical astronomer. Both speak with authority from their own fields and both are interested in the anthropic principle (the idea, proposed by people who are not themselves Christian believers, that the universe exists so that human beings can exist...). Gingerich and Polkinghorne thus work immediately at the interface between their faith and their secular disciplines. It is perhaps particularly appropriate that this volume should begin and end with their contributions. This is the place of Christian mission, which both offers to the world and listens to it.

In another way, it is appropriate too that one of the final respondents should be Jack Dodd. An agnostic among the Christians, he has one of the last words! This is at least a token that Christians should not just engage in debate amongst themselves regardless of their expertise, but should be open to outside voices too. Just how well the Church responds to the challenge of people like Dodd may mark how it will be measured in the time to come. How does it stick to its own faith without becoming impervious to truths made known from outside its own fold — truths which, some might argue, come ever new from the hand of God? How does it listen to that which is new without surrendering the faith of the apostles, and changing to accommodate the whims of the times? At one point during the symposium, Emerton quoted Dean Inge's famous remark: "The Church who is married to the spirit of this age will be a widow in the next." A trust that God is the source of all truth and will comfort the Church in discomforting it seems essential. We should not abandon what makes Christianity unique but neither should we close our ears to the world as if all we ever hear are siren voices. The God of all creation will not lead us astray.

Themes

The division drawn above is, of course, too tidy to be true. Not only is it too limited to do justice to the variety of interests and knowledge of the speakers, but they were not bound within such divisions. Certain questions tended to crop up time and again.

Scientism

The scientific imperialism mentioned above came in for much criticism from many quarters. For many of the speakers, it was science's arrogant assertion of its own omnicompetence that stood in the way of further dialogue. For many, too, the universe was seen as calling out for an explanation from beyond itself.

Divine action in the world

Is divine action to be understood as intervention, interaction, interruption or something else? Is God entitled to act in the world? If there is a hesitation to affirm this amongst Christians, is it based on an obsolete (Deist) view of the universe: namely that it exists as a closed continuum of cause and effect? That is, even if God had set everything in motion once upon a time with a kick-start, it is illegitimate to put his spoke in now. This topic came up repeatedly, not just in the symposium debates, but in the public lectures as well.

The problem of evil

This issue was connected to divine action in the world. Is it possible to draw a clear distinction between natural evil such as earthquakes and volcanos, and moral evil such as humans killing one another? What is the responsibility of God, or of us, for either? If suffering occurs through both, can the first be seen as necessary, and part of the package-deal of creation that enables us to be here discussing it? There was much talk of the ragged edges of creation. Is this truly the best of all possible worlds, so that we should stop complaining about God and make the best of it, and work to ameliorate suffering as best we can?

Freedom and determinism

Is it true that classical physics (of Newton, and maybe Einstein too) was fundamentally determinist, whilst quantum mechanics opens the way to freedom? What does it mean to draw a distinction between an open and a closed system, both in scientific models and in their relation to the question of divine action in the world, and to allow for the possibility of newness, a genuinely non-determined future? Culturally, we see a world of increased knowledge but also one that confronts us with our apparent impotence in the face of world problems — problems such as poverty that overwhelm us with their enormity and apparent insolubility. Can humans truly be free?

Reductionism and humanity

Relativity speaks at a macrocosmic level, quantum mechanics at a microcosmic level. Are epistemological principles at one level applicable to another? Sometimes human beings seem to exist somewhat uneasily between the telescopic and the microscopic levels of scientific thought. Is there a scientific way of thinking about ourselves that respects our uniquely personal characteristics? Can we speak at a human level that avoids either a reduction of humanity into "things" or flight from the scientific for a dualistically conceived world of the arts?

The limits of knowledge

Is there a contribution possible here from the theology and literature debate? Some might argue that post-modernism stands as a fundamental challenge to science. The methodological debate is here central. If our knowledge is personal, are we limited to our own perspective rather than some Olympian viewpoint *sub specie aeternitatis*? If so, is this something to grieve over? If we acknowledge the particular contingency of our viewpoint, what does this mean for "certainty", for the possibility of dialogue with others, for changing our own minds over things? Is this growth or just alteration? In other words, how can we speak of "truth"?

Moreover, if all knowledge is personal, with all that implies about the partiality of claims of truth, does this not affect the way we should talk about it? Does it not affect the way we do science or engage in dialogue — or indeed write books about it? Perhaps it affects our view of the relationship between generality and particularity so that story-telling becomes a valid part of the enterprise.

Thinkers

As well as certain themes, particular names tend to appear often as well. Hume's devastating critique of natural theology has given all subsequent thinkers on this subject due pause. Pascal's famous saying: "The heart has its reasons of which reason knows nothing", makes a number of appearances to set against Cartesian rationalism. Laplace's classical "science can explain everything" viewpoint embodies all that is objectionable about that outlook. Contemporary debaters such as Hawking, Sagan and Dawkins are recurrently mentioned as are ideas much in the air at the moment — the anthropic principle and the multiple worlds' interpretation or multiple universes' interpretation of it. Particular phenomena of quantum mechanics, such as the particularly puzzling Einstein-Podolsky-Rosen effect, came in for discussion. It was also remarked that our conversations took place at the time that Michael Crichton's *Jurassic Park* was hitting New Zealand. This work's own anti-scientistic, anti-modernist espousing of chaos theory might be seen to be particularly apposite in the circumstances of the debate.[13]

Synopsis

Due to the complexity of much of the material in this book, the synopsis of the papers below, in large part, avoids commentary, trying instead to let the various offerings speak for themselves. As will be immediately evident, there was plenty of disagreement between speakers, notably on methodological issues. This liveliness of debate bodes well for the future.

Owen Gingerich's paper is entitled, "Is there a role for natural theology today?" The response he gives to the question he sets himself is fundamentally "Yes" — as part of an overall Christian vision of the cosmos. However, he is at pains to indicate that specific evidence for design, however convincing to one coming from a fundamentally Christian position, might not necessarily persuade anyone else. It is from the viewpoint of faith that the available data can be interpreted as "impressive evidences of design and purpose". Teleology in science is currently very unpopular: "Reductionism is the name of the game ... the current philosophical orthodoxy [is of] the non-directed nature of evolution." Gingerich presents a picture of the current scientific understanding of the early universe, taking it back as close to the beginning as 10^{-43} second. He provides awesome examples of what has come to be known as the anthropic principle, the notion that the universe has to be exactly the way it is so that humanity can now exist to exclaim in wonder at it. The extreme fine-tuning that lies in the original conditions of the universe means that "like the Little Bear's porridge, this universe is just right". Similarly, he argues that life has evolved on earth in an unlikely way, so that the "perfect timing of this complex configuration of circumstances" has given celebrated pause to the atheism of people such as Fred Hoyle.

Gingerich argues that all this amazing evidence does not add up to proof as such, but that it does paint a particular picture of the universe which is certainly consonant with Christian faith. Thus,

---

13. This is more evident in the novel by Michael Crichton (London: Random House, 1991) than in the 1993 film directed by Steven Spielberg.

science is more a matter of coherence than proof. There is a
particular place for rhetoric as that which persuades people of the
coherence of a particular vision. Arguments and evidence by
themselves are insufficient. For one thing, what seems to us to be a
remarkably unlikely coincidence may be explained by a
subsequently-developed scientific theory — the inflationary
hypothesis about the expansion of the early universe being a good
example. Gingerich sees Johannes Kepler as a superb instance of a
person who was both a believing Christian and a creative scientist,
and argues that "indeed the very motivation of scientific research can
stem from a desire to trace God's handiwork".

The response by Stephen May concurs with Gingerich that no
knock-down proof for the existence of God will ever be found.
What is more at issue is a coherent vision of the universe. Whilst
Gingerich understands the age and size of the universe as fitting in
with a Christian understanding of the anthropic principle, other
atheistic interpretations continue to affect popular culture. H. G.
Wells' pessimistic humanism was grounded on a vision of the
insignificance of life in a vast cosmos. More recent works by
authors such as Douglas Adams and Terry Pratchett draw their
inspiration from this and quantum mechanics to assert a defiantly
absurdist vision of human existence.

In her response, Nancey Murphy compares two models of
epistemology. The first, which has now been largely abandoned, is
deductive and based on indubitable axioms moving linearly by
certain, deductive steps. The alternative model is an inductive one,
based on empirical knowledge. This distinction has had historical
significance for theistic arguments: "Proofs came to be seen by most
to be impossible, and the argument from design became prominent
as a merely probable argument beginning with experience". She
proposes, as an alternative to the linear model of knowledge,
Lakatos' model of a web of belief — distinguishing between beliefs
near the edge of the web correlated to experience, and more
theoretical or logical ones near the core-centre. (Murphy expounds
this interpretation at greater length in her own main paper.) For her,
"arguments such as Gingerich's allow us to build a more coherent
Christian world-view. These same findings, instances of apparent
intelligent design, create inconsistencies within an atheistic worldview." Like Gingerich, she thinks that this is indeed a rhetorical

task and comments that "some of the proponents of an atheistic worldview have been much more effective rhetorically than the Christians have been". Design is indeed in the eye of the beholder, insofar as particular examples may not be sufficient to trigger changes in our entire worldview. Data are always theory-laden. Nature is properly to be interpreted in the light of revelation, as a sequel to it. It is thus that the Books of Nature and Scripture are to be understood.

However, science is not to be left in the realm of "mere opinion". Rational judgment between competing systems is involved. There is a vital need for Christians to be involved in the secular world, to be "bilingual".

Both Stephen May and Nancey Murphy instance David Hume and the multiple worlds interpretation of the anthropic principle to show that the most apparently knock-down evidence for design in the universe need not necessarily point in that direction. We could simply happen to live in the particular universe — out of a multitude of universes — in which humans have evolved. We lack the perspective to see how logical, or illogical, our existence really is.

Norma Emerton's paper, "Arguments for the existence of God from nature and science", gives an historical overview of the subject. Emerton details some of the sources for the classical arguments, concentrating mostly on the cosmological and teleological ones and pointing out their "hidden dangers".

She identifies a common root for these arguments, one shared by Jewish, Muslim and Christian traditions in the Middle Ages, particularly around the twelfth century. Here, equally shared, is the intellectual debating partner of Aristotelian philosophy. Maimonides, Anselm, Peter Lombard and Aquinas are all major figures of this period. Aquinas differs from his contemporary, Bonaventure, in arguing that reason by itself cannot bring one to God. Emerton argues that Aquinas, like Augustine, wanted to avoid the danger of being trapped theologically in a particular worldview. "The interaction of theology and natural philosophy must respect the integrity of both disciplines. Thomas, like Augustine, believed that philosophical and theological truths both proceeded from the God of truth and could not ultimately be in conflict." Emerton argues that the early Church Fathers took the argument from design from Stoics such as Cicero, thus importing into Christian theology a danger of pantheism.

In the sixteenth and seventeenth centuries the scientific revolution brought a new attitude to the natural world: it was seen increasingly as an object of study in itself. Scientists such as Robert Boyle identified examples of design in the natural world whilst being wary of pantheism. John Webster too scented peril, seeing natural theology as a threat to revealed theology as well as a boon to science. With the Deists, natural theology became natural religion and supplanted revealed theology. "Scientific rationalisations of creation in terms of chemistry, atomism, or Newtonian astronomy [by such as the Deist William Whiston] were intended to serve the same purpose as the argument from design ... to increase the credibility of belief in God as Creator by showing that it was compatible with physical processes and with the reasoning of natural philosophy." This approach has a very modern ring to it!

However, in the seventeenth and eighteenth centuries the argument from design was sharply criticised on philosophical grounds, notably by Hume. Despite this, natural theology increased in popularity, particularly with William Paley, but attention shifted away from cosmology towards biology. To this development Charles Darwin produced a stunning rebuff. Whilst his own attitude to teleology was ambiguous, Darwin effectively demolished the traditional argument from design.

For Emerton, Stephen Hawking's well known argument, that God is unnecessary because there is nothing for him to do, misses the point. Yet the God of the gaps is still being evoked, particularly at a popular and/or emotional level — despite devastating philosophical rebuttals. Darwin's theory of natural selection did the vital damage. This was more a matter of content than method: the facts were convincingly explained in a way that did not require God. Twin dangers are to be seen in "the opposite extremes of pantheism and deism". The first derives from Stoicism, the second from a clockwork notion of God.

John Stenhouse's response argues that the present anti-theistic nature of much modern science derives more from culture and history than logic. The seventeenth-century wars of religion left a bitter memory. The Enlightenment was born in a period characterised by widespread religious bigotry, intolerance and persecution. In addition, proponents of the anti-theistic school such as Huxley had a wide agenda, including the control of education. The Church was often identified with reactionary and conservative forces, against which atheistic science could claim to be revolutionary and progressive. For Stenhouse scientism, "the scientific imperialism that claims there is no reality beyond science and the natural", needs to be fundamentally challenged before any Christian apologetics can be undertaken successfully. This requires engagement with the historical issues.

In his response John Polkinghorne identifies three main points in Emerton's paper: natural theology is a limited exercise; its claims are vulnerable to alternative explanation; and it is ambiguous because of evil and suffering in the world. Nevertheless, a new natural theology has arisen from the ashes of the old. More modest and appropriate, it is the work of scientists rather than theologians. For Polkinghorne, as for Gingerich, its claims are of insight rather than proof: "It trades in intellectually satisfying understanding rather than in logically coercive demonstration. It does not claim that atheists are stupid but rather that they explain less." The laws of nature are insufficiently self-explanatory, but rather point beyond themselves. The new natural theology points not to specific occurrences within the world but to its fabric as a whole, whose ground rules cry out for an explanation beyond themselves. This new natural theology takes account of the imperfection of creation by arguing that God gives it a place to make itself. "A world allowed to make itself will necessarily have blind alleys and ragged edges ... The flawedness of the world is acknowledged and understood, not as signifying a botched job by its 'rude, infant' Creator but as a necessary price of its divinely-bestowed independence." For Polkinghorne the revival of natural theology is grounded on "the search for sufficient reason and for an adequate response to the deep rational beauty of the world in which we live". He sees natural theology neither as an apologetic strategy nor "a preliminary warming-up exercise", but as a "modest but indispensable component in the great search for the knowledge of God and of his ways with his creation".

Nancey Murphy's paper, "What has theology to learn from scientific methodology?" develops a thesis based on the methodology of Imre Lakatos. She begins by arguing that

Stephen May

"Christian tradition is still trying to recover from the advent of modern science". There is an epistemological crisis "yet to be resolved", resulting from the development of a new theory of knowledge. She regards it as promising that modern epistemological theory has moved away from foundationalism towards holism. Instead of knowledge being based on independent, unverifiable but unquestionable presuppositions, it is now generally accepted that theory is inseparable from data, presuppositions from that which they support. For Lakatos, the basic units of appraisal in science are not the paradigms of Thomas Kuhn but "research programmes". Murphy endeavours to show that theological research programmes may be justified according to these new canons of scientific understanding.

Murphy finds parallels to Lakatos' description of the four elements of a research programme (the hard core, the auxiliary hypotheses, the data, and theories of instrumentation) in theology. For her the raw material for theology is scripture and, above all, religious experience. She argues that in theology theories of interpretation of scripture operate very much as theories of instrumentation do in science. In terms of religious experience, two main points are made. First, against accusations of circularity, she instances the similar circular nature of scientific thinking, for example, Boyle's Law. This circularity is "virtuous" rather than "vicious".

Secondly, she argues that publicly observable criteria are necessary for theological data to be meaningful. The mystics Catherine of Siena and Teresa of Avila developed such criteria in humility and charity. Judged by a consensual community, these can provide appropriate ways of judging the authenticity of claimed religious experience. Thus, the theory of discernment here too functions as theories of instrumentation do in science, making judgments possible regarding consistency and reliability. Similarly, there is a falsifiable element to such experiences. Another criterion for judgment would be progress in explaining novel facts; this could also be used "to arbitrate among competing theologies within Christianity as well".

For Murphy, such criteria are necessary if theology claims "*knowledge* of a reality independent of the human subject". In this way she sees her own work as part of an attempt to turn theology away from the "subjective turn" in modern liberal theology.

The responses by Grant Gillett and John Puddefoot express substantive concerns about the main thrust of Murphy's paper. Gillett questions what he sees as Murphy's claim that "observation may act as a gold-standard for objectivity or truth". He interprets Wittgenstein's objection to private language differently from Murphy: to say "I think I am in pain but could you please check for me" is patently absurd. To argue that all truth derives from public observation is inadequate.

In addition, Gillett argues that a method appropriate to the impersonal, objective, and detached natural sciences falls drastically short when dealing with the irreducibly personal and interpersonal nature of the human and theological sciences. Here, we not only know but are known: "[this] ontological fact ... cannot help but change our epistemology at a very deep level". As psychology needs to avoid a mechanical reduction of its scope (thinking of action "as events associated with physical objects that happen to be people"), so theology too has to take seriously issues of intentionality. God, who is personal, must be regarded with an epistemology appropriate to persons. Faith is "the appropriate epistemic ground for knowledge of God ... God's subjectivity must come to us and speak or breathe into us before we can begin our task of knowing."

Puddefoot's response agrees with Murphy about the inadequacy of foundationalism, but wonders whether she herself has sufficiently escaped from it. He argues that if theology seeks empirical verification, it apes a method not only alien to its own subject matter, but incorrect in any context. He wishes to take the theory-laden nature of data more seriously. We can never "climb out of our minds", attaining an Olympian standpoint from which to judge the truth objectively. To do so would deny an essential aspect of theology and general human existence — risk. Communal verification of experience is helpful, but it has no place for the dissenter or prophet, whose message "must either conquer or die". He argues that while any claim to self-authentication is bogus, so too is the desire for a certainty stretching beyond the sheer coherent persuasiveness of a vision. When applied to theology, the empirical method becomes "an attempt to know God without the involvement of God in the process". Although indeed, "it is necessary to show that the discipline of theology aims at knowledge of reality independent of the human subject", we can never know if we truly achieve this. Science ought not to pride itself on being superior to ethics or art or literary theory in this regard: it has no privileged access to reality, and for theology to try and share such an illusion would be to lead both astray.

John Puddefoot's own paper is entitled "The relationship of natural order to divine truth and will". For him, it is pivotal that if the world is made by God, it embodies God's rationality and intentions, however hard they may be for us to discern. Our very difficulty in this regard would be consistent with a deep structure created by God, stretching beyond our understanding. Thus our failure to grasp these easily would witness not to a failure on God's part but to the requirement of a growth in our own conceptions of rationality. Puddefoot argues that his paper follows a hermeneutical rather than an apologetic task. He concurs with Michael Polanyi that "the deepest reality is possessed by higher things that are least tangible". Moreover, the rationality of the universe is not self-evident from within, but derives from a higher ordering principle beyond it. It is the mistake of scientific imperialism to think that science can accurately describe its own boundary conditions.

For Puddefoot, the tendency in science is to speak in general, impersonal, objectivist terms which are an adequate description of neither life, nor scientific existence, nor theology. The universal language of critical scientific thought and metaphysics alike is inadequate to deal with the particularity and ambiguity of concrete existence. Rather than theology being "the down-trodden poor relation of modern scholarship", it actually should provide "the highest level of description to which we aspire". For Puddefoot the only possible contradictions between theological and scientific accounts of the world derive from poor theology, creationism, or a scientific imperialism that insists that what science is capable of talking about is all that is worth talking about. "Science comes into conflict with theology when it believes itself able to specify the kinds of things that are possible in the world." He instances the working of a computer to illustrate the idea that, from within a system, external operation may indeed appear unintelligible, a "miracle". Science itself is based on the faith that rationality goes beyond our current "clear and distinct ideas", but unfortunately tends to seek for objective grounds for truth that avoid the necessary uncertainty of personal knowing.

Puddefoot attempts to develop the theme of particularity in science, partly as a helpful way of cementing the harmony between it and theology. For him, the ambiguity and openness of the world goes some way at least to explaining the suffering in the world — like parents who cannot anticipate where having children will take them but who are committed to the project in a covenantal way. There is no set of absolute criteria available to humanity either in science or art. Science works "because it is applied to systems and by organisms which already know what they are doing". Science and theology embody skills: "Theology is no better or worse than science, for its equipment is frail and imprecise human language, and its limitations are imposed as much by human imagination as by human reason." For Puddefoot, a post-critical way of thinking about science opens up much richer and harmonious possibilities of dialogue with theology.

In his response John Honner argues that there are some tensions inherent in Puddefoot's paper, including a discrepancy between his ostensive basis and actual content. For Honner, Puddefoot expresses strong reservations about the healthiness of science, but also utilises it to suggest a way forward for epistemology when it suits his purposes. He notes what he describes as Puddefoot's "very neat and original reworking of the design argument" based on "the ambiguous intelligibility of reality". However, Puddefoot's remarks about the incarnation as revelatory of God are essential in unfolding the rationality of such an argument, which would otherwise leave us with a teasing and malicious God. For Honner, there are signs of a certainty in Puddefoot's paper which seems to militate against his expressed aim. He sees the relation of grace and nature to be basic, and expresses some confusion as to Puddefoot's "highly dialectical approach".

Owen Gingerich's response is in some ways more exegesis than criticism. He underlines transcendence and deconstruction as underlying themes in Puddefoot's paper. He notes that transcendence can only be known as unknowable as it reveals itself. The influence of deconstruction can be seen in Puddefoot's emphasis on particularity as opposed to generality. Gingerich refers these themes to his own attempt, alongside colleagues in the American Scientific Affiliation, to produce a public television series in the United States on the nature of science from a Christian perspective. For him, Puddefoot is aligned with John Polkinghorne in his emphasis on the incarnation, the place where "God has directly entered the world and revealed Godself to the world, [giving] us a hope and confidence that our human understanding can indeed encompass much of the construction of the natural world."

Carver T. Yu's paper "The principle of relativity as a conceptual tool in theology" addresses the "spectre of relativism which is haunting the present age". Yu's first concern is to dispel what he regards as a common popular misunderstanding of relativity, namely that it leads to relativism. For him, it is significant that Einstein wished he had called the theory of relativity the theory of invariance. To interpret the theory of relativity to mean that truth is only true "for you" or "for me", and that there is no conversation about absolute truth possible between us, is to drastically misunderstand it. It is not true that every frame of reference is absolutely relative to itself, but rather that everything is relative to the absolute speed of light. It is not absolutes that are wrong — it is the *wrong* absolutes.

However, "the postulate of the constant velocity of light goes against our intuition ... We are shocked to find that what we consistently regarded as constant actually changes ... We are therefore led to the impression that ... we are left with no universal standards. Perhaps it is here that many feel driven to relativism. Yet it is also here that a deeper invariant structure of nature is being revealed to us." Yu expounds in detail the scientific understanding of relativity, and then attempts to apply his findings to the realm of theology. As he notes, this is not without difficulty, particularly because the God of whom we speak addresses us. Nevertheless, Yu argues that this itself provides its own equivalence of invariance. For him, invariance in theology includes conceiving God as transcendent, as Creator and as incarnate. Since the incarnation is the place where God has given Godself to be known, to look elsewhere for God is to ignore the invariant revelation which is true for all people in all frames of reference.

Yet, as Yu has already argued in relation to physics, there is another side of invariance — the particular situations wherein particular people relate to the invariant measuring rod. As such, we must not absolutise our own frames of reference, nor find absolutes in the wrong location. There is an appropriate place for particularity and contextuality in theology. Drawing on his own legacy, Yu suggests that Asian theology needs to examine its inheritance from the West to see whether absolutes have been misplaced.

Lloyd Geering interprets relativity rather differently to Yu. For him, the debate between theology and science requires a radical rethinking on the part of the former. He does not see the trap of relativism as being as significant as absolutism, which he regards as more dangerous and enticing for the Church. For Geering, the invariant analogue to the speed of light in theology is not God, but "the basic human condition ... the quest for meaning" — humanity's religious sense. He regards Yu's starting points of transcendence and *creatio ex nihilo* as neither sufficiently public nor neutral for a debate with science. For him, theology does not dispense enough with unnecessary beliefs. It is of the essence of the Judaeo-Christian faith to be committed to relativism, and relativity encourages us "to live in the absence of all absolutes".

Norma Emerton's response questions the extent to which one can validly draw inferences from physical science for theology. "It is one thing to say that Einstein's relativity theory has implications for epistemology, or that it is compatible with Christian doctrine, or that it offers insights that are valuable to theology. It is quite another thing to suggest that its method could be imitated or even appropriated by theology." For her, quantum mechanics shows some of the problems involved in such linkage. She notes the way in which Einstein never reconciled himself to the problems it raises regarding causality and indeterminacy.

Emerton also raises questions about the relation of knowledge of God in creation and redemption. She expresses some doubt whether Asian theologians will have any greater success than their western forerunners in providing a formulation of the faith.

John Polkinghorne's paper, "Theological notions of creation and divine causality", analyses areas of consonance between theology and science, and develops ideas more briefly expressed in his response to Emerton's paper. He begins by saying that in science we recognise that in order to be faithful to our object of study we have to speak of it in ways which may at first be counterintuitive. Polkinghorne describes himself as a "bottom-up thinker", finding in religious experience an anchor for the theological notions of creation and providence. Like Peter Berger, he sees signals of transcendence in the creative order. These include such deep-seated human intuitions as hope. Although the popular perception is that "scientific discovery has disposed of religious beliefs [in many areas, with] the unrelenting laws of nature [affording] no room for divine manoeuvre within the network of causality", for Polkinghorne both science and the world it investigates cry out for an explanation beyond themselves. Moreover, science "purchases its success by narrowing its vision". The fact that the world is moral as well as physical "becomes intelligible if the world is a creation".

So too, the Christian doctrine of creation is consonant with "the unreasonable effectiveness of mathematics" as well as with metaquestions from science itself such as the anthropic principle. "Science cannot explain the laws which are the foundation of its own explanatory endeavour." Polkinghorne regards the creation explanation of the anthropic principle as being "of equal coherence and ... greater economy" than the many worlds interpretation.

Like Arthur Peacocke, Polkinghorne sees God as "the Great Improviser". Here "the shufflings of chance are the explorations of creation's potentialities. The interplay of chance and necessity is a *creatio continua*." Polkinghorne regards this view as explaining, to some extent, the imperfect nature of the universe. "A universe able to explore its own God-given potentiality ... will inevitably be a universe with ragged edges and painful malfunctions." Polkinghorne sees this as a free-process defence in relation to physical evil, parallelling the free-will defence in relation to moral evil. Thus science helps theodicy to make physical evil intelligible. "A world allowed to make itself cannot be a world free from pain and suffering." Nevertheless, he acknowledges that an "ultimate Christian response looks to the Cross of Christ".

Polkinghorne argues in relation to the doctrine of providence that a top-down causality is entirely compatible with bottom-up thinking. "It is conceivable that God interacts with his creation in such a way as to bring about particular outcomes on particular occasions, whilst still respecting those gifts of otherness and independence that he has conferred upon his creation." Polkinghorne sees chaos theory's insight into intrinsically unpredictable behaviour as more helpful in this regard than quantum theory's emphasis on uncertainty. For him divine action will always be "contained within the cloudiness of unpredictable process". Moreover, he is happy to adopt the insight of process theology that "in such a world even God does not know the unformed future, for it is not yet there to be known".

Polkinghorne declares that he nails his colours to the mast by asserting his belief in human free will. In his response, Jack Dodd identifies clearly his agnostic faith. He differs from Polkinghorne as to the status of truth in scientific modelling of reality. Dodd differentiates various views of God in Polkinghorne's paper. For him, "What many people call prayer, I call *trying to think things out carefully*." He sees pain as a "natural characteristic developed as part of the evolutionary process for the survival of the species". What Polkinghorne sees as signals of transcendence, he regards as evolutionary traits. The notion of a God who responds to prayer has no evidence to support it, and Dodd sees no necessity to posit the hand of God acting in providence. Whilst it is entirely natural to want to know why things exist, he sees no reason why one has to believe in a God. "To say 'God made it so', and do nothing because we think we have answered the question, would not be human." Indeed, it would not be scientific.

For Dodd, the central tenet of the scientific method is the principle of simplicity enshrined in Ockham's razor. Although as a "sceptical atheistic scientist", he too is "at a loss to explain why it is all so", he sees no reason to resort to God to explain creation. Rather, for him, it is humanity who has created God.

The response by Carver Yu has three appreciations and three reservations. He appreciates Polkinghorne's emphasis on the "continuity, convergence and consonance" between scientific rationality and the rational order intrinsic to the personal world. For him it is significant that "To understand the universe in its wholeness, one cannot see the physical in abstraction from the personal." Moreover, it is important to note that theology does not act to fill a gap in scientific knowledge, but rather that "the notion of creation becomes intelligible and relevant ... as something in consonance with what the universe itself is pointing to or something which scientists feel compelled to appreciate". Lastly, Yu refers to Polkinghorne's argument that Christianity explains the universe with greater economy of effort than alternatives: this is in consonance with Ockham's razor, too!

In terms of reservations, Yu questions whether the experiential anchorage for creation and providence lies primarily in religious life. Does this not do violence to the idea of a dialogue between science and theology wherein it might be argued that one moves "between two experiential anchorages to see consonance between [them]". Also, one might ask whether the refusal to ask a metaquestion about the fine-tuning of the universe is due simply to "rational laziness"; it may simply be because of tough-mindedness. Lastly, whilst Yu appreciates the emphasis on an open universe, he asks why a universe able to make itself will *inevitably* be full of pain and suffering. He asks Polkinghorne to explain a little further "the inner relation between free process and the possibilities of painful malfunction".

Challenges

It was the physical sciences that were largely discussed at the symposium. The main reason for this was simply the fact that one conference could not cover everything. However, it could also be argued that these are currently more amenable to discussions with theology. This is not because they are softer or easier than the biological or human sciences: it should be readily evident from this volume that this is not the case. Rather, there have been extraordinary developments over the last hundred years that have made the conversation with theology far more open, exciting and constructive than has been possible in the past. To some extent, it might be argued, this is because they have had to reflect more thoroughly on their methodology — a methodology that has shown some remarkable changes. It might be asked: is this as much the case in the biological or social sciences? T. F. Torrance, for one, thinks that the latter need to make more progress here, dispensing with inappropriate dualisms derived from the past.[14] So here is a challenge for another symposium.

With whom does the dialogue take place? To assert, as some of my own more provocative students did, that it occurs properly

---

14. For example, *God and Rationality* (London: Oxford University Press, 1971) p. 105.

between Christians and atheist scientists, assumes that the only true scientists are atheists! Yet, if mission is to be taken seriously, this engagement is necessary too. It is not good if the debate is internal only to the Christian world — or sub-culture. It was for this reason that speakers at the symposium were not restricted to orthodox believers alone.

One of the key words running through this symposium was integrity. We should show integrity in both disciplines — theology and science. We should show integrity in not trying to avoid apparently unpalatable facts or theories from science — discarding those that do not fit in with our prejudices. Similarly, however, some of those at the symposium argued that we should never sell Christianity down the river in this dialogue either. We have to do justice to our own traditions. It is in the creative tension between theology and science that growth is possible.

A further task for theology, therefore, might be to develop the doctrine of the Trinity in relation to science. Is the discussion with science to be couched at a merely theistic level such that a Unitarian might feel happy with our pronouncements, or is there something specifically Christian that might be said? Does the Holy Spirit have a significant role in creation, and how might that affect epistemology and ontology? Is our knowledge of the world fundamentally different from that of God insofar as we are left to interpret the world whereas, according to certain theologies, God is *self-interpreting*. If so, might it be argued that God makes Godself known in such a way that we are given a sure grasp on reality — something not grounded on our own hermeneutical skills? Does such a view do adequate justice to the interrelation between the human subject and the revelation — even if that is made known through the supremely active divine subject? Or does God act in science too, through the Spirit, to lead us into all truth? Do we need to develop a scientific theology of Word and Spirit as the two hands of God?

These questions are raised here to indicate some possible directions for further discussion. This is an enormously fruitful area of debate, as the richness of the contributions below shows. They should provide much food for thought.

1

Is there a role for natural theology today?

Owen Gingerich

Discussions on the role of purpose and design as they pertain to the universe have employed philosophers and scientists for millennia. Specific analogies may endure with vigour for centuries:

> In crossing a heath, suppose I pitched my foot against a *stone,* and were asked how the stone came to be there; I might possibly answer that, for any thing I knew to the contrary, it had lain there forever: nor would it perhaps be very easy to show the absurdity of this answer. But supposing I had found a *watch* upon the ground, and it should be inquired how the watch happened to be in that place; I should hardly think of the answer which I had before given, that for any thing I knew, the watch might have always been there. Yet why should not this answer serve for the watch as well as for the stone? Why is it not as admissible in the second case, as in the first? For this reason, and for no other, namely, that when we come to inspect the watch, we perceive that its several parts are framed and put together for a purpose ... The mechanism being observed (it requires indeed an examination of the instrument, and perhaps some previous knowledge of the subject, to perceive and understand it; but being once, as we have said, observed and understood), the inference, we think, is inevitable, that the watch must have had a maker: there must have existed, at some time, and at some place or other, an artificer or artificers, who formed it for the purpose which we find it actually to answer; who comprehended its construction, and designed its use.[1]

---

1. William Paley, *Natural Theology; or, Evidences of the Existence and Attributes of the Deity Collected from the Appearances of Nature* (first edition 1803, quoted from Edinburgh: William Whyte, 1816) pp. 5-7.

Whether you have read this passage before or not, I am sure you all recognise it as the famous argument from design that introduces William Paley's *Natural Theology; or, Evidences of the Existence and Attributes of the Deity Collected from the Appearances of Nature.* Paley's work, written nearly two hundred years ago, continues to have its modern repercussions, as witnessed by the title of the bestseller from the Oxford biologist Richard Dawkins, *The Blind Watchmaker.* Dawkins writes, "When it comes to complexity and beauty of design, Paley hardly even began to state his case."[2] But he also declares that Paley's argument "is wrong, gloriously and utterly wrong",[3] and the subtitle of his book boldly states: *Why the evidence of evolution reveals a universe without design.*

As an astronomer, I have always been intrigued by some of the astonishing details of the physical world, to say nothing of the intricacy and complexity of the biological domain. To me, looking out at the universe through the eyes of faith, these data have seemed to be impressive evidences of design and purpose. I propose to sketch briefly the modern scientific scenario of the creation of the universe, the origin of the elements, and the evolution of our terrestrial environment, pointing out several wonderful episodes where it appears, on the face of it, that a designing hand has been at work. Yet science today eschews any hint of design or purpose in its descripton of the world. Thus my scientific scenario, as promised in the announced title of my paper,[4] will be grist for two more specific questions: dare a scientist believe in design? And, is there a role for natural theology today?

That it is unfashionable in scientific explanations today even to hint at purpose or design is made clear repeatedly, and not just in such avowedly atheistic polemics as exemplified by Dawkins' subtitle. Reductionism is the name of the game. Typical is a recent statement in *Scientific American:* "It is difficult to understand the brain because, unlike a computer, it was not built with specific

---

2. Richard Dawkins, *The Blind Watchmaker* (London: W.W. Norton, 1987) p. 21.

3. Dawkins, *op. cit.* p. 5.

4. "Modern cosmogony and Biblical creation" - see my article with this title in *The World Treasury of Physics, Astronomy, and Mathematics,* Timothy Ferris, editor (Boston: Little, Brown & Co., 1991) pp. 378-94.

purposes or principles of design in mind. Natural selection, the engine of evolution, is responsible."[5]

Three years ago *Science* magazine carried a report on the toxins of certain cone shells, which I happened to notice because my wife and I are avid shell collectors. A supplementary news article titled "Science digests the secrets of voracious killer snails" remarked that "the great diversity and specificity of toxins in the venoms of the cone snails are due to the intense evolutionary pressure on the snails to stop their prey quickly, since they can't chase it down".[6]

Very promptly a letter to the editor objected that this language implied that some real pressure was driving the snails to develop the toxins.

> The reality is that those snails that produced toxins that immobilised their prey quickly tended to obtain food more often than those possessing slower-acting or no toxins, and thus over time the population of cone shells became dominated by those possessing the fast-acting agents. There was no pressure! In the vernacular, "If it works, it works; if it don't, it don't."[7]

The response shows clearly the current philosophical orthodoxy about the non-directed nature of evolution. It also typifies the enormous change of view that has occurred over the past century with respect to the wonders of the biological world.

What is now seen as the zigzag, largely accidental path to amazing organisms with astonishing adaptations was in earlier times routinely interpreted as the design of an intelligent Creator. The long neck of the giraffe, which so well adapts the creature to an environment where food is available high off the ground, would have been seen, in William Paley's words, as a "mark of contrivance, in proof of design, and of a designing Creator".[8] "Who gave white bears and white wolves to the snowy regions of

---

5. Gerald D. Fischbach, "Mind and brain" *Scientific American* (September, 1992) p. 48.
6. Marcia Barinaga, "Science digests the secrets of voracious killer snails" *Science* 249 (20 July 1990) pp. 25-51.
7. James L. Carew, "'Purposeful' evolution" (letter) *Science* 249 (24 August 1990) p. 843.
8. Paley, *op. cit.* chapter 5, section 5, p. 61.

the North, and as food for the bears the whale, and for the wolves, birds' eggs?" asked Johannes Kepler two centuries earlier.[9] "Great is our Lord and great his virtue and of his wisdom there is no number!" he exclaims in answer, "Use every sense for perceiving your Creator." Even Jean Jacques Rousseau, not best known as a theist, declared:

> It is impossible for me to conceive that a system of beings can be so wisely regulated without the existence of some intelligent cause which affects such regulation ... I believe, therefore, that the world is governed by a wise and powerful Will.[10]

The notion of design suggests the existence of a goal-directed or end-directed process, what can aptly be termed teleology. Ernst Mayr, a leading evolutionist who has written very clearly on the modern philosophy of evolution, wisely remarks that it is futile to attempt to clarify the concept of teleology without discriminating between different types of end-directed processes. There are some kinds of inanimate natural processes that do have an end point, for example, and there are also goal-directed processes in genetically controlled organisms.

> The third category, organic adaptness, is not directed toward an end but rather an adaptation to the environment in the widest sense of the word, acquired during evolution, largely guided by natural selection. The fourth teleology, the cosmic one, is not supported by scientific evidence.[11]

So much then, for a role for the Creator in modern biology. "Man was not the goal of evolution, which evidently had no goal",

---

9. Johannes Kepler, *Harmonies of the World* in *Great Books of the Western World* 16 (Chicago: Encyclopedia Britannica, 1952) p. 1085.
10. J. J. Rousseau, *Profession of Faith of a Savoyard Vicar* (1765) quoted in Alan Lightman and Owen Gingerich, "When do anomalies begin?" *Science* 255 (1992) pp. 690-695.
11. Ernst Mayr, "The ideological resistance to Darwin's theory of natural selection" *Proceedings of the American Philosophical Society* 135 (1991) pp. 123-39, especially p. 131.

wrote G. G. Simpson in a more visceral fashion. "He was not plan-
ned, in an operation wholly planless."[12]

Yet, despite the articulate denials of cosmic teleology by the
leading evolutionists of our age, there still remain enough
astonishing details of the natural order to evoke a feeling of awe —
beginning with the remarkable scenario that the cosmologists have
woven together concerning the earliest moments of the universe.
During the past two decades knowledge of the world of the
smallest possible sizes, the domain of particle physics, has been
combined with astronomy to describe the universe in its opening
stages. The physics ultimately fail as the nucleo-cosmologists push
their calculations back to Time Zero, but they get pretty close to the
beginning, to 10^{-43} second. At that point, at a second split so fine
that no clock could measure it, the entire observable universe is
compressed within the wavelike blur described by the uncertainty
principle, so tiny and compact that it could pass through the eye
of a needle. Not just this room, or the earth, or the solar system,
but the entire universe squeezed into a dense dot of pure energy.
And then comes the explosion. "There is no way to express that
explosion," writes the poet Robinson Jeffers:

All that exists
Roars into flame, the tortured fragments rush away from each other
    into all the sky, new universe
Jewel the black breast of night; and far off the outer nebulae like
    charging spearmen again
Invade emptiness.[13]

It is an amazing picture of pure and incredibly energetic light
being transformed into matter, and leaving its vestiges behind.
"But," you may well ask, "how do we know this story is plausible?
Or is it just a strange kind of science fiction?" I have not time here
to outline the systematic steps, starting with the ancient Greek
astronomers, in laying out the scale of ever larger reaches of
the cosmos, and culminating in our own century with the

12. George Gaylord Simpson, *The Meaning of Evolution* (New York: Mentor
    Edition, 1951) p. 143.
13. Robinson Jeffers, *The Beginning and the End and Other Poems* (New York:
    Random House, 1963) p. 3.

measurements of the realm of galaxies, where the distances are so vast that they are reckoned in millions and billions of light years. Added to this is the remarkable discovery that the more distant the galaxy, the faster it is rushing away from us. These data arrived on the scene just as the cosmologists had begun to speculate on the large-scale properties of the universe, and out of this confluence of theory and observation arose the concept of the expansion of the universe. It was a picture of quite awesome beauty: from a super-dense state "all that exists roars into flame, the tortured fragments rush away from each other into all the sky". What is more, given the rate of expansion and the distances of the galaxies, we can calculate backwards to the time when they were back together, "crushed in one harbour" in Robinson Jeffer's phrase. That comes out about ten to twenty billion years ago, a time that can be interpreted as the age of the universe itself.

Let us, for a moment, run time backwards in our mind's eye and enquire what happens as the universe is squeezed back together and its density increases. The total of the mass and energy remains the same, but the temperature rises as the matter-energy is compressed. Finally the temperature becomes so high, and the mean energy of the components so great, that the presently-known laws of physics no longer apply. This happens when we are a split second from squashing the universe into nothingness.

Now let us run the clock forward again. In the first few minutes things happen much faster than we can possibly describe them. In the first microseconds the high-energy photons vastly outnumber particles of matter, but there is a continual interchange between the photons and heavy particles of matter and antimatter. Einstein's famous $E=mc^2$ equation helps describe how the energy of the photons is converted into mass and vice versa. By the end of the first millisecond, the creation of protons and antiprotons is essentially finished, and the vast majority has already been annihilated back into photons. As the universe loses its incredible compression, the average energy per photon drops, and during this first second electrons and antielectrons (called positrons) are repeatedly formed and annihilated, finally leaving about one hundred million photons of light for every atom — a ratio that still remains.

The thermonuclear detonation of the universe is now on its way, and in the next minute fusion reactions take place that build up deuterium and helium nuclei. After the first few minutes the explosive nuclear fireworks are over, but the headlong expansion continues, and the cosmic egg gradually cools. The left-over radiation, redshifted into the microwave region of the spectrum, is ours to observe, and those photons have been observed by looking out in every direction into space, the fossil evidence of the primeval fireball of the Big Bang. "If you're religious, it's like looking at God," declared astronomer George Smoot in an over-enthusiastic response to the especially accurate data from the COBE satellite. This observed background radiation is one piece of evidence supporting the contemporary scientific picture of creation. The other is the observed abundances of helium and of deuterium, which match well the predicted amounts that would be formed in that cosmic explosion.

This picture by itself seems quite mind-boggling, but there is something else that astrophysicists began to notice a few decades ago. The universe seems quite finely balanced between the outward energy of expansion and the inward pull of gravitation. Had the universe exploded with somewhat greater energy, it would have thinned down too fast for the formation of galaxies and stars, the astrophysists concluded. Had the energy been somewhat less, gravity would have quickly got the upper hand and would have pulled the universe back together again in a premature Big Crunch. Like the Little Bear's porridge, this universe is just right.

Let me be just a little more specific. According to this scenario, only two elements — hydrogen and helium — are produced in any abundance in the Big Bang itself. In order to get the carbon, oxygen, and iron needed for the formation of life, a very long period of cooking in stellar interiors — some billions of years — is required. So, to have a life-bearing universe, it must be very old and very large. It sometimes seems a little intimidating to be on such a small speck of a planet in such vastness of space, but according to our modern understanding, this immensity is a requirement for us to be here. Not just that: it looks as if the entire universe has been tuned (shall I say designed?) for the emergence of intelligent life. And these facts have not escaped notice. The evidence of design appeared so striking that cosmologists even gave it a name: the anthropic principle. The initial energy balance of the universe and many other details were so extraordinarily right that it seemed that the universe had been expressly designed to produce intelligent, sentient beings. Such was the original context that led to the anthropic principle.

Later I want to return to the idea of the energy of the universe being so finely balanced, but first I wish to examine two other evidences of design.

Let us consider the complex interaction between the earth's atmosphere and intelligent life on our planet. From what astronomers have deduced about solar evolution, we believe that the sun was perhaps 25% less luminous several billion years ago. Today, if the solar luminosity dropped by 25%, the oceans would freeze solid to the bottom, and it would take a substantial increase beyond the sun's present luminosity to thaw them out again. Life could not have originated on such a frozen globe, so it seems that the earth's surface never suffered such frigid conditions. As it turns out, there is a good reason for this. The earth's early atmosphere, formed from the outgassing of volcanoes, included large amounts of carbon dioxide and water vapour. Such an atmosphere would have produced a strong greenhouse effect, something that has been so much in the news that I hardly have to explain it. It can be understood more readily with a locked car parked in the sun on a hot summer day than with a greenhouse. When you open the car, it is like an oven inside. The glass lets in the photons of visible light from the sun. Hot as the interior of the car may seem, it is quite cool compared to the sun's surface, so the reradiation from inside the car is in the infrared. The glass is quite opaque for those longer wavelengths, and because the radiation cannot get out, the car heats up inside. Similarly, the carbon dioxide and water vapour partially blocked the reradiation from the early earth, raising its surface temperature above the mean freezing point of water.

Over the ages, as the sun's luminosity rose, so did the surface temperature of the earth. Had the atmosphere stayed constant, our planet would now have a runaway greenhouse effect, something like that found on the planet Venus, and the earth's oceans would have boiled away leaving a hot, lifeless globe. How did our atmosphere change over to oxygen just in the nick of time? Apparently the earliest widely successful life-forms on earth were the so-called blue-greens, single-celled prokaryotes, which survive to this day as stromatolites. Evidence for them appears in the pre-Cambrian fossil record of a few billion years ago. In the absence of predators, these algae-like organisms covered the ocean shelves, extracting hydrogen from the water and releasing oxygen to the air. Nothing much seems to have happened for over a billion years. However, about a billion years ago the oxygen content of the atmosphere rose rapidly, and then a series of events, quite possibly interrelated, took place.

- Eukaryotic cells, that is, cells with their genetic information contained within a nucleus, originated. This allowed the invention of sex and the more efficient sharing of genetic material, and hence a more rapid adaptation of life-forms to new environments.
- More complicated organisms breathing oxygen, with its much higher energy yield, developed.
- The excess carbon dioxide was converted into calcite in the structure of these creatures and ultimately into great limestone beds, thus making the atmosphere more transparent in the infrared and thereby preventing the oceans from boiling away in a runaway greenhouse effect as the sun brightened.

The perfect timing of this complex configuration of circumstances is enough to amaze and bewilder many of my friends who look at all this in purely mechanistic terms. Can we not see here the hand of a designer? Just as with the energy balance of the earth and the anthropic principle, the atheists have been obliged to come to terms with this almost miraculous survival of life on earth. In fact, you can now read about the Gaia hypothesis, the connectedness of the physical and biological realms, as if by giving it a name, it becomes a mechanical necessity.

Let me turn to one final example. One of the first scientists to consider how the environment itself made life possible was the Harvard chemist L. J. Henderson. Early in this century, after Darwin's emphasis on the fitness of organisms for their various environments, Henderson wrote a fascinating book titled *The Fitness of the Environment*, which pointed out that the organisms themselves would not exist except for certain properties of matter.[14] He argued for the uniqueness of carbon as the chemical basis of life, and everything we have learned since then, from the nature of the hydrogen bond to the structure of DNA, reinforces his argument. But today it is possible to go still further and to probe the origin of carbon itself, through its synthesis deep inside evolving stars.

I do not intend to give a course in stellar evolution, but I need to sketch briefly how stars spend their lives in order to explain where elements like carbon and oxygen come from. Most of the time stars get their energy by converting hydrogen into helium. But when the available hydrogen has been exhausted, the core of the star pulls together under the irresistible tug of gravity, the temperature increases, and finally the formerly inert helium becomes a fuel, fusing into carbon and later into oxygen. If the star is massive enough, a whole sequence of higher elements will be generated.

Eventually, however, there comes a place in the periodic table where the atoms no longer yield up nuclear energy for powering the star; instead, they demand energy. This happens when the chain has gone about a quarter of the way through the list of elements, approaching the element iron. When the star has burned the atoms to this point, it swiftly falls into bankruptcy, and the star is about to become a supernova. Gravity resumes its inexorable grasp, and within a split second the core of the star collapses, squashing the electrons and protons into a dense sphere of neutrons. On the rebound, the neutrons irradiate the lighter atoms, and in a colossal overshoot, they build up the heavier elements including gold and uranium. From the cosmic debris come the building blocks for future stars and planets, and even for you and me. We are, in a sense, all recycled cosmic wastes, the children of supernovae.

Now back to carbon, the fourth most common element in our galaxy, after hydrogen, helium and oxygen. Carbon is made in the cores of stars long before they reach the supernova stage although it is the later explosion that spews the element back into space

---

14. Lawrence J. Henderson, *The Fitness of the Environment* (New York: Macmillan, 1913).

DILBERT®

By Scott Adams

4|17|99   © 1999 United Feature Syndicate, inc.

Wednesday
APRIL
17

DILBERT®
By Scott Adams

Tuesday
APRIL
16

where it becomes available for a subsequent generation of stars and planets. A carbon nucleus can be made by merging three helium nuclei, but a triple collision is tolerably rare. It would be easier if two helium nuclei would stick together to form beryllium, but beryllium is not very stable. Nevertheless, sometimes before the two helium nuclei can come unstuck, a third helium nucleus strikes home, and a carbon nucleus results. And here the details of the internal energy levels of the carbon nucleus become interesting: it turns out that there is precisely the right resonance within the carbon to help this process along.

Let me digress a bit to remind you about resonance. You have no doubt heard that opera singers such as Enrico Caruso could shatter a wine glass by singing just the right note with enough volume. I do not doubt the story, because in the lectures at our Science Center at Harvard, about half a dozen wine glasses are shattered each year using sound waves. It is necessary to tune the audio generator through the frequency spectrum to just the right note where the glass begins to vibrate — the specific resonance for that particular goblet — and then to turn up the volume so that the glass vibrates more and more violently until it flies apart.

The specific resonances within atomic nuclei are something like that, except in this case the particular energy enables the parts to stick together rather than to fly apart. In the carbon atom, the resonance just happens to match the combined energy of the beryllium atom and a colliding helium nucleus. Without it, there would be relatively few carbon atoms. Similarly, the internal details of the oxygen nucleus play a critical role. Oxygen can be formed by combining helium and carbon nuclei, but the corresponding resonance level in the oxygen nucleus is 0.5% too low for the combination to stay together easily. Had the resonance level in the carbon been 4% lower, there would be essentially no carbon. Had that level in the oxygen been only 0.5% higher, virtually all of the carbon would have been converted to oxygen. Without that carbon abundance, neither you nor I would be here now.

I am told that Fred Hoyle, who together with Willy Fowler found this remarkable nuclear arrangement, has said that nothing has shaken his atheism as much as this discovery. Occasionally Fred Hoyle and I have sat down to discuss one or another astronomical or historical point, but I have never had enough nerve to ask him if his atheism had really been shaken by finding the nuclear resonance structure of carbon and oxygen. However, the answer came rather clearly about a decade ago in the Cal Tech alumni magazine, where he wrote:

> Would you not say to yourself, "Some supercalculating intellect must have designed the properties of the carbon atom, otherwise the chance of my finding such an atom through the blind forces of nature would be utterly minuscule." Of course you would ... A common sense interpretation of the facts suggests that a superintellect has monkeyed with physics, as well as with chemistry and biology, and that there are no blind forces worth speaking about in nature. The numbers one calculates from the facts seem to me so overwhelming as to put this conclusion almost beyond question.[15]

A few years ago I used the carbon and oxygen resonance in a lecture at a university in the American Midwest, and in the question period I was interrogated by a philosopher who wanted to know if I could quantify the argument by Bayesian probabilities. Now I will confess that, at the time, I had not a clue that Bayesian statistics meant evaluating a proposition on the basis of an original probability and new relevant evidence. But even knowing how to handle that would hardly have enabled me to perform a convincing calculation, that is, a probability so overwhelming as to be tantamount to a proof that superintelligent design was involved in the placement of the resonance levels.

Clearly my petitioner was daring me to convince him, despite the fact that I had already proclaimed that arguments from design are in the eyes of the beholder, and simply cannot be construed as proofs to convince sceptics. Furthermore, in posing his question he had already pointed out the quicksands of using numerology to prove the existence of divine order in the cosmos. So now I hasten to dampen any notion that I intended the resonance levels in carbon and oxygen nuclei to demonstrate how to *prove* the existence of God. Even William Paley, with his famous watch and his conclusion that it pointed to the existence of a watchmaker, said:

---

15. Fred Hoyle, "The Universe: Past and Present Reflections" *Engineering and Science* (November, 1981) pp. 8-12, especially p. 12.

> My opinion of Astronomy has always been that it is not the best medium through which to prove the agency of an intelligent creator; but that, this being proved, it shows, beyond all other sciences, the magnificence of his operations.[16]

For me, it is not a matter of proofs and demonstrations, but of making sense of the astonishing cosmic order that the sciences repeatedly reveal. Fred Hoyle and I differ on lots of questions, but on this we agree: a common-sense and satisfying interpretation of our world suggests the designing hand of a superintelligence. Impressive as the evidences of design in the astrophysical world may be, however, I personally find even more remarkable those from the biological realm. As Walt Whitman proclaimed, "A leaf of grass is no less than the journey work of the stars."[17] I would go still farther and assert that stellar evolution is child's play compared to the complexity of DNA in grass or mice. Whitman goes on, musing that:

> The tree toad is a chef-d'oeuvre for the highest,
> And the running blackberry would adorn the parlors of heaven,
> And the narrowest hinge in my hand puts to scorn all machinery,
> And the cow crunching with depress'd head surpasses any statue,
> And a mouse is miracle enough to stagger sextillions of infidels.

Hoyle, by his allusion to biology, seems to agree that the formation of, for example, DNA is so improbable as to require a superintelligence. Such biochemical arguments were popularised about forty years ago by Lecomte du Noüy in his book *Human Destiny*. Du Noüy estimated the probability of forging a 2000-atom protein as something like one part in 10^{321}. He wrote:

> Events which, even when we admit very numerous experiments, reactions, or shakings per second, need an infinitely longer time than the estimated duration of the earth in order to have one chance, on the

---

16. Paley, *op. cit.* chapter 22.
17. Walt Whitman, "Song of Myself" stanza 31, in *Leaves of Grass* (1891-2 edition).

average, to manifest themselves can, it would seem, be considered as impossible in the human sense.[18]

To study the most interesting phenomena, namely Life and eventually Man, we are, therefore, forced to call on anti-chance, as Eddington called it; a "cheater" who systematically violates the laws of large numbers, the statistical laws which deny any individuality to the particles considered.[19]

The game plan for evolutionary theory, however, is to find the accidental, contingent ways in which these unlikely and seemingly impossible events could have taken place. The evolutionists do not seek an automatic scheme — mechanistic in the sense that Newtonian mechanics is determined — but some random pathways whose existence could be at least partially retraced by induction from the fragmentary historical record. But when the working procedure becomes raised to a philosophy of nature, the practitioners begin to place their faith in the roulette of chance and they find du Noüy and Hoyle an aggravation to their assumptions about the meaninglessness of the universe.

Despite the reluctance of many evolutionary theorists such as Ernst Mayr who states that "cosmic teleology must be rejected by science... I do not think there is a modern scientist left who still believes in it",[20] there does seem to be enough evidence of design in the universe to give some pause. In fact, scientists who wish to deny the role of design have taken over the anthropic principle. They have turned the original argument on its head. Rather than accepting that we are here because of a deliberate supernatural design, they claim that the universe simply must be this way *because* we are here; had the universe been otherwise, we would not be here to observe ourselves, and that is that. Such is almost precisely the view enunciated by Stephen Hawking in his inaugural lecture as Lucasian Professor at Cambridge University — an illustrious chair once held by Isaac Newton — and a view of nature

---

18. Lecomte du Noüy, *Human Destiny* (New York: Longmans, Green & Co., 1947) p. 35.
19. *Ibid.* p. 38.
20. Mayr, *op. cit.* p. 131.

repeated by Hawking in his best-selling *A Brief History of Time.*[21]
As I said, I am doubtful that you can convert a sceptic by the
argument of design, and the discussions of the anthropic principle
seem to prove the point.

So this leads back to my central question: is there a role for
natural theology today? If you can convert sceptics, what is its
use? Is it all mere rhetoric? And I would answer, "Of course it
is rhetoric, but rhetoric is not *mere* rhetoric." In the twelfth
century, logic and rhetoric were equally esteemed components of
the medieval curriculum. In some pursuits logic was more suitable,
whereas in others, such as ethics, rhetoric led the way. In the
following century, the time of Thomas Aquinas, logic began to gain
the ascendancy. Today, common opinion places logic on a
pedestal, while "mere rhetoric" is a term of opprobrium.

Actually, surprisingly little in science itself is accepted by
"proof". Let us take Newtonian mechanics as an example. Newton
had no proof that the earth moved, or that the sun was the centre of
the planetary system. Yet, without that assumption, his system did
not make much sense. What he had was an elaborate and highly
successful scheme of both explanation and prediction, and most
people had no trouble believing it, but what they were accepting as
truth was a grand scheme whose validity rested on its coherency,
not on any proof. Thus, when a convincing stellar parallax was
measured in 1838 or when Foucault swung his famous pendulum at
2 am on Wednesday 8 January 1851, these supposed proofs of the
revolution and of the rotation of the earth did not produce a
sudden, newfound acceptance of the heliocentric cosmology. The
battle had long since been won by a persuasiveness that rested not
on proof but on coherency, and what persuaded people of that
coherency was the cogency of the essentially rhetorical arguments
mustered in its favour.

Now if we understand that science's great success has been in
the production of a remarkably coherent view of nature rather than
in an intricately dovetailed set of proofs, then I would argue that
a belief in design can also have a legitimate place in human
understanding even if it falls short of proof. What is needed is a

21. Stephen Hawking, *A Brief History of Time* (New York: Bantam Books,
1988) p. 125.

consistent and coherent worldview and, at least for some of us, the universe is easier to comprehend if we assume that it has both purpose and design.

Just as I would try to persuade you that the awesome details of the natural world make more sense and have more coherence in a theistic framework, there are those who polish their rhetoric to make the contrary case, as Dawkins puts it, to allow atheists to be intellectually fulfilled.[22] Dawkins gives a lively and articulate defence of natural selection as the agent that has very gradually led to sentient, questioning beings. When I saw the subtitle of his book, *Why the evidence of evolution reveals a universe without design*, I guessed quite wrongly that he introduced some empirical evidence against the role of design. He might, as Darwin frequently did, have defended the notion of imperfect design, or he might have argued from the stupefying percentage of species that have gone extinct, that if a designer was at work, he was at best clumsy and inefficient. But no, Dawkins seems to feel that by defending the view that a mechanistic process could have brought about humankind, his case against design had been made. But we can look at the same data and come to opposite conclusions. He is no more able to *prove* the non-existence of a Creator than I, by arguments from design, can prove the existence of a super-intelligent Designer and Creator. It is as if people from a far different age or culture were to hear what they might take as a cacophony of sounds, but to us that same onrush of notes would be a Mozart symphony. We hear the same notes, but come to opposing interpretations. I would like to think that hearing the sounds as a Mozart symphony is closer to reality. With respect to natural theology, it is not a tight logical deduction but, in Pascal's memorable words, "the heart has its reasons that reason does not know".[23]

I, having made the leap of faith, find the arguments from design very illuminating; nevertheless, there are two issues worth facing before giving even a qualified endorsement to a modern-day natural theology. On the one hand, there has been a persistent

---

22. Dawkins, *op. cit.* p. 6.
23. Blaise Pascal, *Pensées* in *Great Books of the Western World* 33 (Chicago: Encyclopedia Britannica, 1952) p. 222.

criticism that arguments from design will cause scientific investigators of Christian persuasion to give up too easily. If the resonance levels of carbon and oxygen are seen as a miracle of creation, would a Christian physicist try to understand more deeply why, from the mechanistic view of physics, the levels are that particular way and not in some other configuration? Might it not be potentially detrimental to the faith to explain a miracle? On the other hand, what if the scientific explanation changes, and an argument suddenly loses its efficacy? Is faith now undermined?

Consider once more the design of the Big Bang, the observation that the universe seems so closely balanced between too much and too little energy of expansion. During the past decade this narrow balance has been the focus of ever greater attention, and cosmologists versed in the intricacies of the general theory of relativity found that the situation was more acute than they had earlier imagined. If the universe has too little energy to expand forever, its global geometry corresponds to what mathematicians call Riemannian or spherical space. If it has an excess, the global geometry is called Lobachevskian or hyperbolic space, and if it hangs in the balance in between, the familiar Euclidian geometry holds and the space is referred to as flat even though the universe has more than two dimensions. The wonderful discovery was that in the very earliest stages of the expansion, the universe had to be incredibly flat to maintain its present near-flatness. Even a tiny departure one way or the other would cause a runaway situation that would bend the space one way or the other. And — hold your breath — the flatness required was one part in 10^{60}, that is, one followed by sixty zeros. To the cosmologists, this looked like more than just good luck or a superintelligent designer who tuned the universe this way. It seemed that some fundamental property *required* the universe to be this way. I will not go into the splendid scenario called inflation that was schemed up to make this happen. It would derail us to consider its technical aspects or some of its fascinating ramifications, such as the fact that this theory cannot be empirically demonstrated and simply must be believed because of its beauty. But in a sense it punctures the notion of a Creator who, with a kind of cosmic roulette, picks just the right starting conditions to enable us to arrive on the scene. Of course, it can make us turn in awe at a Designer who built the inflationary epoch into the plans for creation, and perhaps all we have to worry about is whether, in fact, the Designer had a choice in the matter.

If natural theology is mistakenly viewed as a source of proof for the divine in the universe, then inevitable changes in scientific ideas pose a serious threat. However, if natural theology deals with hints and coherencies, not proofs and forced convictions, then I think it is on safe and reasonable ground. But what about the other criticism, that belief in design could deter investigators from pushing their inquiries to the limit? In other words, dare a scientist believe in design?

There is, I shall argue, no contradiction between holding a staunch belief in supernatural design and being a creative scientist, and perhaps no one illustrates this point better than the seventeenth-century astronomer Johannes Kepler. He was one of the most creative astronomers of all time, a man who played a major role in bringing about the acceptance of the Copernican system through the efficacy of his tables of planetary motion.

Now one of the principal reasons Kepler was a Copernican arose from his deeply held belief that the sun-centred arrangement reflected the divine design of the cosmos: the sun at the centre was the image of God, the outer surface of the star-studded heavenly sphere was the image of Christ, and the intermediate planetary space represented the Holy Spirit. These were not ephemeral notions of his student years, but a constant obsession that inspired and drove him through his entire life.

Today Kepler is best remembered for his discovery of the elliptical form of the planets' orbits. This discovery and another, the so-called law of areas, are chronicled in his *Astronomia nova*, truly the New Astronomy. In its introduction he defended his Copernicanism from the point of view that the heavens declare the glory of God:

> I implore my reader not to forget the divine goodness conferred on mankind, and which the psalmist urges him especially to consider. When he has returned from church and entered on the study of astronomy, may he praise and glorify the wisdom and greatness of the Creator ... Let him not only extol the bounty of God in the preservation of living creatures of all kinds by the strength and stability of the earth, but also let him acknowledge the wisdom of the Creator in its motion, so abstruse, so admirable.

If someone is so dumb that he cannot grasp the science of astronomy, or so weak that he cannot believe Copernicus without offending his piety, I advise him to mind his own business, to quit this worldly pursuit, to stay at home and cultivate his own garden, and when he turns his eyes toward the visible heavens, (the only way he sees them), let him with his whole heart pour forth praise and gratitude to God the Creator. Let him assure himself that he is serving God no less than the astronomer to whom God has granted the privilege of seeing more clearly with the eyes of the mind.[24]

A detailed study of Kepler's life reveals an evolution of ideas on a number of topics, such as whether planets have "souls" that guide them. He had grown up in an age when philosophers still attributed heavenly motions in part to the individual intelligences of the planets, and, in his first, youthful treatise, he endorsed the idea of animate souls as moving intelligences of the planets. But by the time of his mature work he could flatly state that "I deny that celestial movements are the work of Mind". However, on his views of God as a geometer and of a universe filled with God's geometrical designs, Kepler was unwavering.

Kepler's life and works provide central evidence that an individual can be both a creative scientist and a believer in divine design in the universe, and that indeed the very motivation for the scientific research can stem from a desire to trace God's handiwork. As you might guess, my admiration for Kepler is almost unbounded!

In reflecting on these questions I have attempted, in a somewhat guarded way, to delineate a place for design both in the world of science and in the world of theology. As Kepler once said of astrology, the stars impel, but they do not compel.[25] There is persuasion here, but no proof. However, even in the hands of secular philosophers the modern mythologies of the heavens, and the beginnings and endings implied in the Big Bang, give hints of ultimate realities beyond the universe itself. Milton Munitz, in his

---

24. Slightly abridged and modified from my translation in *Great Ideas Today 1983* (Chicago: Encyclopedia Britannica, 1983) pp. 321-22.
25. Kepler elaborates this idea in book IV, chapter 7 of his *Harmonice mundi* (1619).

closely argued book *Cosmic Understanding*,[26] declares that our cosmology leads logically to the idea of a transcendence beyond time and space, giving the lie to the notion that the cosmos is all there is, or was, or ever will be.

Munitz, in coming to the concept of transcendence, describes it as unknowable, which is somewhat paradoxical, since if the transcendence is unknowable then we cannot know that it is unknowable. Could the unknowable have revealed itself? Logic is defied by the idea that the unknowable might have communicated to us, but coherence is not. For me, it makes sense to suppose that the superintelligence, the transcendence, the ground of being in Paul Tillich's formulation, has revealed itself through prophets in all ages, and supremely in the life of Jesus Christ.

To believe this requires the acceptance of teleology and purpose. But I think that the philosophers might rightfully point out that purpose transcends design, that is, there can be purpose without design; God could work God's purposes even in a universe without apparent design, or with designs beyond our finite comprehension. It would be possible to be a theist and a Christian even in the absence of observed design.

Nevertheless, just as I believe that the Book of Scripture illumines the pathway to God, so I believe that the Book of Nature, with its astonishing details — the blade of grass, the *Conus geographus* (with its lethal harpoon), or the resonance levels of the carbon atom — also suggests a God of purpose and a God of design. And I think my belief makes me no less a scientist.

To conclude, I turn once again to Kepler who wrote:

> If I have been allured into brashness by the wonderful beauty of thy works, or if I have loved my own glory among men while advancing in work destined for thy glory, gently and mercifully pardon me: and finally, deign graciously to cause that these demonstrations may lead to thy glory and to the salvation of souls, and nowhere be an obstacle to that. Amen.

---

26. Milton K. Munitz, *Cosmic Understanding: Philosophy and Science of the Universe* (Princeton University Press, 1986).

Response by Stephen May

On the rear cover of my copy of Richard Dawkins' book *The Blind Watchmaker* the blurb runs: "A brilliant and controversial book which demonstrates that evolution by natural selection — the unconscious, automatic, blind, yet essentially non-random process discovered by Darwin — is the only answer to the biggest question of all: Why do we exist?"[1]

It has been said, "Of that of which one cannot speak, one must remain silent."[2] This applies to physicists and biologists who confuse different kinds of questions, physics with metaphysics, the nature of the universe with its transcendental origin, and perhaps the way systems work with their purpose. It applies no less to theologians whose knowledge of biology remains extremely thin after forty years of life on this planet — and whose inclinations have always lain more in the direction of astrophysics. Accordingly, I was delighted to be invited to respond to Owen Gingerich, a noted *astronomer*! If I am rather overawed to be discussing the details of the first three minutes of the universe's life, let alone what lay beyond the apparently accepted epistemological limit of 10^{-43} second, then it is with even more trepidation that I come to discuss the mechanics of natural selection.[3]

I am grateful for the lucidity and simplicity with which Gingerich makes his argument. I see this as a model of communication in any field whatsoever quite apart from that of a scientific one which has, perhaps somewhat unfairly, been regarded as being somewhat incomprehensible and inaccessible to lay people. The clarity of his

1. Richard Dawkins, *The Blind Watchmaker* (London: Penguin, 1986).
2. Ludwig Wittgenstein, *Tractatus Logico-Philosophicus* 7. I am somewhat misusing Wittgenstein here, to mean rather "that of which one is not qualified to speak, one *ought* to remain silent"!
3. Willem B. Drees, "Quantum cosmologies and the 'Beginning'" *Zygon* 26:3 (September 1991) pp. 373-396, 374, on the epistemological limit of Planck time.

argument reminds me of that of C. S. Lewis, surely a model to be emulated anywhere in terms of Christian communication.

I have very few arguments with the general drift of Gingerich's paper. My comments will be more directed, therefore, to elaboration of some of the themes he raises, as well as a few question marks to others that he mentions. I am pleased, for example, that his basic response to the question "Is there a role for natural theology today?" seems to be "maybe". That is, it is not seen as an independent discipline in its own right persuading by its own logic but something that indeed is transparent to the eyes of faith. I myself think that Christians are in some danger if they start looking at particular scientific discoveries as substantiating their own positions at a merely neutral or dispassionate objective level of debate. However, I do not particularly wish to engage in this discussion — it is discussed elsewhere in this book at greater length.

I think here of what C. S. Lewis wrote in a 1958 paper and originally entitled "Shall we lose God in outer space?" This paper was subsequently republished under the title "Religion and Rocketry". Lewis writes that during his time he had heard two quite different arguments against his religion put forward in the name of science. First, when he was a youngster:

> People used to say that the universe was not only not friendly to life but positively hostile to it. Life had appeared on this planet by a millionth chance as if at one point there had been a breakdown of the elaborate defences generally enforced against it. We should be rash to assume that the leak had occurred more than once. Which just showed the absurdity of the Christian idea that there was a Creator who was interested in living creatures.[4]

Lewis then goes on to explain the alternative point of view, generally the more popular one, both in his latter days and in ours. According to this, everybody seems to have decided the universe is probably

> quite well provided with habitable globes and with livestock to inhabit them. Which just showed equally well the absurdity of

---

4.   See C. S. Lewis, *Fern-seed and Elephants* (Glasgow: Fontana/Collins, 1975) pp. 86-95. The extracts are from pp. 86-87.

Christianity with its parochial idea that humanity could be important to God ... Each new discovery, even every new theory, is held at first to have the most wide reaching theological and philosophical consequences. It is seized by unbelievers as the basis for a new attack on Christianity; it is often and more embarrassingly, seized by injudicious believers as the basis for a new defence.

Lewis' argument is that when the popular hubbub has subsided and the novelty has been chewed over by theologians, scientists and philosophers, "both sides find themselves pretty much where they were before".

I say this in no way to minimise the discoveries that are brought to us. I am reminded of the name of a new journal which has been set up in association with the Templeton Foundation and dedicated to what is called Humility Theology.[5] When I first saw this title I thought it a rather strange one in connection with science but it is, of course, quite right. As Karl Barth wrote in a rather different context about the subject of theology, those who have ceased to find themselves amazed in wonder at their topic have lost it altogether.[6]

As an adolescent, I remember going out into the garden of my home in Britain, having just read C. S. Lewis' novel *Perelandra,* which is about life on the planet Venus. I gazed up at the starry sky, overwhelmed by the glory of the heavens, thinking how, seeing this, could anyone not believe in God? Subsequently, I uttered this statement to a hardened atheist who seemed less than wholly impressed. I would now no longer state the remark quite like this, any more than I would use any other of the classical arguments for

---

5. John M. Templeton, *The Humble Approach: Scientists Discover God* (London: Collins, 1981). The journal is called *Progress in Theology.*
6. Karl Barth, *Evangelical Theology: An Introduction,* Grover Foley, translator (Glasgow: Collins/Fontana, 1963) pp. 61-62. Barth differentiates theological from scientific wonder, arguing that the former alone is perpetually starting again at the beginning, and thus is forever surprised. Nevertheless, he writes that "it has been justly said that ... Socratic amazement is the root of all true science" (p. 62). Einstein wrote that science was based on an "awe" before a mystery we would never understand. From *Out of My Later Years,* p. 60, quoted in T. F. Torrance, *Theological Science* (London: Oxford University Press, 1969) p. 184.

the existence of God. However, I do believe that they quite properly do make part of an overall pattern of understanding the universe.

This is how I see Gingerich's plea for coherence — as a major sign of the truth of a vision. Indeed, I think Christianity proposes a coherent and convincing picture of the universe. Rather than being scared at the discoveries of science, we should see these as new ways in which God leads us into the fullness of truth. Moreover, they themselves are part of that convincing Christian vision of the cosmos. This vision is not only moral and aesthetic, it is scientific as well. Science does not pose a threat to faith but an opportunity to expand its understanding.[7]

I am glad that Gingerich did not, however, see these extraordinary apparent evidences of design in the cosmos as knockdown arguments. For one thing, as he points out, subsequent discovery might unveil rational scientific reasons for what seems at present an extraordinarily unlikely coincidence of events. I think here of what is being touted in some quarters as "complexity theory" according to which the most incredibly sophisticated systems can appear to be spontaneously self-organising.[8] One might again look at Darwin's theory of evolution and the way in which it is argued to explain, according to various principles following the laws of natural selection, what we might otherwise regard as highly improbable according to mere chance. The danger of such an approach is that perpetually threatening any kind of God-of-the-gaps approach.

Alternatively, one cannot minimise the desire on the behalf of non-Christians to find any evidence or theory to suit their own views either. Some are more up front about this procedure than others. Steven Weinberg in his book *The First Three Minutes* roundly declares that "some cosmologists are philosophically attracted to the oscillating cosmological model, especially because, like the steady

---

7. "Religion without science is blind. Science without religion is lame" — Albert Einstein, *Ideas and Opinions* (Souvenir Press, 1973) p. 55. John Polkinghorne suggests an improvement in his *Science and Creation: the Search for Understanding* (London: SPCK, 1988) pp. 97-98.

8. Michael D. Lemonick, "Life, the universe and everything" *Time* (22 February 1993) pp. 42-43. This seems to be a development of chaos theory.

state, it mostly avoids the problem of genesis".[9] One wonders at times of people such as Stephen Hawking with his famous comments regarding cosmogenesis in *A Brief History of Time*,[10] as well as all those devisors of ten-dimensional vacuums which translate themselves automatically into existence, whether they too are strongly affected by those presuppositions. The notion that the reason why there is "something rather than nothing" is because "nothing is unstable", is a beautiful way of appearing to ridicule the whole classical Christian notion of *creatio ex nihilo*. There is no need for creation — as the universe, according to certain mathematical laws, can translate *itself* into existence.[11]

The extent to which Steven Weinberg's own philosophical predispositions affect his vision are shown in the concluding pages of his book:

> It is very hard to realise that our world is just a tiny part of an overwhelmingly hostile universe ... The effort to understand the universe is one of the very few things that lifts human life a little above the level of farce and gives it some of the grace of tragedy.[12]

I would like to use this quotation as a way of transferring to another part of my response. I would like to recall some astronomical predecessors of Gingerich's in the United States. There is actually some dispute in the sources here about who had

9. Steven Weinberg, *The First Three Minutes: A Modern View of the Origin of the Universe* (Glasgow: Fontana, 1978) p. 148. This point is also made by Stanley L. Jaki in his *Cosmos and Creator* (Edinburgh: Scottish Academic Press, 1980) pp. 21-25.

10. Stephen Hawking, *A Brief History of Time* (London: Bantam, 1988) pp. 122 ff., 175; also the inflammatory remarks of Carl Sagan in the Introduction that it is "a book about God ... or perhaps about the absence of God ... (because there was) nothing for a Creator to do" (p. x). See also the review by M. W. Poole in *Science and Christian Belief* 2:1 (April 1990) pp. 66-67.

11. This is a popular modern notion. See Sten F. Odenwald, "A modern look at the origin of the universe" *Zygon* 25:1 (March 1990) pp. 25-44; here p. 35 quoting Frank Wilczyk in J. S. Trefil, *The Moment of Creation: Big Bang Physics from before the First Millisecond to the Present Universe* (New York: Scribner's, 1983) p. 206.

12. *Op. cit.* p. 149.

the honour of the first discovery. According to one version it
was a Professor Farrell of Mt. Jennings Observatory, Chicago,
according to another it was a Professor Harold Pierson of Princeton
Observatory. Unfortunately for the sake of continuity with
Gingerich's own posts at Harvard and the Smithsonian Institute, it
was not averred of either of those places.[13] The date was the 31
October 1938. According to both my sources, on this date in the
early evening, the aforementioned gentlemen observed incandescent
gas explosions occurring at regular intervals on the surface of the
planet Mars. At this point perhaps you have picked up the fact that
these predecessors of Professor Gingerich are merely fictional. I am
referring to the famous 1938 broadcast by Orson Welles' Mercury
Theatre group of H. G. Wells' *The War of the Worlds*. These
observations are the prelude to the invasion of earth by the Martians.
The gas explosions mark the propulsion of invading Martian
cylinders from huge guns. What, you may ask, does all this have to
do with an esteemed, and highly prestigious, theology and science
conference? (Quite apart from a particular astronomical observation
reference.) The answer I would like to suggest is the particular
vision of the cosmos and the place that humans have within it that is
shown in this particular work.

   In H. G. Wells' original 1898 version the first Martian cylinder
falls on Horsell Common near Woking; Orson Welles' version
commenced in Grover's Mill, New Jersey and this time it is not
London that is evacuated but New York. The broadcast is notorious
as having caused thousands of people to flee in panic from the
threatened area whilst others took to the fields with shotguns to
valiantly resist the invading Martians — thus endangering the local
chicken population ... According to the reports, millions huddled
round their radio sets in terror. There were broken legs, mis-

---

13. The film reconstruction, *The Night that Panicked America,* concentrates
    upon Pierson who was played by Orson Welles himself. The original CBS
    radio broadcast (extracts from which were used in a BBC programme, *The
    Shadow Knows: the Sound of Orson Welles)* attributes the first to the
    Jennings Observatory. The film version mentions a Professor Maurice of
    McGill University, Toronto as supporting the observations. The occasion
    of the broadcast was Hallowe'en Eve. Many believed the play to be real
    throughout despite repeated announcements to the contrary.

carriages and a narrowly-averted attempted suicide.[14] After the event of the radio broadcast, which was delivered with extraordinary verisimilitude — including radio broadcasts interrupting dance music and so forth — Orson Welles apologised profusely saying that panic had certainly not been part of his original intention. Later in his life he admitted that this apology had not been wholly sincere ... H. G. Wells' *War of the Worlds* has had an active life. There have been many subsequent versions including the George Pal film of 1953 and, more recently, the Geoff Wayne rock musical.[15] The *War of the Worlds* has become a hoary literary ancestor to hundreds of almost always inferior alien contact and invasion stories. I want to argue, however, that the themes which it expresses resonate deeply in the minds of contemporary humanity.

One commentator describes these themes as a combination of the Pascalian fear of the void, on the one hand, and Darwinian evolution on the other.[16] Another ponders upon the novel's evocation of a Huxleyan cosmic pessimism[17] and it is described by yet another as a Darwinian fable.[18] Briefly, the plot involves the elderly race of

---

14. I. F. Clarke, *Voices Prophesying War: Future Wars, 1763-3749*, second edition (Oxford University Press, 1992) pp. 86-87. A social science team was set up to study the panic. Barbara Leaming in her *Orson Welles* (London: Weidenfeld and Nicholson, 1985) pp. 159-63 attributes much of the effect of the broadcast, written by Welles and Howard Koch, to the former's originality and flair.

15. Narrated by Richard Burton, this CBS double album has a distinguished cast and some effective dramatic music, highlighting in particular the remorseless will of the invaders, their intellects "vast and cool and unsympathetic". In most respects, it is a strikingly faithful and powerful version of the 1898 original which was published by William Heinemann (quotations here from the London Pan version of 1975). Mark Hillegas in his *The Future as Nightmare: H.G. Wells and the Anti-Utopians* (Carbondale and Edwardsville: Southern Illinois University Press, 1967) p. 23, comments that in the 1890s popular interest in Mars as the abode of life was, because of Schiaparelli's earlier discovery of the "canals", so intense that it "amounted to a mania".

16. Mark Rose, *Alien Encounters: Anatomy of Science Fiction* (Cambridge: Harvard University Press, 1981) pp. 69-71.

17. Hillegas, *op. cit.* p. 24.

18. Rose, *op. cit.* p. 69. See also Clarke, *op. cit.* p. 84, and B. Stableford, *Scientific Romance in Britain, 1890-1950* (London: Fourth Estate, 1985) p. 63. Wells makes this even clearer by comparing the Martian colonisation

Martians who evolved into near-bodiless brains and are dying on the planet Mars. They observe Earth and decide to take it over so that they may survive on the more youthful planet. Wells is at pains to contrast the fate that stands over humanity with the complacent way in which it moves about what he describes as "its petty affairs". The cylinders are shot from guns on Mars and land around London. Rapidly the Martian invaders overwhelm the surrounding area, destroying anything that resists them with a heat ray and killing black smoke. The Martian Red Weed then begins to take over the planet rapidly as well. It is the beginning of the end of humanity. However, in the end the Martians are slain, not by resisting earth people, but by bacteria. This is the signal for a thousand stories in which invading aliens succumb to the common cold.

Wells has a number of different themes in this work. One of them that also appears in several of his early works is:

> The terrible fragility of civilisation, of all that we consider humane, when seen in the larger context of such brutal natural forces as the evolutionary process.[19]

Here it is not accidental that the Martians with their enormous brains bear an astonishing similarity to the hero's own vision of humanity in the year one million. Humanity, according to this model, will develop into the very alien race that is here destroying it.[20] Again we see an enormous contrast between the insignificance of humanity and the hugeness of the universe. As has been pointed out, Wells transfers to the Martians the physical attributes often attributed to the physical cosmos: vastness, coldness, indif-

---

of the Earth to the European extermination of the Tasmanians as one of humanity's "own inferior races" (*The War of the Worlds* p. 11).

19. Rose, *op. cit.* p. 69.
20. Rose, *op. cit.* p. 76; Wells, *op. cit.* p. 135. Their hypertrophied brains and atrophied bodies are evolutionary adaptions, except with the result that, "without the body the brain would, of course, become a mere selfish intelligence, without any of the emotional substratum of the human being" (p. 136). Rose contends that the metaphorical point made here is a "moral one in which the Martians represent the eternal danger of cold reason divorced from human being" (p. 76). They are, as it were, proto-Daleks!

ference.[21] However, just as the Martians act to reduce humanity to insignificance, so too are they themselves relativised by bacteria. At the very beginning of the book Wells writes of the Martians' own observations:

> as men busied themselves about their affairs they were scrutinised and studied, perhaps almost as narrowly as a man with a microscope might scrutinise the transient creatures that swarm and multiply in a drop of water. With infinite complacency men went to and fro over this globe about their little affairs, serene in their assurance of their empire over matter. It is possible that the infusoria under the microscope do the same.[22]

Yet it is the same bacteria that are the nemesis of the Martians. The human tragedy is actually turned into the tragedy of the Martians. There is an extraordinary passage in the chapter called Dead London, the very climax of the book, in which the last Martian is heard by the hero as he succumbs to his conqueror. The Martian has been wailing "Ulla, ulla, ulla!". But, as the cry ceases, the narrator states directly that the wailing represented a kind of companionship. "By virtue of it London had still seemed alive and the sense of life about me had upheld me."[23] He is now overwhelmed by sheer desolation. The Martians, alien, incomprehensible, remorseless, indifferent as they are (and as superior to humanity "as [human minds] are to the beasts that perish"[24]), are a precious oasis of life in the universe. They too are wiped out — by bacteria. And bacteria itself is a form of life, but one that is even then dwarfed by the vastness of space.

Throughout the work Wells highlights the inconsequentiality of humanity and the irrelevance of its view that it is itself important. In pursuit of this aim, the provincial curate "whose inability to transcend his inappropriate religious conceptions results in madness" is a significant figure. Mark Rose comments:

---

21. *Ibid.* p. 71.
22. *Ibid.* p. 79.
23. *Ibid.* p. 178.
24. *Ibid.* p. 9.

limited in our understanding of things by the pettiness of our lives, we all find it difficult to come to grips with a truly indifferent universe; one neither arranged on a human model nor constructed on a human scale.[25]

This extraordinarily rich work is open to more interpretations than I have mentioned.[26] Why I discuss it here is in relation to the themes of the paper. These I see as concerning the significance of humanity in the universe. What Wells portrays is in its way a convincing and persuasive vision. It is one that perhaps has a greater hold over minds now than ever before. It is one to which ideas of the anthropic principle justly give pause.

Gingerich ends his paper with a quotation from Kepler. It is ironic, perhaps, that Wells at the start of his most opposite work begins with a quotation also from Kepler: "But who shall dwell in these worlds if they be inhabited? Are we, or they Lords of the world? And how are all things made for men?"[27]

The scope of Gingerich's paper is truly enormous, genuinely exciting and thought provoking. I have chosen merely to concentrate on one or two particular themes. I have written here about the notion of coherence and a persuasive vision. I believe indeed that, as Christian apologists, we can do nothing more than present our vision of the world, believing in the persuasive power of the Holy Spirit.

Yet there are other visions around. There is the rationalist, scientistic vision still given expression by people such as Carl Sagan. I am glad that Gingerich has a proposal to produce a Christian alternative to Carl Sagan's *Cosmos* series.[28] I salute this enterprise and wish it well. That this scientism is still prevalent is

---

25. *Ibid.* p. 75.
26. Rose, for example, argues that we could consider the Martians as "a metaphorical projection of the capitalistic industrial system of the late nineteenth century, here conceived as a social machine created by a ruthless economic reason that sucks the lifeblood out of human beings" (*op. cit.* p. 76). I.F. Clarke, *op. cit.* pp. 84-85 emphasises the themes of colonisation and technological advances in warfare. Most commentators highlight the contemporary fears of invasion from Germany, both in 1898 and 1938.
27. *Op. cit.* p. 8. Wells attributes this to *The Anatomy of Melancholy*.
28. "Space, time and beyond: the place of God in the cosmos", Valparaiso University, 12 October 1992.

very clear. An episode of the vastly popular *Star Trek: the Next Generation* televised in New Zealand some six months ago and entitled "Who watches the Watchers?" gave expression to this very vision to an extraordinary degree. Here the captain of the Starship Enterprise was taken as a god, the Overseer, by the unfortunate, benighted inhabitants of one particular planet and he had to spend a good deal of time convincing them that this view was erroneous. Belief in supernatural beings was described as "cultural contamination". It was something that they were described as having previously outgrown along with believing "that the stars controlled their fate or the spirits of the dead hound the living".[29]

On the one hand that kind of scientistic rationalism is still prevalent. On the other, we have the ravages of post-modernism. Here I want to raise a question about Gingerich's stress on coherence. It is unexceptionable, I think, in what he has written in this book but in some of his previous publications, I was a little concerned in *case* the model of coherence which he was presenting as a way in to understanding truth could be seen as a denial of correspondence. I feared lest his emphasis on scientific models rather than truth might give hostages to fortune at this point.[30] Post-

---

29. The writers of this episode, Richard Manning and Hans Beimler, give every appearance of being wholly unaware of the irony in this statement (episode 152, aired in the USA during the week of 16 October 1989). As in the original *Star Trek* series, though more noticeably here, there is no chaplain on board ship, only a doctor who serves the same pastoral role - in the new series with the aid of a New Age counsellor and a sympathetic alien who runs the bar. All these caring roles are played by women. In 1993 the men still have the more energetic, cerebral roles. This episode seems wholly compatible with the philosophy of the creator of *Star Trek,* Gene Roddenberry (see interview in *Starlog* 100, November 1985, pp. 18-20). By contrast some of the *Star Trek* actors are theists, for example, Leonard Nimoy, *I am not Spock* (New York: Ballantine, 1975) pp. 107, 115. The famous Vulcan salute is based on an Orthodox Jewish blessing, shaped from the Hebrew letter *Shin*, standing for *Shaddai*, "Almighty".

30. For example, in "Let there be light: Modern cosmogony and biblical creation" in *Is God a Creationist?: the Religious Case Against Creation-Science,* R.M. Frye, editor (New York: Scribner's, 1983) pp. 119-137. "It is an interlocked and coherent picture, a most workable explanation, but it is not ultimate truth ... All of science is in a sense hypothetical. But the tapestry is all of a piece, and it cannot be shredded easily ... it is the coherency of the picture and the systematic procedures for getting there - not

modernism, in its own way, is quite keen on coherence but a
coherence that is of a self-enclosed world that does not bear a
relationship to any external truth, to any world "out there". Post-
modernists are fond of quoting Wittgenstein's language games in
this regard. I wonder at times which is the greater danger or enemy
— if one can speak in such militaristic ways: scientistic rationalism
or post-modernism? Perhaps they are merely opposite sides of the
same coin.

The post-modernist vision in its own way has popular adherence
and influence. To pursue the model of science fiction here as
indicative of this cultural presence one can refer to the popular works
of, for example, Douglas Adams in his *Hitchhiker's Guide to the
Galaxy* or Terry Pratchett. In one of the latter's most recent works,
Lords and Ladies (1992), one of his central characters is a Reader in
Invisible Writings at the Unseen University. Pratchett's Discworld
novels are set on a flat circular world resting on the backs of four
elephants which themselves stand on a great turtle swimming
through space. On this world it is not science but magic that works.
The Reader in Invisible Writings is a young wizard in the High
Energy Magic research building who speaks learnedly of rubber
sheets with weights on them, wormholes, parallel universes,
"accidentally ripping the fabric of reality", the multiverse and the
Discworld equivalent of quarks.[31] In a footnote this particular issue
is explained to us:

---

the final truth - that science is all about" (pp. 132-133). Yet elsewhere
Gingerich rightly criticises, I think, the creationists for trying to have
evolution presented in biology textbooks as a mere hypothesis. He writes
that this was "precisely the tactic the Inquisition adopted with Copernicus'
book: they made it acceptable by making it appear hypothetical. I expect the
creationists will have as much success as the Holy Congregation of the
Index did". See "The Galileo affair" *Scientific American* 246 (August,
1982) pp. 118-127. I do not think it necessary to believe that we have
access to ultimate truth to believe we genuinely speak truly in science. I do
not see coherence as contrary to correspondence but a strong pointer to it.

31. Terry Pratchett, *Lords and Ladies* (London: Victor Gollancz, 1992) pp. 40-
41, 62, 50-51. Pratchett has now written fourteen Discworld novels, all of
them bestsellers.

the *thaum*, hitherto believed to be the smallest possible particle of magic had been successfully demonstrated to be made up of 'resons' or reality fragments (literally, 'thingies'). These themselves have five flavours known as up, down, sideways, sex appeal and peppermint.[32]

Quantum is a star here. As Pratchett writes significantly at one point: "everybody may be right all at the same time, that's the thing about quantum".[33]

I refer to this book to show the way in which it seems to me certain strongly subjectivist, relativist and indeed absurdist conclusions *are* popularly drawn from the world of quantum mechanics. The multiple-worlds interpretation so beloved of nontheists is another major player in this book. Ultimately, it seems to me that if one strongly desires not to believe in God one will find any kind of ingenious reason not to. The multiple–worlds interpretation certainly seems considerably further fetched than a merely theistic explanation. And yet we cannot logically prove that it is wrong. One might extrapolate from Hume here to argue along the following lines: the reason the universe looks as if it has been designed is because *if* we existed in a universe which had arisen by chance to this level of complexity then it *would* look as if it were designed, wouldn't it?[34]

Finally let me return to the work of Douglas Adams yet again. He is famous for having given the ultimate answer to "life, the universe and everything" as 42.[35] It is not so well known that in a later work of his this question — the meaning of life, the universe and everything — is formulated more precisely as: "what is six multiplied by nine?"[36] The discrepancy between this question and

32. *Ibid.* p. 97.
33. *Ibid.* p. 109. My point here is that Pratchett reveals the popular understanding of quantum mechanics, that it opens the door to belief in absolutely anything.
34. David Hume, *Dialogues on Religion.* (1779) in *Hume's Dialogues concerning Natural Religion* Norman Kemp, editor (Oxford: The Clarendon Press, 1935).
35. Douglas Adams, *The Hitch-Hiker's Guide to the Galaxy* (London: Pan, 1979) p. 135.
36. Douglas Adams, *The Restaurant at the End of the Universe* (London: Pan, 1980) p. 184. See also the prologue to this book: "There is a theory which

the answer 42 summarises Adams' view of the universe. At the beginning of this paper I quoted C. S. Lewis as he answered accusations that the Christian view was absurd. Here we have a glorying in the absurd that comes from the denial of God. Yet this absurdist conclusion seems to accompany a certain rationalism. In another of Adams' works, *The Restaurant at the End of the Universe*, one of his heroes is put into a torture machine designed to reduce any victim to gibbering imbecility. This is known as the total perspective vortex. Adams writes:

> When you are put into the vortex you are given just one momentary glimpse of the entire unimaginable infinity of creation and somewhere in it a tiny little marker, a microscopic dot on a microscopic dot, which says "you are here".

His conclusion is that the one thing human beings cannot afford is a sense of proportion.[37] Part of C. S. Lewis' retort to this is to argue that human beings are inveterate poets. They automatically turn enormous variations in size into a qualitative as well as a quantitative difference. He considers this as illogical as regarding somebody five feet high as having more value than somebody three-and-a-half feet high. The same principle applies. He argues that it is indeed ourselves who impute to the universe this awesome quality. "The silence of the eternal spaces terrified Pascal, but it was the greatness of Pascal that enabled them to do so."[38]

---

states that if ever anyone discovers exactly what the Universe is for and why it is here, it will instantly disappear and be replaced by something even more bizarre and inexplicable." On turning over the page, one reads: "There is another theory that states that this has already happened."

37. *Ibid.* pp. 59, 64.
38. "Dogma and the Universe" (1943), republished in *God in the Dock* (Glasgow: Collins/Fontana, 1979) p. 31. The quotation is from Pascal's *Pensées* 206; however the whole argument is central to Pascal's thought of humanity balanced between the enormities of scale in both directions. See also the excellent chapter on Pascal by John Cruickshank in a book edited by him, *French Literature and its Background: Book 2 - the 17th Century* (Oxford University Press, 1969) pp. 50-65, especially p. 60. Cruickshank quotes Sir Arthur Eddington: "In the case of our human friends we take their existence for granted, not caring whether it is proven or not. Our relationship is such that we could read philosophical arguments designed to

What we are discussing here is the relationship of humanity to the cosmos and the place of God and the doctrine of creation in all this as well. H. G. Wells emphasises the sheer loneliness of planets in the observer's telescope compared to the vast empty black spaces that surround this spot of life. "Few people realise the immensity of vacancy in which the dust of the material universe swims."[39] He repeatedly reminds us of "unfathomable darkness of empty space" and the "infinite remoteness" of stars. Yet the word infinite is surely here a metaphorical exaggeration.

Another contributor to this book, John Polkinghorne, has written that "when you look at all those trillions of stars you shouldn't be daunted at the thought of them being there, because if they weren't there, you wouldn't be here to be dismayed by them."[40] The multiple worlds interpretation gives a different view of the same evidence. According to it, the reason why we are amazed at the extraordinarily complex and apparent design of the universe is because we exist in one (perhaps the only one) of all the possible parallel universes in which humanity has arisen to be amazed at it. One might say: you pays your money and you takes your choice.

What then is humanity's place in the universe?

> When I look at your heavens, the work of your fingers, the moon and the stars that you have established;
> What are human beings that you are mindful of them, mortals that you care for them?[41]

---

prove the non-existence of each other, and perhaps even be convinced by them - and then laugh together over so odd a conclusion. I think it is something of the same kind of security we should seek in our relationship with God. The most flawless proof of the existence of God is no substitute for it; and if we have that relationship the most convincing disproof is turned harmlessly aside" (p. 62). See also C. S. Lewis, *The Problem of Pain* pp. 1-4.

39. *Op. cit.* p. 13.
40. John C. Polkinghorne, *God in a Scientific World* (West Watson Lectures, 1990) p. 5.
41. Psalm 8:3-4.

Christians believe that humanity is at home in the universe. It has been made for us — if not alone for us. We matter because God, the creator of this vastness, has become a human being. We do not need to be afraid of size. (As Lewis has said, this is a false concept anyway.) The *real* total perspective vortex is that which we see in Christ, that reassures us that we are important, that we do matter and that God has saved us and that there are far more important priorities than just size and that God has solved those problems (of sin) too. The moral element of the universe is one of its essential characteristics. I would like to conclude with another prayer. Here, not one of Kepler's, but one of my own:

> Heavenly Father, we thank you that you have given us this whole unimaginably vast universe as a remembrance of your far greater incomprehensibility. Yet we remember that the hands who made all this hold us forever in the embrace of Christ. Amen.

Response by Nancey Murphy

I find myself in a rather awkward position in being assigned to comment on Owen Gingerich's paper "Is there a role for natural theology today?" As is well known, the usual procedure in responding to an academic paper of this sort is to make a few conciliatory and flattering remarks about the paper, and then proceed to tear it to pieces. My embarrassment is caused by the fact that I agree with nearly everything the author says here. But it would be both boring and counter to the mores of the academic subculture for me to go through, paragraph by paragraph, and comment only that what the author says is true.

Fortunately, I did find three words to which I will take exception. But I shall not reveal what they are just yet. Rather, my plan is to concentrate on the epistemological aspects of his paper because my area of competence is epistemology, not science. I shall first lift out of the text the epistemological assumptions upon which Gingerich's conclusions, regarding design arguments and natural theology, are based. I will expand and defend them in a way that Gingerich has not been able to do in his paper. Then, I shall make my "vicious" criticism.

Let me take several sentences from Gingerich's paper, then explain how they fit with our current best epistemological theories:

- Arguments from design are in the eyes of the beholder, and simply cannot be construed as proofs to convince sceptics (p. 40).
- I am doubtful that you can convert a sceptic by the argument of design, and the discussions of the anthropic principle seem to prove the point (p. 43).
- [Natural theology is rhetoric], but rhetoric is not *mere* rhetoric (*ibid.*).
- [Speaking of the Copernican theory] The battle had long since been won by a persuasiveness that rested not on proof but on coherency, and what persuaded people of that coherency was the cogency of the essentially rhetorical arguments mustered in its favour (*ibid.*).

- Belief in design can also have a legitimate place in human under-standing even if it falls short of proof. What is needed is a consistent and coherent worldview and, at least for some of us, the universe is easier to comprehend if we assume it has both purpose and design (p. 43-44).

The contrast made several times in the course of this paper between proof and persuasive coherence reflects a recent revolution in our understanding of knowledge. At the beginning of the modern period, geometry still represented the ideal of knowledge. The following are the relevant characteristics of geometrical reasoning.

- Reasoning must begin with *indubitable* premises or axioms.
- Reasoning must be *linear*.
- Each step in the chain of arguments must confer certitude; that is, the reasoning must be *deductive* or demonstrative.

The history of modern epistemology could be described as the gradual and reluctant rejection of two of these ideals: that of deductive reasoning and that of indubitable starting points.   The change was forced simply by the character of empirical knowledge. It was recognised by the British empiricists that reasoning from experience needs to follow inductive rather than deductive patterns. Furthermore, while it is possible to find indubitable beliefs based on experience, for example, reports of sense data such as "I am now being appeared to greenly" when staring at the grass, no kind of reasoning from such a starting point leads to any interesting conclusions.

One consequence of these changes in epistemology was a shift in interests regarding arguments for the existence of God.   Proofs came to be seen by most to be impossible, and the argument from design became prominent as a merely probable argument beginning with experience.

What survived throughout the whole of the modern period was the view that knowledge must be structured by means of linear arguments.   I say "the whole of the modern period" because I believe that the rejection of this assumption, along with the earlier rejection of the other two features of the geometrical ideal, is a change so radical as to mark the end of modern philosophy.[1]

What replaces the linear model of knowledge is called holism. I say more about this in my own paper in this book. Here knowledge is envisioned as being structured like a web or net, where beliefs are connected to one another in various directions, and there is no such thing as a starting point. If we imagine knowledge as like a spider web, where the nodes are the beliefs, we can distinguish between beliefs near the edge and beliefs near the centre. Those near the edge represent the beliefs closely related to experience, and those near the centre are theoretical and logical beliefs.[2] The interconnections among beliefs within the web will be of varying strengths; some will be genuine deductive connections, but most will be weaker than that.

The epistemological task is to seek coherence and consistency within the web without losing touch with experience. The ideal web has plenty of beliefs around the edges — that is, beliefs closely tied to experience. It has no inconsistencies such as beliefs that are in genuine conflict with one another. The interconnections within the web are dense. All beliefs are supported by at least one tie to the others, and ideally by multiple connections. This is our picture of coherence. Changes among beliefs at the periphery, occasioned by new experience, will usually be the stimulus for changes within, either because they simply present new data to be explained or because they create inconsistencies.

There will still be linear proofs in limited regions within the web, such as within formal logic. But the appropriate criteria for judging most beliefs will be coherence and consistency with an entire web of beliefs. It should now be obvious why I agree with Gingerich that fine tuning and the other scientific evidence he has cited should not

---

1. For an explication of this claim, and an account of the consequences of this change for theology, see Nancey Murphy and James William McClendon, Jr., "Distinguishing modern and postmodern theologies" *Modern Theology* 5:3 (April, 1989) pp. 145-168.

2. W. V. O. Quine is to be credited with the invention of the holist model of knowledge. See "Two dogmas of Empiricism" *Philosophical Review* 40 (1951) pp. 20-43, reprinted in *From a Logical Point of View* (Cambridge, MA: Harvard University Press, 1953) pp. 20-46; and W. V. O. Quine and J. S. Ullian, *The Web of Belief*, second edition (New York: Random House, 1978).

be construed as an attempted proof. The way to envision the matter
is this: each of these findings allows for one more connection
between the doctrine of creation and a nexus of beliefs close to
experience. In other words, arguments such as Gingerich's allow
us to build a more coherent Christian worldview. These same
findings, instances of apparent intelligent design, create
inconsistencies within an atheistic worldview. Recall Gingerich's
reference to Fred Hoyle and his shaken atheism.

So in the contest between a Christian (or Jewish or Islamic)
worldview and a naturalistic one, these findings from science
strengthen the one and create anomalies for the other. Yet no one
of them is decisive. No worldview, no web of beliefs, is ever
perfect. We all live with some inconsistencies and with a great deal
of incoherence. So our comparisons need to be in terms of *degree*
of coherence. I often wonder if it is possible to make exact
measurements or comparisons of consistency and coherence within
two competing webs of belief. It is difficult enough when
comparing two limited theories such as competing theories in
physics. When considering something as vast, complex and
variable as the Christian worldview it seems clear that the best
we can do is to give glimpses of the intellectual assets of our
worldview, and help our opponents to recognise the besetting
problems of their own. This, as Gingerich points out, is a rhetorical
task, not a purely logical one. While it involves careful argument
and hard evidence, it also requires rhetorical skill to convey the
beauty, the intellectual satisfaction of living and thinking within
one's worldview.

I am sad to say as a Christian, that some of the proponents of an
atheistic worldview have been much more effective rhetorically than
Christians have been. We have allowed a sharp cleavage to develop
between the scientific appreciation of reality and our theologies.
Thank heaven for discussions such as this where we are beginning
to acquire skill and intellectual resources for bridging that chasm!

Now, what about Gingerich's claim that design is in the eye of
the beholder? This is true in a limited sense. A single scientific fact
does not (ordinarily) give evidence of design apart from a worldview
in which a designer can be conceived. As I have indicated above,
the credibility of the design hypothesis depends on taking seriously a
whole host of other facts and theoretical connections. Thus, to

someone for whom both the notion of a designer and all of the other evidence are in place, something like fine tuning adds an impressive degree of confirmation. For someone whose thinking lacks this background, the expected response should instead be mere puzzlement.

An exception to the claim that isolated scientific facts are not construed as evidence for design is, in fact, the fine-tuning of the cosmological constants. Some scientists with no previous theistic inclinations claim that they have been led to consider the possibility of design. However, as Gingerich notes, there is no rational compulsion to do so. Not only do the various versions of the anthropic principle serve to obviate this conclusion, but there are also a variety of other hypotheses that will get the atheist off the hook. One of these is the hypothesis that there are either an infinity of other universes, or at least vastly many other universes, all with different numbers for the basic forces. Thus it is possible to say that it is simply a matter of chance that this universe is capable of supporting life.

Nonetheless, it is ordinarily true that evidence only becomes evidence in light of a theoretical structure that helps to interpret it. The data upon which the hypothesis of design is based are, like the data for all empirical theories, theory-laden.

This fact leads to a consideration of the role of Scripture in this discussion. Gingerich uses the metaphor of the two books, the Book of Scripture and the Book of Nature, both pointing to God. However, it seems clear to me, based on the considerations I have raised here, that these books ought not be read independently of one another. In fact, the Book of Nature ought to be read as a sequel to the Bible. As with the sequel to a novel, it is important to read the first volume to find out about the characters.

Or, to drop the metaphor, we get our hypothesis of design from revelation. Discoveries like the fine tuning come along later, and their strength as evidence lies in confirming an already-existing hypothesis that already has other confirmation from other realms of experience.[3] Without revelation, we would be at a loss to know

3. For a detailed defence of this claim, see my "Evidence of design in the fine-tuning of the universe" in *Quantum Cosmology and the Laws of Nature: Scientific Perspectives on Divine Action,* Robert John Russell, Nancey Murphy and C. J. Isham, editors (Vatican City State: Vatican Observatory

what we mean by "designer" in such arguments. As Hume pointed out, we might postulate an intelligence behind it all, but in terms of analogies with anything we know, it would be as much like human intelligence as our intelligence is like the rotting of a turnip.[4]

Now, at last, I am in position to make my criticism. Gingerich uses the phrase "leap of faith" to describe his commitment to the Christian worldview (p. 44). These are the three words with which I take issue, because they too easily play into the hands of those who would say that if there is no proof, then there is nothing left but mere opinion, mere faith. I do not mean to attribute this thinking to Gingerich, but it is a way of thinking about epistemological issues that is so common and so pernicious that it is well worth attacking whenever the possibility arises.

Let us return to the issue of how to evaluate competing worldviews. We have recognised that the superiority of one worldview over another cannot be proved, but this does not mean it is impossible to make a rational judgment. Rather, it is that the judgment is too complex to describe in a single paper, perhaps even in an entire book. The best guidance to be found in these matters is that of Alasdair MacIntyre. I will not attempt to summarise here his entire theory on the justification of large-scale traditions, but a part of it involves what he calls "dialectical questioning". To judge a tradition (which we might define for present purposes as a worldview evolving through time) one needs to be bilingual. One needs to be able to use and understand the concepts of each of the traditions as an insider. One needs to be sympathetic to both traditions, and from this insider-outsider position, one can see the strengths and weaknesses of both traditions, and can see when resources from one tradition are capable of solving problems that cannot be solved from within the other.

MacIntyre's favourite example of such a bilingual thinker is Thomas Aquinas. Thomas was sympathetic to both the Christian tradition in its Augustinian form and the Aristotelian tradition, and was able to show that Christianity offered resources for solving

---

Publications, 1993 [distributed by University of Notre Dame Press]) pp. 407-435.

4.   See David Hume, *Dialogues concerning Natural Religion* (1779).

intellectual problems that had not been soluble with Aristotelian categories alone.[5]

Owen Gingerich is also bilingual. He is a sympathetic insider to science and, I presume, to the atheistic worldview that has been developed out of science.[6] Yet he is also a sympathetic insider to the Christian tradition, and to the tentative new natural theology that people involved in dialogues such as this one are in the process of developing.

I, too, am bilingual. I am a sympathetic insider to both Christianity and the naturalistic, empiricist, rationalist worldview that most philosophers inhabit. Bilinguists like us have experienced from the inside the intellectual beauty, the exciting rational coherence and explanatory power of the competitors. In contrast to many of our academic opponents who know the secular worldview but have only partial and often totally distorted views of Christianity, we are in a position to judge between Christianity and these other worldviews. Both Gingerich and I, in our respective papers, are making small contributions to a cumulative argument for the rational superiority of the Christian tradition. But neither of us can come anywhere close to saying it all.

But I, for one, am happy to hear the testimony of a reliable witness who has been to the world of science and reports back that he has seen nothing there that cannot be subjected to the lordship of our God.

---

5. See MacIntyre, *Whose Justice, Which Rationality?* (Notre Dame: University of Notre Dame Press, 1988). For a short account of the justification of large-scale theories, see also "Epistemological crises, dramatic narrative, and the philosophy of science" in *Paradigms and Revolutions: Applications and Appraisal of Thomas Kuhn's Philosophy of Science,* Gary Gutting, editor (University of Notre Dame Press, 1980) pp. 54-74.

6. I want to emphasise that the atheism is not inherent in science. Proponents of atheistic worldviews such as Carl Sagan are creating worldviews by adding a great deal of interpretation and metaphysical speculation to the actual results of science.

2

Arguments for the existence of God from nature and science

Norma Emerton

Traditionally, Christian apologetic has always appealed to the natural world in order to give a reasoned account of God. The cosmological argument reasons that the very existence of the world points to a divine Creator, and the argument from design reasons that the Designer is powerful, wise and good. This is attested in both the Old and the New Testaments, for example, Psalm 19:1, "The heavens are telling the glory of God, and the firmament proclaims his handiwork", or Romans 1:20, "God's eternal power and divine nature ... have been understood and seen through the things he has made." The use of arguments that try to speak about God from the evidence of the natural world is the role of natural theology. It reached its peak in the early nineteenth century with William Paley's book *Natural Theology* with its simple yet forceful argument:

> The marks of design are too strong to be gotten over. Design must have had a designer. That designer must have been a person. That person is God.[1]

In this paper I look at some arguments that have been used at different times in the past. I show what conclusions were drawn from them; and I uncover some of the hidden dangers that lurked under them as well as the obvious support they have given to faith. Finally I shall look at the role of natural theology in today's

---

1. William Paley, *Natural Theology,* Revised and annotated edition (Edinburgh: Chambers, 1849) chapter 23, p. 246.

Christian thought. I make no excuse for examining this topic in a broad historical context. We ignore at our peril our predecessors' insights and mistakes.

In the Middle Ages the monotheistic religions of Judaism, Christianity and Islam all felt the need to have a rational demonstration of their beliefs concerning the existence and nature of God. They all believed in the existence, unity, eternity and incorporeality of God, and in his creation of the universe out of nothing at the beginning of time. It was important for them to be able to uphold these beliefs in terms that were compatible with, and not liable to attack by, the currently favoured Aristotelian philosophy. They all appealed to the cosmological argument, for the existence of the world was an unassailable fact on which to base their reasoning. Probably the best account of Muslim and Jewish arguments was that of the twelfth-century Jewish scholar Moses Maimonides who asserted that the Muslim arguments were based on those of eastern Christian apologists. Two of these were forms of the cosmological argument: that the series of causes of motion and of change in the world cannot be infinite and must terminate in the first cause, God.[2]

In western Christendom a similar process was taking place. In the eleventh century Anselm had advanced the ontological argument for the existence of God: that the existence of the idea of God as that than which no greater can be conceived necessarily involves the existence of God himself. In the twelfth century Maimonides' contemporary Peter Lombard used the cosmological argument to show that a created, changeable world containing bodies, spirits and forms must have an uncreated, unchanging Author from which those entities take their being.[3] The thirteenth-century scholar Thomas Aquinas, influenced by Peter and Maimonides, produced his "Five Ways" demonstrating the existence of God. One was ontological: the existence of partial truth and goodness implies the existence of absolute Truth and Goodness. Three were forms of the cosmo-logical argument: the motions in the world must start from an unmoved Mover, the efficient causes must start from a first Cause, and the world of contingent impermanent creatures must come from

---

2. Moses Maimonides, *The Guide for the Perplexed* 2.1.
3. Peter Lombard, *Sententiarum Libri Quattuor* 1.3 2-5.

a self-existent Creator. Last, the argument from design pointed to an intelligent and beneficent Providence.[4]

Thomas denied that the existence of God was self-evident to reason, but his contemporary Bonaventure believed that rational argument constituted compelling proof for it. On a related topic, the debate whether the world was eternal or had a beginning, Thomas and Bonaventure differed in the same way. Bonaventure held that the non-eternity of the world could be proved rationally, whereas Thomas allowed that both positions could be supported by rational arguments and that the choice between them was based on revelation. This was an important difference in principle — if philosophical reasoning based on the physical world ensured the content of religious belief, theology would be tied to one philosophical or scientific position, or natural philosophy would be absorbed into theology. Many centuries before, in a different context, Augustine had commented on the risk of assuming that biblical interpretation necessitated a single understanding of cosmology. Expecting change and development in scientific theory, he had stressed the importance of not being trapped theologically in one particular worldview.[5] Thomas took a similar attitude. The interaction of theology and natural philosophy must respect the integrity of both disciplines. Thomas, like Augustine, believed that philosophical and theological truths both proceeded from the God of truth and could not ultimately be in conflict.

The argument from design had been popular with the Fathers of the early Church, especially the Latin Fathers. They borrowed the argument from design and examples of design in the world from a pagan author, Cicero. In his book *On the Nature of the Gods* Cicero had expounded the Stoic reasons for belief in providence: divination, the cosmological argument, and a detailed argument from design based on the order and beauty of the heavens, the earth's provision for human needs, and the design of the human body. The Fathers repeated all this, except for divination, and they seemed unconcerned that it was aimed to support Stoic pantheism that identified God and nature. For instance, in the early third century

---

4.   Thomas Aquinas, *Summa contra Gentiles* 1.13 30-35; *Summa Theologica* 1.3 1-5.
5.   Augustine, *De Genesi ad Litteram* 1.18 37, 1.20 40.

Tertullian spoke of the complementarity of natural and revealed theology:

> God must be first known from nature and afterwards recognised from doctrine; from nature by his works and from doctrine by his revealed words.[6]

This gave rise to the notion of God's two books, the Book of the Bible and the Book of Nature, which was popular in the Middle Ages and the early modern period. However, it could be misleading: the Book of Nature, "the heavens telling the glory of God", was interpreted astrologically by some medieval and Renaissance writers as the foretelling of the future by the stars. This had elements of the Stoic emphasis on divination as an argument for divine providence ruling the world. The strict doctrinal stance of the early Church allowed no drift towards Stoicism, but the risk was there and surfaced in later times.

In the Middle Ages, especially in the twelfth century in circles connected with the school of Chartres, there was a change in the view of the natural world. Stoic ideas crept in, and it became acceptable to personify nature and to allow her a semi-independent existence as the governor of the terrestrial world from which God was thought to have withdrawn to heaven. In the Stoic manner, nature became a semi-deity by being linked to divine reason, allowing the entry of a pagan attitude that tended to erode Christian belief. For instance, Bernard of Tours' *Cosmographia* and Alain of Lille's *Complaint of Nature* depicted the creation of mankind as being delegated by God to nature. And whereas Alain combined nature's procreative function with a role as moral guardian, in Jean de Meung's *Romance of the Rose* she sank to being the promoter of sexual licence for whom celibacy was a deadly sin. The Stoic attitude to nature was popular in medieval and Renaissance literature and natural philosophy, and it would have an effect on natural theology.

The scientific revolution of the sixteenth and seventeenth centuries brought about a new attitude to the natural world, which was seen increasingly as an object of study. The view of the world

---

6.   Tertullian, *Contra Marcionem* 1.18.

as God's book took on new relevance. Francis Bacon was one of many who emphasised its value not only as pointing to God but also as elucidating God's other book, the Bible:

> God's two books are ... first the Scriptures, revealing the will of God, and then the creatures expressing his power; whereof the latter is a key unto the former.[7]

Far from weakening the argument from design and the view of the world as God's Book of Nature, the new sciences enhanced and enriched this approach. They added precision and accuracy to the evidence of design both in the heavens and in living creatures including human beings. Bacon did not think that the search for final causes had any place in natural philosophy and he criticised the Stoic approach, derived from Cicero, which emphasised biological trivia and saw the world as created solely for the benefit of mankind. Bacon insisted, however, that the study of physical phenomena in a scientific manner was a way to glorify God in his creation. Thanks to his influence, this attitude became prevalent among English seventeenth-century scientists, and it was also voiced on the Continent by Kepler and others. Robert Boyle, a pioneer in both physics and chemistry, wrote:

> When with bold telescopes I survey the old and newly discovered stars and planets ... when with excellent microscopes I discern nature's curious workmanship; when with the help of anatomical knives and the light of chymical furnaces I study the book of nature ... I find myself exclaiming with the psalmist, How manifold are thy works, O God, in wisdom hast thou made them all! [8]

Boyle was more aware than most of his contemporaries of the ambiguities of natural theology. He recognised the threat of the Stoic assumptions underlying it in its traditional form, and he thought it better to avoid the word 'nature' with its pantheist overtones. He described nature as a semi-deity that was "a danger to

---

7. Francis Bacon, *The Advancement of Learning* (1605) 1.6 16, Arthur Johnston, editor (Oxford, Clarendon Press, 1974) p. 42.
8. Robert Boyle, *Some Motives and Incentives to the Love of God* (1648) in *Works* volume 1, Thomas Birch, editor (London, 1744) p. 167.

religion in general".[9] This was a danger to which some of his contemporaries succumbed, for instance, the Cambridge Platonists Henry More and Ralph Cudworth who were interested in the new sciences although they were not engaged in scientific work themselves. In their use of the argument from design they posited nature as a Stoic type of semi-deity acting as God's agent in the world. They called it "plastic nature" whose function was to "execute that part of providence which consists in the regular and orderly motion of matter".[10] Another hazard, warned against by Bacon, was of accumulating instances of biological design that unbalanced the study of anatomy and physiology, harming their integrity by making natural theology trespass upon them like, in a modern writer's words, "a teleological cuckoo in the nest".[11] Boyle's contemporary John Ray, the botanist, took the argument from biological design to ridiculous teleological lengths in this way in his book *The Wisdom of God Manifested in the Works of the Creation* (1691). Boyle also encountered problems in religious attitudes to natural theology. He saw that it was scorned by unbelievers:

> Undervaluation ... of the study of things sacred is grown rife among ... students of physics ... Our new libertines deny natural theology ... namely the existence and providence of a Deity.[12]

But scientific studies and their theological consequences were mistrusted by some theologians. Boyle remarked that "several divines ... deter men from inquiries into nature, as from a study unsafe for a Christian".[13] Some divines such as Boyle's contemporary John Webster, a puritan physician, saw natural theology as a bonus to science but a threat to revealed theology:

---

9. Robert Boyle, *A Free Inquiry into the Vulgarly Received Notion of Nature* (1666) in *Works* volume 4, *ibid.* p. 381.
10. Ralph Cudworth, *The True Intellectual System of the Universe* (London, 1678) pp. 671, 684.
11. Peter Green, *Alexander to Actium: The Hellenistic Age* (London: Thames and Hudson, 1990) p. 634, referring to Stoic teleology in ancient science.
12. Robert Boyle, *The Excellence of Theology* (1665) in *Works* volume 3, *op. cit.* pp. 405, 410.
13. Robert Boyle, *The Usefulness of Natural Philosophy* (1648) in *Works* volume 1, *ibid.* pp. 429-430.

> What can be discovered of God ... by the power of reason and the
> light of nature, may be handled as a part of natural philosophy
> (unto which it doth belong), because it is found out by the same
> means that the other natural sciences are ... and may be holden
> forth as a means to overthrow atheism ... but not to build up
> anything in religion, nor like a wild boar to enter into the Lord's
> vineyard to root up and destroy it.[14]

In seventeenth- and eighteenth-century England, scientists and
divines alike saw the argument from design as "a means to overthrow atheism". Boyle bequeathed money to fund annual Boyle
lectures "for proving the Christian religion" by the argument from
design. The great English scientist Isaac Newton saw his scientific
work as contributing to the same aim. Referring to his *Principia*, he
said that "when I wrote my treatise about our system, I had an eye
upon such principles as might work with considering men for the
belief of a Deity."[15]

The design of the solar system, of which he was able to give a
mathematical account, the action of gravity, and the atomic theory
of matter, all seemed to him to be forceful arguments from design
for the power, wisdom and beneficence of God. So Newton took
natural theology seriously. He gave it much weight in establishing
our beliefs about God:

> This Being governs all things ... as Lord over all ... The true God
> is a living, intelligent and powerful Being ... He is supreme and
> most perfect. He is eternal and infinite ... He endures forever and
> is everywhere present: and, by existing always and everywhere, he
> constitutes duration and space ... We have ideas of his attributes,
> but ... much less have we any idea of the substance of God. We
> know him only by his most wise and excellent contrivances of
> things and final causes, but we reverence and adore him on
> account of his dominion ... for a god without dominion,
> providence and final causes is nothing else but fate and nature ...
> And thus much concerning God, to discourse of whom from the

---

14. John Webster, *Academiarum Examen* (London: 1653) p. 98.
15. Isaac Newton, *First Letter to Richard Bentley* (1692) in *Newton's
    Philosophy of Nature: Selections from his Writings,* H.S. Thayer, editor
    (New York: Hafner, 1953) p. 46.

appearances of things does certainly pertain to natural
philosophy.[16]

Newton believed that he could carry natural theology even further
and make it a basis for piety and ethics:

> So far as we know by natural philosophy what is the First Cause,
> what power he has over us, and what benefits we receive from him,
> so far our duty towards him, as well as that towards one another,
> will appear to us by the light of nature.[17]

Newton was a religious man but not an orthodox Christian. He
was a Deist, believing in a benevolent but remote God whose
concern was with creation rather than salvation. Those who had
promoted the argument from design in earlier generations had given
more detailed attention to the design of human and animal bodies
than to the heavens. Newton's version of the argument from design
was based on cosmology, and shifted attention away from human
life and needs to the general physical principles of the universe.
This clearly favoured a Deistic outlook, and in the eighteenth century
the argument from design was taken up eagerly by Deists. In their
hands natural theology became natural religion; instead of being
complementary to revealed theology, it supplanted it, as Webster
had feared would happen. The proponents of natural religion, like
Newton, took their doctrine and ethics from natural theology,
dropping revealed doctrines such as the Trinity. In the words of
Alexander Pope's *Essay on Man,* they "look through nature up to
nature's God". Natural religion based on the argument from design
was held by eighteenth-century opponents of Christianity such as
Lord Shaftesbury and Joseph Priestley in England, and Voltaire and
Rousseau in France. Leibniz put his finger on the risk of Stoicism
in the argument from design when he commented:

---

16. Isaac Newton, *Mathematical Principles of Natural Philosophy,* General
    Scholium, second edition (London, 1713) *ibid.* pp. 42-45.
17. Isaac Newton, *Opticks* Query 31, fourth edition (London, 1730) *ibid.* p.
    179.

Mr Newton and his followers have an extremely odd opinion of
the work of God ... This God will be very like the Stoic God, who
was the whole universe.[18]

The cosmological argument and the argument from design
were not the only ways in which scientific study influenced
Christian belief. Of all doctrines, the creation of the world by God
was the most obviously linked to natural philosophy, and scientific
disciplines seemed to offer support. Chemistry claimed to be able to
explain the creation narrative of Genesis 1 in a material fashion as a
separation of chemical substances out of chaos. Even crude
medieval alchemy had been pressed into service for this. With the
more sophisticated sixteenth- and seventeenth-century chemistry of
Paracelsus and his followers this process developed into a style of
reasoning by which chemistry seemed to vindicate the Bible and the
Bible to vindicate chemical theory. On a small scale, the chemist in
his laboratory claimed to re-enact God's action at the creation.
Alchemical and Paracelsian chemical theory brought with it some
underlying pagan assumptions, particularly Gnostic and Hermetic
beliefs such as uncreated matter and a dualistic worldview. It was
greeted with alarm by many orthodox writers who clung to the
medieval Christianisation of Aristotelian natural philosophy.

The use of chemistry to explain the creation had no appeal for
Boyle, but he turned to atomism to perform a similar function. He
held, as did Newton, that God had wrought the world into its
present form by creating atoms endowed with certain properties
of size, shape, weight and motion, from which the fabric of the
universe was constructed. There were also several attempts to
reinterpret the creation story in terms of Newtonian astronomy,
which caused an outcry among the orthodox. The most ingenious
of these was made by Newton's successor, the Deist William
Whiston in his *New Theory of the Earth* (1696). He explained that
the creation narrative of Genesis 1 referred to the origin of the solar
system only, not the whole universe, by means of a cometary
hypothesis. All these scientific rationalisations of creation in terms
of chemistry, atomism or Newtonian astronomy were intended to

---

18. G.W. Leibniz, *First and Fifth Letters to Samuel Clarke* in *Leibniz'
    Philosophical Writings,* G. Parkinson, editor, Mary Morris, translator
    (London: Dent, 1973) pp. 205, 230.

serve the same purpose as the argument from design. They aimed to increase the credibility of belief in God as Creator by showing that it was compatible with physical processes and with the reasoning of natural philosophy. But as we have seen, they often assumed a doctrine of God that fell short of full Christian orthodoxy because of a leaning towards Stoic, Gnostic or Deistic views.

In the seventeenth and eighteenth centuries the argument from design was coming under sharp criticism on a philosophical level. Descartes warned against imagining that human beings can understand God's purpose in creating the world; like Bacon, he ridiculed the notion that the world was created solely for the benefit of mankind. Spinoza insisted that nature has no purpose and that final causes were mere fabrications of the human mind. Atheists such as Baron d'Holbach and David Hume poured scorn on the notion that there was any design at all in a world which had such a mixture of good and evil; it was self-contained with no need of a Creator. D'Holbach made the point that it was a misuse of natural history to quarry it for the argument from design, and that natural theology did not prove the existence of God but only ignorance of nature. The cosmological argument was mere self-delusion, according to Hume, in which Christians became enamoured with the offspring of their own brain. Kant, too, held natural theology to be invalid, and he replaced the argument from design by the argument from human conscience.

In spite of Stoic overtones, the link with Deism, mistrust from orthodox divines, and philosophical censure, natural theology continued to increase in popularity throughout the eighteenth and early nineteenth centuries. However, orthodox Christian interest shifted away from Newtonian arguments concerning the design of the heavens, back to the more old-fashioned and theologically safer arguments drawn from the design of human and animal bodies. Willian Paley's *Natural Theology* of 1802 was a resounding success. It was closely modelled on John Ray's *Wisdom of God Manifested in the Works of the Creation* written in 1691, and it copied Ray's excessively teleological approach to biology. It is symptomatic of the post-Deism position that the orthodox Paley wrote eighteen chapters on biology and only one on cosmology. After Paley, the *Bridgewater Treatises* joined the Boyle lectures in defending the Christian faith by means of natural theology.

In spite of the continuing popularity of the argument from biological design in the nineteenth century, a challenge was at hand: Charles Darwin's theory of natural selection. So long as species were held to be fixed and unchanging, the suitability of living creatures to their environment could easily be seen as evidence of God's original design. Adaptation by evolution of species through the survival of favourable random variations was much harder to interpret as design, though not impossible. Darwin himself, though he was no longer a Christian, used such language from time to time. He ended *The Origin of Species* (1859) with these words:

> To my mind it accords better with what we know of the laws impressed on matter by the Creator, that the production and extinction of [species] should have been due to secondary causes ... From the war of nature ... the production of the higher animals directly follows. There is grandeur in this view of life ... that whilst this planet has gone cycling on according to the fixed law of gravity, from so simple a beginning endless forms most beautiful and most wonderful have been, and are being, evolved.[19]

In the same passage he urged a view as optimistic as Paley's:

> We may look with some confidence to a secure future ... As natural selection works solely by and for the good of each being, all corporeal and mental endowments will tend to progress towards perfection.

Darwin's later book, *The Descent of Man* (1871), posed even more of a challenge to traditional Christian views. But towards the end of this book, too, he presented evolution as compatible with some sort of belief in providence, though not with Paley's argument from design:

> I am aware that my conclusions ... will be denounced by some as highly irreligious. But ... the birth both of the species and of the individual are equally parts of that grand sequence of events, which our minds refuse to accept as the result of blind chance. The understanding revolts at such a conclusion, whether or not we

19. Charles Darwin, *The Origin of Species* (London: John Murray, 1859) chapter 14, pp. 488, 490.

are able to believe that every slight variation of structure ... and other such events, have all been ordained for some special purpose.[20]

As a young man Darwin had much admired Paley's writings, but in a memoir of 1876 he wrote:

> The old argument from design in nature, as given by Paley, which formerly seemed to me so conclusive, fails now that the law of natural selection has been discovered ... There seems to be no more design in ... natural selection, than in the course which the wind blows. Everything in nature is the result of fixed laws.[21]

There was no longer room for the traditional form of the argument from design.

We have followed the fortunes of various arguments from the physical world that have been used to buttress Christian faith, even though they cannot conclusively prove it: the cosmological argument, the argument from design, and attempts to show that the biblical account of the creation of the world is compatible with current scientific theories. Does the history of their use give us any help towards the use of such arguments today? The pure cosmological argument can stand in spite of changing fashions in scientific theories. The existence of the world, then as now, is an incontrovertible fact. Whether the world is self-sufficient or needs a cause outside itself will always be a subject of debate. We have a modern example of this in Stephen Hawking's book *A Brief History of Time*. However, Hawking errs in supposing that creation is necessarily incompatible with an eternal universe:

> So long as the universe had a beginning, we could suppose it had a creator. But if the universe is really completely self-contained, having no boundary or edge, it would have neither beginning nor end: it would simply be. What place, then, for a creator?[22]

---

20. Charles Darwin, *The Descent of Man* (London: John Murray, 1871) chapter 21, pp. 395-396.
21. Charles Darwin, *Autobiography,* Religious Belief, Gavin de Beer, editor (Oxford University Press, 1983) pp. 50-51.
22. Stephen Hawking, *A Brief History of Time* (London: Bantam Press, 1988) p. 141.

Creation means total dependence on a divine creator, either with a beginning (as Christians have held) or eternally (as in Neoplatonism) as Augustine and Aquinas knew. By thinking that a scientific theory can rule out belief in a creator, Hawking is here making the same mistake (though in the opposite direction) as Bonaventure did in thinking that he had proved the beginning of the world.

This brings me to the historic use of scientific theories to validate the biblical creation story. To most religious believers and scientists such a procedure is discredited, but we should not think that it does not exist nowadays. It was in common use in the earlier part of this century among religious people, and when the Big Bang was established as the likeliest scientific cosmological theory many believers, including the Roman Catholic Church, saw it as vindicating the Christian belief in creation. Some religious people, not necessarily fundamentalist, think that with a little adjustment on both sides Genesis 1 and evolutionary theory could be united. The God of the gaps is still being evoked. High-level philosophical and theological arguments should not make us ignore popular views of this kind. There is an important principle at stake: preserving the integrity of both theology and science, and it needs to be explained to well-meaning but confused believers.

I want to give more attention to the argument from design. I believe it is very powerful on an emotive, non-intellectual level, and this is not to be despised. Modern Christians in the West have tended to lose one aspect of it that Cicero and the Fathers acquired from Plato: the value of beauty as a pointer to God. Cicero said that "If any man cannot feel the power of God when he looks upon the stars, then I doubt whether he is capable of any feeling at all."[23] Augustine and Basil similarly waxed lyrical about the beauties of earth and sky, which seemed to them to shout the praise of the Creator. We lose at our peril the sense that beauty leads to worship. It is not incompatible with rational argument.

What about the argument from design appealing to reason? It carries with it a subtext of Stoic pantheism, as Boyle realised. In Christian terms one can understand this as divine immanence carried to extremes. By putting on nature the whole emphasis and weight of

---

23. Cicero, *On the Nature of the Gods* 2.55, Horace McGregor, translator (Harmondsworth: Penguin Books, 1972) p. 145.

argument, design could be seen as inherent in nature rather than as imparted by the Creator, thus opening the way for nature to be seen as what Boyle called a "semi-deity". This point of view is still widespread, for instance, in James Lovelock's Gaia hypothesis, in the views of many green environmentalists, and in much alternative science and New Age thinking. Although it is not always rationally articulated, it must be taken into account when natural theology is discussed.

Another subtext of the traditional argument from design was Deism, the opposite of pantheism, which one can understand as divine transcendence carried to extremes. The corollary of the old belief in fixed species was that design was imparted once for all at the creation. Once this was done, the creator would have no need to intervene again (although Newton held that this might be necessary because of instabilities caused by gradually diminishing motion). It was Cicero who originated Paley's favourite comparison of the world to a clock whose intricate mechanism implied the existence of an intelligent maker. The God of Deism was a clockmaker whose work did not need continual winding up. It is noticeable that this is the God presupposed by Hawking. The "natural religion" of Deism — the belief in a Creator God together with a simple moral code — is widely held at the present day and passes for Christianity among many, perhaps even most, people.

The argument from design has been attacked from different directions. The attitude of some Christians, such as Boyle's contemporary Webster, that natural theology is a dangerous rival to revealed theology, is by no means dead. Opposition to natural theology is characteristic of Karl Barth and his school, among others. Further attacks come from outside the Church. We have looked at the argument against design in, for example, the suffering, disaster and waste of life in the world; the admission of human ignorance of the cosmic purposes of God; the accusation of partiality in choosing only favourable evidence of design; and the lack of respect for the integrity of science in burdening it with teleology. These criticisms were, and are, valid. But they did not destroy the argument from design. The vital damage was done by Darwin's theory of natural selection, that is, by a different explanation of the facts, not by an attack on the method. Chance and necessity had to be taken into account: chance in the random appearance of variations, and necessity in the fixed laws that governed their survival and breeding. Would chance and necessity leave any room for design?

One of the old forms of the argument from design is dead, with its accumulations of anatomical and physiological details thought to be unchanged since creation. But natural theology is far from dead, and in its renewed and revised form it has gone back to cosmology, though not the same cosmology that Newton put forward "for the belief of a Deity". One new variety of the argument from design — not necessarily a religious one — is the anthropic principle, which in its strong form carries some of the old Stoic and Christian connotations, for instance, that the world was designed to be the home of mankind. Another is the attempt to make sense from a Christian viewpoint of the roles of chance and necessity, which are necessary to molecular biology as well as to Darwinian natural selection. The new natural theology is not just a support to traditional Christian beliefs. It carries with it an obligation to rethink the expression of those beliefs in a way that will do justice to the insights of both science and revealed theology and respect the integrity of both.

The new natural theology will be wise if it pays attention to the problems of the old. As we have seen, the opposite extremes of pantheism and Deism are still alive and thriving, and both of them in different ways are strongly linked to the argument from design. Natural theologians have to tread a path between them. It is easy to see the new natural theology only as an inner-theological exercise or an intellectual exploration of the interactions of science and religion. It is both of these, and basic questions must come first. But Boyle and Newton were right in seeing the cosmological argument and the argument from design as useful tools for apologetics, "for the belief of a Deity". The sense of wonder at the beauty and order of the natural world is an obvious starting-place for belief in God. And the Fathers were right, too, in seeing the beauty of earth and sky as a stimulus to worship. Natural theology has important roles to play in all these approaches: the science and theology debate, apologetics, and spirituality. There can be fruitful cross-fertilisation between them which the insights, and even the errors, of the past can help us to achieve.

Response by John Stenhouse

Norma Emerton's paper compressed the history of natural theology and its relations with revealed theology from antiquity to the present in an admirably clear, concise and illuminating way. The point to which I wish to draw attention is how theistic the dominant conception of nature remained during the scientific revolution. The great names — Copernicus, Brahe, Kepler, Galileo, Bacon, Boyle and Newton — were generally religious believers, and most were Christians. Johannes Kepler, for example, found in nature not just the God of theism but the Holy Trinity. Galileo, who has often been presented as a secular martyr of science, seems to have been a believing Catholic, who felt he could teach the Church a thing or two not just about science but about theology as well. Isaac Newton's theological views are more difficult to pin down.

Emerton argues that Newton was a Deist, but I am not entirely convinced. Matter in itself was lifeless and inert, Newton believed, and God was immediately and actively present everywhere in the universe, responsible for the regular workings and occasional adjustments of the cosmic machinery. As he put it in the *General Scholium:* "God ... is everywhere present ... He is omnipresent not *virtually* only, but *substantially* ... In him are all things contained and moved."[1] Yet there is a sense of distance and remoteness about Newton's God. Anything that detracted from God's absolute sovereignty and dominion, including the divinity of Christ, was to be abandoned as far as Newton was concerned. Historians have sometimes used such evidence to argue that he was a sceptical scientific rationalist before his time, but, as with Galileo, remaking Newton in the image of modernity will not do. He wrote the *Principia* to refute scepticism and atheism, not to advance them. And yet, although his emphasis on the radical sovereignty of

---

1. Isaac Newton, *Sir Isaac Newton's Mathematical Principles of Natural Philosophy and His System of the World,* Andrew Motte, translator, Florian Cajori, editor (Berkeley: University of California Press, 1934) p. 547.

God looks orthodox enough, the deep spiritual and pastoral concerns which informed Calvin's doctrines of divine sovereignty and providence are largely absent. Newton's God is a ruler to be obeyed. Though scientifically sound and socially useful, Newtonianism was spiritually and pastorally impoverished.[2] Since nature was for Newton the basis of piety and ethics, his admirer Alexander Pope in his *Essay on Man* drew the conclusion which many others came to: "whatever is, is right". The social Darwinism of the nineteenth century was one outcome of the "cosmic toryism" of the eighteenth.

Leap from the seventeenth to the late twentieth century, however, and we enter a different world. Leading scientists articulate atheism with assurance. Take the American astronomer Carl Sagan's TV series and book *Cosmos*, whose opening line reads: "The cosmos is all there is, there was, or ever will be".[3] Nobel prize-winning French biochemist Jacques Monod declares in *Chance and Necessity* that humankind is godless and alone in "an alien world ... as indifferent to his hopes as it is to his sufferings or his crimes".[4] According to the influential American sociobiologist E. O. Wilson, scientific materialism is the only intellectually respectable option. Stephen Hawking informs readers of his best-selling *A Brief History of Time* that the universe simply is, and that the Creator is an unneccessary postulate.

Why in the modern West is science so widely perceived to suggest the non-existence of God, especially of the Christian God? This is a crucial question, because unless scientism — that is, the scientific imperialism which claims that there is no reality beyond science and the natural — can be effectively challenged, no form of theology, natural or revealed, can begin to get off the ground. An historical understanding and critique of scientism is thus a

---

2. For a fuller discussion see the interesting essay by Gary B. Deason, "Reformation theology and the mechanistic conception of nature" in *God and Nature: Historical Essays on the Encounter between Christianity and Science,* David C. Lindberg and Ronald L. Numbers, editors (Berkeley and Los Angeles: University of California Press, 1986) pp. 167-191.

3. Carl Sagan, *Cosmos* (New York: Random House, 1980) p. 4.

4. Jacques Monod, *Chance and Necessity: An Essay on the Natural Philosophy of Modern Biology,* Austin Wainhouse, translator (New York: Alfred A. Knopf, 1971) p. 160.

fundamental task for Christian apologetics. My argument in the rest of this paper is that the rise of modern scientism has far less to do with new understandings of nature than with culture, and with historical developments over the last three centuries whose significance for the history of science-and-theology has been poorly understood. In analysing the rise of scientism I shall treat it with the hermeneutic of suspicion normally reserved for religion. I must point out, in parenthesis, that I am deliberately ignoring that large group of thinkers whose views on the relations between science and theology are substantially continuous with those of the great minds of the scientific revolution. It is those who broke with the theistic tradition whose outlook I want to discuss.

My approach to the history of science may provoke objections. Most are familiar with the idea that the study of theology can be brought down to earth, related to concrete historical contexts in illuminating ways, without reducing theology to anthropology (Feuerbach) or sociology (Durkheim). Theology can incorporate insights from all the sciences, natural and human, without abandoning critical realism — the belief that God is, and is not merely a reified projection of humanity or society. There may be more resistance to the claim that science cannot adequately be understood unless it is thoroughly historicised — systematically related to the changing cultural contexts in which scientific knowledge has been produced. Science is about understanding nature, the objection might run, and so understanding the cultural context in which natural knowledge is constructed is irrelevant. Yet if the metaphysical character of modern science has been profoundly informed by cultural developments, then it must systematically be historicised, otherwise we will understand neither it, nor its changing relationship with theology. Once this is done, we may be in a position to contextualise and to demythologise the scientism of modernity. We may arrive at a more productive post-modern phase in the relations between science and theology, one in which science and theology are both seen as humanly constructed forms of knowledge *and* as sources of knowledge of the divine. If adequately historicised, dogmatic anti-theological scientism may appear to be less an irresistible consequence of scientific enlightenment, than a contingent, problematic and ideological process.

The Enlightenment of the eighteenth century is the place to start. It is certainly possible to overstate the gulf between Christianity and enlightened thought. In England, Scotland, North America and parts of the Continent the Enlightenment developed mainly as an attempt to simplify and rationalise Christian belief within established forms of piety. Yet during this period there began the attack on "stupidity, Christianity and ignorance", as David Hume put it. Why were the most radical enlightenment thinkers so hostile to orthodox Christian belief? Why did the rise of atheism, agnosticism, deism and natural religion become so compelling at this time? Had science and Christianity suddenly ceased being compatible in the way that they were for the great figures of the scientific revolution? These are questions which Emerton does not discuss in detail, but the Enlightenment illustrates the point that treating science and theology as essentially cerebral, cognitive enterprises has limitations when it comes to understanding their changing historical relationship.

If the most radical enlightenment thinkers wanted nothing to do with Christian theology, few were prepared to dispense with God entirely. Voltaire, who was a deist, was probably more representative than materialists like Baron d'Holbach or agnostics like Hume. Voltaire found Newton's Supreme Being both intellectually necessary and socially useful; unbelief was alright for aristocrats and intellectuals, but only the fear of hell would stop the servants from stealing the silver.

Voltaire also illustrates a more important point. Science was a club wielded by the enlightened to batter the orthodox. Here are the beginnings of the characteristically modern sense of antagonism between science and Christian theology. As Denis Diderot put it: "Do you see this egg? With it you can overthrow all the schools of theology, all the churches of the earth."[5] Yet, as this example suggests, the origins of the Enlightenment's hostility toward orthodoxy owed little to science.

Appalled by the bloody wars of religion of the seventeenth century, enlightened thinkers continued to be disgusted by the bigotry, superstition and intolerance of established Churches in the eighteenth. In 1762, for example, Jean Calas, a Huguenot

---

5. Quoted in Francois Jacob, *The Logic of Life: A History of Heredity*, Betty E. Spillman, translator (New York: Pantheon Books, 1973) p. v.

merchant, was tortured and executed in the Catholic city of Toulouse for murdering his son, who wanted to convert to Catholicism. Voltaire was convinced that the son had actually committed suicide, and that the father was an innocent victim of Catholic bigotry. "Écrasez l'infame!" became his battle cry. The Enlightenment's attempt to reconstruct the world on the basis of nature rather than revelation was motivated by revulsion at the behaviour of the orthodox, and by the faith that science and reason would build a cooler, safer world.

Science was being forged into a weapon against Christian theology for reasons which had little to do with a cool concern for scientific truth. The tendency of the established Churches in Britain and Europe to identify with the established order, to identify the cause of Christ with that of Caesar, and to advance the former with the weapons of the latter, rebounded with a vengeance. If Protestants and Catholics were going to butcher each other for the sake of Christian truth, the philosophers, for the sake of humanity, would destroy the faith which fired such fanaticism.

Things were different in England, of course. The English had little liking for sceptical philosophers, especially after the bright promise of the French Revolution drowned in blood. The conservative English Enlightenment talked not of science-versus-religion but of science-and-religion. As Emerton pointed out, William Paley's *Natural Theology*, the *Bridgewater Treatises*, and the Boyle lectures set the tone for the first half of the nineteenth century in the "holy alliance" between science and religion. Yet even in England Christian theologians did not have it all their own way. In the 1830s and 1840s, especially in London, atheistic and materialistic evolutionary doctrines were popularised by radicals in an attempt to undermine the Anglican Establishment's control of science and medicine. Radicals satirised the *Bridgewater Treatises on the Power, Wisdom and Goodness of God in the Creation* as the Bilgewater Treatises.[6] In England, too, science became antitheistic for political reasons.

Then along came Darwin who demolished the traditional form of the argument from design in *The Origin of Species* (1859). At least

---

6. A. Desmond, *The Politics of Evolution: Morphology, Medicine, and Reform in Radical London* (University of Chicago Press, 1989).

this is what most historians have assumed until recently. In fact most scientists in the English-speaking world, while they were converted to evolution, did not abandon natural theology, but found in the great panorama of evolution new evidence of the power and wisdom of God. The idea that science triumphed over Christianity in the war over evolution is a myth which has been abandoned by most historians of late nineteenth-century culture. The foremost champions of Darwin in both the United States and New Zealand, for example, were Christians: Asa Gray at Harvard, who was a moderate Calvinist, and F.W. Hutton at the University of Otago, who was a devout Anglican.[7]

Emerton dealt with Darwin's views, which saw him gradually abandon nominal Christian faith for agnosticism later in life. Darwin has often been presented as a paradigm case of scientific discovery destroying Christian belief. It was never that simple. He had lots of misgivings about Christianity which had nothing to do with science. During the voyage of the Beagle he began to doubt the historicity of the Old Testament, which contained "a false history of the world" and depicted God as a "revengeful tyrant". He condemned as "damnable doctrine" the idea that unbelievers such as his own freethinking father would be sent to hell. Jim Moore has argued that the final nail in the coffin of Darwin's Christianity was not his science but the tragic death of his beloved daughter Annie.[8]

Darwin's colleagues were also alienated from Christianity for reasons which went well beyond science. T. H. Huxley, for example, the world's first self-styled episcopophage (bishop-eater), declared war on "theology and parsondom" after *The Origin of Species*. His anti-theological animus was aroused partly by the desire to defend the integrity and autonomy of science. In the late 1850s he engaged in a fierce controversy with Richard Owen, a pillar of the Establishment, over the physiological uniqueness of humans. Attempting to safeguard human uniqueness and dignity, Owen argued that the human brain had a lobe called the

---

7. John Stenhouse, "Darwin's Captain: F.W. Hutton and the nineteenth-century Darwinian debates" *Journal of the History of Biology* 23:3 (Fall, 1990) pp. 411-442.

8. J. Moore, "Of love and Ddath: why Darwin 'gave up Christianity'" in *History, Humanity and Evolution: Essays for John C. Greene*, J. Moore, editor (New York: Cambridge University Press, 1989) pp. 195-229.

hippocampus minor which apes did not possess, and that this set humans definitively above the lower animals. Huxley knew that the hippocampus was not unique to humans, and mercilessly exposed Owen's errors. How could science progress if the orthodox were allowed to adulterate facts to save their own religious preconceptions? But there was more to Huxley's crusade than the freedom of science. Huxley and colleagues such as J. D. Hooker and the physicist John Tyndall set out to wrest control of British science and education from the Anglican Establishment. Scientific naturalism and religious agnosticism — a term coined by Huxley — were weapons in their campaign. They were as intent on intellectual and cultural dominance as on the autonomy of science.[9] Soon Huxley was preaching lay sermons and, as Pope of the "church scientific", was sending out "disciples" to the uttermost ends of the earth, including Dunedin.

The Continent was even more polarised than England. Darwin's chief champion in Germany was the biologist Ernst Haeckel, and he was outraged at the way established Churches had colluded with the state to oppose the liberal revolutions of 1830 and 1848. With the hopes of middle class intellectuals for greater political power crushed, criticism of Christianity became the beginning of all criticism, in science as surely as in philosophy and theology. In 1863 Haeckel told the Congress of German naturalists at Stettin that, since evolution proved that change was the dynamic of history, scientists must overthrow the "tyrants and priests" who stood in the way of German emancipation and freedom. His popular scientific works continued the assault on Christianity, which he detested for detracting from German national unity and for promoting compassion for the weak which encouraged racial degeneration. Scientific naturalism, sometimes of an overtly pagan variety, became popular among the German middle and working classes well into the twentieth century.[10]

---

9.   F.M. Turner, "The Victorian conflict between science and religion: A professional dimension" *Isis* 69 (1978) pp. 356-376.

10. On Haeckel see Frederick Gregory, *Scientific Materialism in Nineteenth Century Germany* (Dordrecht: Reidel, 1977) and Daniel Gasman, *The Scientific Origins of National Socialism: Social Darwinism in Ernst Haeckel and the Monist League* (New York: American Elsevier, 1971). On Darwin's German popularisers see Alfred Kelly, *The Descent of Darwin:*

Interestingly, and contrary to the propaganda of the apostles of rationalism, zealous Christians had no monopoly on scientific error. In the 1860s T. H. Huxley, at the beginning of his campaign against the Church ecclesiastical, placed under the microscope some alcohol-preserved specimens of mud dredged up from the North Atlantic sea-bed. He discovered an extremely primitive form of living protoplasm which he named Bathybius Haeckelii, in honour of Ernst Haeckel. To Huxley and Haeckel, both antagonists of Christianity for different reasons, Bathybius was religiously as well as scientifically useful; it was the "missing link" between the inorganic and organic worlds, which proved that life might easily and naturally be generated from non-life. Unfortunately it was shown that Bathybius was not a primitive living organism at all. The preserving alcohol had caused some of the chemicals in the mud to precipitate. Bathybius Haeckelii was calcium sulphate in colloidal form.[11] This story is not designed to suggest that Huxley and Haeckel were poor scientists. Nor is it designed to defend the God of the gaps idea of their Christian opponents. It illustrates two points: that orthodoxy had no monopoly on scientific error, for militant anti-Christianity could also lead zealots up the garden path; and that the aggressive scientism of Huxley and Haeckel was motivated by much more than the disinterested pursuit of natural knowledge.

The chequered career of Darwinism in France shows how misleading it is to abstract science and theology from their contexts. As we saw in the French Enlightenment, France had long been polarised over religion, and biology was caught up in the ideological warfare in the nineteenth century. The preface with which Clémence Royer introduced the French translation of *The Origin of Species* (1862) illustrates the point. The choice she offered readers was between the "rational revelation" of progressive science and the obsolete revelation of Christianity. Evolution fared better in the 1870s, however, with the establishment of the Third Republic, which adopted a strongly secular ideology. This new regime purged

---

The Popularization of Darwinism in Germany, 1860-1914 (Chapel Hill: University of North Carolina Press, 1981).

11. Nicolaas A. Rupke, "Bathybius Haeckelii and the psychology of scientific discovery" *Studies in History and Philosophy of Science* 7 (1976) pp. 53-62.

the University of Paris of scholars with clerical leanings, and even moderate scientists with Catholic sympathies were watched, especially if they used their teaching positions to criticise secular values. Scientific institutions, on the other hand, could and did become aggressively secular. One member of the Paris school of anthropology in 1878 argued that Christ's behaviour could be explained on the hypothesis that he suffered a bad case of meningitis.[12]

The natural sciences thus acquired a secular and anti-theological character in many parts of the Old World. Their secularity can partly be explained as a legitimate demand for the freedom of scientific enquiry. But there was more to it than that. The anti-theological animus of scientists and popularisers of science had an ideological dimension. Science was caught up in the warfare between state Churches which identified with the established political order, and scientists, alienated from the Churches, who turned science into an ideological weapon with which to attack Christianity. Theologians and biblical scholars were caught up in these struggles. The naturalistic lives of Jesus of biblical scholars like D. F. Strauss and Ernest Renan are cases in point. The dead hand of nineteenth-century positivism still lies heavy upon western theology. The social sciences which were established in the late nineteenth century — anthropology, sociology and psychology — imbibed the positivistic atmosphere of the period. All of these developments undermined the intellectual popularity of Christian theism, and their legacy for the modern western mind can scarcely be underestimated.

The two-books tradition, which had remained vital up until the nineteenth century, was a casualty of the conflict. The Book of Nature supplanted the authority of the Book of Scripture. Since many scientists were intent on not finding anything like the Christian God in nature, fewer educated westerners took natural or revealed theology seriously. In an age when science was revered not only for banishing the metaphysical obscurantism and religious bigotry of the past, but also as blessing the West with its extraordinary wealth, power and dynamism, the transcendent God of Christian theology

---

12. J. H. Brooke, *Science and Religion: Some Historical Perspectives* (Cambridge University Press, 1991) pp. 297-303. This is an excellent general reference.

seemed dispensable. Whereas in the early seventeenth century Kepler found the Trinity in nature because he brought it there, more and more twentieth-century scientists, bringing atheism or agnosticism, read those into nature. Carl Sagan's *Cosmos* and Jacques Monod's *Chance and Necessity* became the Bilgewater Treatises, the natural atheology, of the twentieth century.

The antitheistic character of much modern science, then, had its roots in culture, not nature. If natural and revealed theologies are to be taken seriously by those beyond the dwindling Christian subcultures of the West, the first task of Christian apologetics is to understand and to challenge scientism, which remains an obstacle to any form of theology.

Response by John Polkinghorne

One of the benefits of the study of history is to remind ourselves of
the mistakes of the past in the hope that we shall then avoid errors in
the present. Norma Emerton's clear and interesting paper is, in part,
a cautionary tale to which contemporary participants in the science-
religion debate need to pay attention. She issues at least three
warnings about natural theology.

It is a limited exercise. One could define natural theology as the
attempt to learn something of God by the exercise of reason and the
inspection of the world. Such a general form of inquiry could only
yield, at best, certain general forms of conclusion. In particular, the
God it describes would be something like the cosmic architect or the
great mathematician. He would certainly not be the God and Father
of our Lord Jesus Christ, who is encountered in altogether a more
specific and personal realm of experience. Such limited theological
insight is not to be despised, particularly in an age which finds any
kind of theistic belief problematic, but reliance on it alone would
only yield deism, which so easily degenerates into atheism.[1]

*Natural theology's claims are vulnerable to alternative
explanation.* The death blow delivered by Darwin to Paley makes
the point with devastating clarity. We need to heed the warnings of
Augustine and Aquinas against tying theology too closely to current
science. Even more fatal would be a God of the gaps strategy. We
have learned not to make claims such as "only the direct intervention
of God could bring living beings out of the inanimate matter". Yet,
carefulness should not induce intellectual paralysis. After all,
Augustine and Aquinas used the insights of their time, Platonism
and neo-Aristotelianism respectively, to considerable theological
effect.

It is an ambiguous exercise. We need to acknowledge the
criticism of Hume against too blithe an interpretation of the world as

1. See M. J. Buckley, *At the Origins of Modern Atheism* (Yale University
Press, 1987).

beneficially designed. Natural theology must take cognisance of the dark side of the story and seek to fit that also into its scheme of understanding.

I believe that we can heed these warnings and still find a useful role for natural theology. I believe that we are living at a time when there is a considerable revival of natural theology taking place. This is mostly at the hands of scientists, rather than the theologians, and it is pursued as much by those who stand outside any conventional religious traditions[2] as by those who stand within them.[3] People are struck by the rational beauty of the universe and by its delicately balanced fruitful history in a way which suggests to them that there is some intelligence behind it all. There seems more to tell than the scientific story alone can articulate. This new natural theology is not only revived. It is also revised in certain significant ways.

First, its claims are of insight, not proof. Its instincts are to side with Aquinas against Bonaventure. It trades in intellectually satisfying understanding rather than in logically coercive demonstration. It does not claim that atheists are stupid but rather that they explain less. Hume essentially asked, why not treat the universe itself as brute fact and not appeal to a God beyond it? The answer seems to be that the laws of nature, in their fruitful order and beauty, are not sufficiently self-explanatory to provide a comfortable starting point for explanation. Rather they point beyond themselves. Science raises metaquestions of a natural theological kind. One example is the "unreasonable effectiveness of mathematics", by which we have power to penetrate the rational structure of the world, even in regimes far from everyday experience and counterintuitive to our expectation. The universe seems shot through with signs of mind.

Secondly, it points to the fabric of the world and not to occurrences within it. It is science's role to explain physical process, the way in which life and humanity came to be. But the anthropic principle tells us that such fruitfulness is only possible in a very particular kind of universe, with very precise laws and specific force

2.   See P. W. Davies, *God and the New Physics* (London: Dent, 1983);   F. Hoyle, *The Intelligent Universe* (London: Michael Joseph, 1983).

3.   See Hugh Montefiore, *The Probability of God* (London: SCM Press, 1985); J. C. Polkinghorne, *Science and Creation* (London: SPCK, 1988) chapters 1 and 2.

strengths.[4] I personally subscribe to what I have called the "moderate anthropic principle", namely, that this is an interesting observation that calls for an explanation.[5] Natural theology provides one such rational explanation. In other words, the new natural theology is concerned, not with a God of the gaps, but with the significance of the ground rules which control any and every kind of happening in our universe. Our knowledge of these rules will deepen and change, but I do not think that the insight that it is only a universe of a very specific kind which is capable of evolving carbon-based life will disappear.

Thirdly, it acknowledges that creation involves a kenosis of divine power. An evolutionary universe is to be understood theologically as one which is allowed by its creator to make itself. Here is a positive interpretation of the role of chance in cosmic history: the shuffling operations of happenstance are the means for activating and realising the God-given potentiality with which matter has been endowed.[6] We catch here a glimmer of an answer to the problem of theodicy. A world allowed to make itself will necessarily have blind alleys and ragged edges.[7]

This new natural theology answers some of the classical criticisms of David Hume. The flawedness of the world is acknowledged and understood, not as signifying a botched job by its "rude, infant" Creator, but as the necessary price of its divinely-bestowed independence. Because we point to a cosmic fabric endowed with fruitfulness, and not to occurrences within history, there is an appeal to something which has no human analogue, rather than to limited human experience of creativity. We are not as anthropomorphic in argument as Hume supposed.

Behind this revival of natural theology lie two intellectual desires to which Emerton draws our attention and which are completely natural to the scientist: the search for sufficient reason and for an adequate response to the deep rational beauty of the world in which

4. See John Leslie, *Universes* (London: Routledge, 1989).
5. J. C. Polkinghorne, *Reason and Reality* (London: SPCK, 1991) chapter 6.
6. A. R. Peacocke, *Creation and the World of Science* (Oxford University Press, 1979) chapters 2 and 3; Polkinghorne, *Science and Creation, op. cit.* chapter 4.
7. See J. C. Polkinghorne, *Science and Providence* (London: SPCK, 1989) chapter 5.

we live. They motivate the exercise, but it will only be successful as a theological exercise if it keeps in close touch with the general body of theological thinking. Only in that way will we avoid the mistakes of the later eighteenth century. I value natural theology, not just as an apologetic strategy nor as a preliminary warming-up exercise prior to the real thinking, but as a modest but indispensable component in the great search for the knowledge of God and of his ways with his creation.

3

What has theology to learn from scientific methodology?

Nancey Murphy

Introduction

I believe it is fair to say that the Christian tradition is still trying to recover from the advent of modern science. Popular views of the warfare between science and religion stress clashes between specific scientific theories (Copernicus' or Darwin's) and specific Christian doctrines. However, I believe that science has presented a much more serious challenge to theology *indirectly* through changes in our understanding of knowledge. The development of scientific method at the beginning of the modern period had dramatic effects on epistemology, and theology's inability to account for itself in the terms of that new epistemology has been devastating. Consequently, the theology of the modern period has been much preoccupied with the question of theological method. Furthermore, there may be no intellectual discipline wherein one finds less agreement on how to proceed.

So I am suggesting that modern empiricist accounts of knowledge have created a crisis for theology, a crisis yet to be resolved. There is, however, good news. The inability of theologians to give an account of theological reasoning that squares with modern canons of rationality has been as much the fault of inadequate theories of knowledge as the fault of theology. It is only within the past thirty years that theories of scientific reasoning have become sophisticated enough to make it meaningful to ask whether theology can measure up to them. I claim that, given an adequate account of scientific reasoning, it can be shown that theological reasoning does, or at least could, meet exactly the same criteria. If I can make my case, this will be a very important result, both for apologetic purposes and for the sake of providing some stimulus and guidance for discussions of theological method.

It is not possible to make a thorough assessment here of the possibilities for a scientific theology — I shall only be able to sketch the outlines of such a proposal in this paper.[1] I begin with a brief account of recent developments in epistemology and philosophy of science, and then address some of the thornier issues involved in showing that theology fits these current canons of reasoning.

Recent advances in epistemology

The most significant recent development in theory of knowledge is the change from foundationalism to holism. Foundationalism is the view that if knowledge is to be knowledge at all it must be justified on the basis of assertions that cannot themselves be called into question lest there be an infinite regress of justifications. Different candidates have been proposed for a class of such "basic beliefs", beginning with Descartes's clear and distinct intuitions.

In philosophy of science, the foundational assertions were first taken to be descriptions of sense-data. However, philosophers quickly concluded that foundationalism will not work in science. If one begins with incorrigible sense-data, the logical gulf between the foundation and the next storey of the structure (knowledge of material objects) is too broad to span. If instead one begins at a more common-sense level with ordinary scientific facts, then the indubitability required by the classical foundationalist doctrine has already been lost. The neopositivist philosophers of science were willing to live with this chastened version of foundationalism. Karl Popper described facts in science as being more like pilings driven into a swamp than like a solid foundation.[2]

Ronald Thiemann has provided an interesting analysis of how foundationalism affected theology in the modern period, looking specifically at the way Scripture has been pressed into service to provide the foundation, a use for which many have found it ill-

---

1. For a more adequate account, see my *Theology in the Age of Scientific Reasoning* (Ithaca and London: Cornell University Press, 1990).
2. Karl Popper, *The Logic of Scientific Discovery* (New York: Harper, 1965).

suited.[3] In fact, I believe one could do a tidy job of summing up the history of modern theology by looking at answers to three questions. First, what proposals have been made regarding foundations for religious knowledge? Secondly, what are the problems with each of these proposals, and thirdly, in light of failure to find an adequate foundation, what moves have been made to side-step the whole issue?

Looking at the history in these terms, modern theologians fall roughly into three camps: those whose foundation is biblical, those whose foundation is experiential, and those who claim that theology does not belong in the category of knowledge at all. For the biblicists, the question always arises: how do you know that what you take to be revelation really is? Apologists from Locke to American Fundamentalists have turned to miracles and fulfilled prophecies. Karl Barth simply said (if I may be permitted a caricature), "don't ask".

The problem for the experientialists has generally been much like that of the sense-dataists in science: for the positivists it was how to make the leap from private, inner experience to a real *world*, external to the perceiver. For experientialists in theology, it is the problem of how to make the leap from private, inner experience to a real *God,* external to the believer.

The change from foundationalism to holism can be expressed as a change in dominant metaphors for thinking about knowledge. In his landmark article "Two dogmas of empiricism" Willard Quine proposed a new metaphor for understanding knowledge to replace the "building" images of foundationalism.[4] He suggested that the structure of knowledge is more like a web or net, where beliefs likely to be changed in the face of "recalcitrant experience" are near the edges; theoretical and logical beliefs, nearer the centre. When problems arise, in the form of inconsistency, there are usually any number of changes that can be made. These decisions will generally be made on a pragmatic basis: how best to restore consistency without disturbing other regions of the network.

---

3. Ronald Thiemann, *Revelation and Theology* (University of Notre Dame Press, 1985).
4. Willard Quine, *Philosophical Review* 40 (1951) pp. 20-43. Reprinted in *From a Logical Point of View* (Cambridge: Harvard University Press, 1953) pp. 20-46.

Holist accounts of scientific reasoning

Quine's image of knowledge as a net or web is suggestive, but perhaps it leaves too much to the imagination. For a more manageable account of holist epistemology, let us turn to philosophy of science. Thomas Kuhn's analysis of paradigm change is the best-known of holist accounts of science.[5] However, the work of a less-known philosopher, Imre Lakatos, turns out to be clearer and easier to apply to the theological task.

For Lakatos, the units of appraisal in science are not paradigms, but "research programmes". These are vast networks of theories and data, which are unified by a central theory, called the "hard core", since it is the one part of the network not subject to change over time. Between the core theory and the data lies a belt of "auxiliary hypotheses". These include lower-level theories that apply the core theory in various domains, theories of instrumentation, and initial conditions. Lakatos called this the protective belt because scientists will make changes here in order to restore consistency between the core theory and anomalous data, thus protecting the core from falsification. Thus it is more accurate to say that a research programme is an evolving series of theoretical networks, where the core theory stays the same and the belt of auxiliary hypotheses is modified and amplified to take account of an increasing domain of data.[6]

How does this holist view of the structure of scientific knowledge differ from foundationalism? First, it deals with larger structures of scientific thought. Quine would say that it is the whole of our belief system that faces the tribunal of experience. Lakatos and other current philosophers of science concentrate on the testing of large networks of theory. In either case, this is much different from the sentence-by-sentence justification seen in most foundationalist accounts.

---

5. See Thomas Kuhn, *The Structure of Scientific Revolutions,* second edition (University of Chicago Press, 1970).
6. See Imre Lakatos, "Falsification and the methodology of scientific research programmes" in *The Methodology of Scientific Research Programmes: Philosophical Papers* 1, John Worrall and Gregory Currie, editors (Cambridge University Press, 1978) pp. 8-101.

Secondly, and this cuts more to the heart of foundationalism, holists deny the epistemic independence of the foundation from that which it supports. They claim that facts are theory dependent in at least three senses: first, the meaning of factual statements is partially dependent on theory. So, for example, measurements of mass may stay the same in the change from Newtonian to relativistic physics, but the very meaning of the word 'mass' has changed. Secondly, holists recognise that sometimes the weight of theory will lead to the rejection of experimental results.

Finally, theory is almost always involved in the production of experimental results. A very simple example: measurement of temperature with a thermometer assumes some understanding of the thermometric properties of matter — the rising and falling of a column of mercury would be meaningless without the association of temperature with some other directly measurable quantity. These associations, historically empirical, now increasingly theoretical, which are employed in constructing the experimental apparatus and in justifying the use of data thereby produced, are called theories of instrumentation.

The consequence of this dialectical relation between theory and data is that the justification of a research programme is always somewhat circular. One accepts the research programme as a whole because it is better corroborated by its facts than the competitors are by their own somewhat different sets of data, but the facts themselves have been produced, recognised, and interpreted with the aid of theories ingredient in the research programme, and can only be accepted as facts if these theories are assumed to be true. Recognition of this factor in scientific knowledge will turn out to be quite important when we raise the question of the confirmation of theories in theology.

To see how Lakatos' description of a research programme fits theology we need to consider four elements: the hard core, the auxiliary hypotheses, the data, and the aforementioned theories of instrumentation.

Core theories

The hard core of a scientific research programme is a theory so
central to the entire project that to give it up is to give up the entire
programme. It makes a claim about the general character of the
aspect of reality under investigation; in so doing it ties together all of
the more specialised theories within the programme. Lakatos says
that the hard core of a scientific research programme is often so
abstract as to count as metaphysical. A good example of this is
Descartes's corpuscular theory of matter, which served as the hard
core for early modern physics.

The hard core of a research programme in systematic or doctrinal
theology, therefore, will most likely be one's non-negotiable and
most general understanding of God and of God's relation to the
created order. The doctrine of the Trinity functions nicely as a core
theory for classical orthodoxy, since all of the rest of the Christian
doctrines can be unified by means of their direct or indirect relation
to one of the persons of the Trinity.

There are, of course, other starting points for systematic
theology. Wolfhart Pannenberg has agreed that the statement "The
God of Jesus Christ is the All-Determining Reality" functions as
the core of his developing programme. "God is the God of the
oppressed" might be seen as the core of Latin-American liberation
theology. *Sola gratia* must figure as the organising principle of
Martin Luther's vision of Christianity; and likewise the sovereignty
of God is a unifying theme for the Reformed tradition.

Auxiliary hypotheses

The rest of the theories in a scientific research programme are called
auxiliary hypotheses, and they bear most of the explicit theoretical
content of the programme. The auxiliary hypotheses in systematic
theology, then, will be the remainder of the Christian doctrines:
theories of the Church, of the person and work of Christ, and so on.
These doctrines are elaborated differently in different programmes.
The differences will be due, in large part, to differences in the hard
cores of the programmes. Consider two versions of the doctrine
of the work of Christ: substitutionary atonement depends on the
doctrine of the divinity of Christ, which is contained implicitly in a

triune conception of the nature of God; the liberationists' very different account of the work of Christ is equally dependent on their core assumption about the character and purposes of God.

Data for theology

The objection critics are most likely to raise to the project of likening theology to science is to argue that there is no parallel to scientific data. Theologians might reply that the scriptures are treated as data by most theologians, and that there are other sources of data from history, from religious experience, and perhaps others as well.

So the problem is not the absence of anything that *functions* for the theologian as the data do for scientists; but it may be instead that scriptural texts and religious experiences seem *defective* when compared to scientific data.

Scripture

The problem with taking Scripture as a source of data for theology is this: why should these texts be taken to provide reliable evidence regarding the nature and purposes of God rather than evidence merely of Israel's and the early Church's beliefs about God? To meet this objection we need to return to the concept from philosophy of science of theories of instrumentation. Just as the kinetic theory provides justification for taking thermometer readings as a genuine source of knowledge about certain physical processes, we have in theology a theory (or doctrine) of revelation, which serves as a theoretical justification for taking the scriptures as a reliable source of knowledge about God. So, in theology, in place of theories of instrumentation, we incorporate theories of *interpretation*. In particular, we have theories about the nature of the texts that tell us how to make proper use of them in our science of God. Note that different theological programmes with different understandings of the *nature* of revelation will employ the texts differently. If revelation means divine dictation, we take our 'scripture readings' differently than we do if revelation is through salvation history, or through personal encounter with the Word. As David Kelsey has noted, the manner in which Scripture functions to authorise theological proposals is dependent upon a prior judgment about the manner in which God is present to the community — "a single, synoptic, imaginative judgment" in which the theologian attempts to "catch up what Christianity is basically all about".[7]

Religious experience

A great deal more needs to be said about the use of Scripture as a source of data for theology — all the questions about interpretation and historical accuracy, and so forth. However, I shall not pursue these issues here. If we are looking for parallels between theology and science, the more interesting possibility for theological data is religious experience, since we tend to equate confirmation of theories with empirical or experiential confirmation.

There has been a long debate within Christianity regarding the evidential value of religious experience: do Christians' visions and other experiences provide genuine knowledge of God? In particular, can we learn anything new from these experiences, or do they inevitably only confirm the recipient's preconceptions (or biases) about God? In order to make clear the difference that recent philosophy of science makes to this debate, I shall summarise some older arguments against the evidential value of religious experience, and then show how the current developments described above provide answers to these objections.

One common objection is that religious experience is essentially private and subjective. It is contrasted with data for science, which are public and replicable and, in that sense, objective. Let us call this the subjectivity problem.

The second problem with religious experience is what I shall call the circularity problem. It was stated succinctly by Alasdair MacIntyre in a 1955 article entitled "Visions".[8] MacIntyre's argument can be summarised as follows: Visions are taken by the recipient to convey information about something other than the experience itself — in most traditions, about God. However, we could never know from any such experience that it had the character of being a message from God unless we already had knowledge of

---

7. David Kelsey, *The Uses of Scripture in Recent Theology* (Philadelphia: Fortress Press, 1975) p. 159.

8. In *New Essays in Philosophical Theology,* Antony Flew and Alasdair MacIntyre, editors (London: Macmillan, 1955) pp. 254-60.

God, and knowledge, as well, about how messages from God were to be identified. "The decisive evidence for the divine", he says, "would then be anterior to the experience and not derived from it, whereas what we are concerned with here is how far the experience itself can provide such evidence."[9] In other words, to argue from a religious experience to a claim about God is circular, since one needed to have knowledge beforehand that God exists, and also about how God communicates.

In addition, MacIntyre argues that it may be thought that to treat a vision as a sign of the invisible is to accept in the realm of religious belief a procedure we are accustomed to employ elsewhere. So, for example, we infer unseen fire from smoke, approaching trains from signals. But the case of religion is not the same. We can infer unseen fires from smoke because we have seen fires producing smoke in the past. But we have no experience of the causal connection between God and any visions God might produce.

Here is an example that nicely illustrates MacIntyre's worry. Catherine of Siena, a fourteenth-century mystic, called her book *The Dialogue* because in it she posed questions to God and then wrote (or recorded) long passages that were supposed to be God's replies. One of these replies is to a question about how to distinguish between experiences that come from God and those that do not:

> Now, dearest daughter ... I will say something about what you asked me concerning the sign I said I give the soul for discerning the visitations she may receive through visions or other consolations. I told you how she could discern whether or not these were from me. The sign is the gladness and hunger for virtue that remain in the soul after the visitation, especially if she is anointed with the virtue of true humility and set ablaze with divine charity.[10]

So Catherine would say that she can recognise when a religious experience is from God by these signs: if it is from God, it produces gladness, hunger for virtue, humility, and charity.

---

9. *Ibid.* p. 256. MacIntyre's argument is expressed in terms of visions, but it would apply equally to other kinds of purported experiences from God.

10. Suzanne Noffke, translator and editor, *Catherine of Siena: The Dialogue* (New York: Paulist Press, 1980) p. 198.

Now, MacIntyre would ask Catherine: "How do you know that those are reliable signs?"

Catherine: "Because God told me so."

MacIntyre: "How do you know it was God who told you that?"

Catherine: "Well, the experience produced gladness, humility, charity."

So you see the problem.

The subjectivity and circularity problems reinforce one another. Some authors have pointed out that religious experience is nearly always interpreted in terms of the categories of the religion it is taken to confirm: Catholic Christians have experiences of Christ or the Virgin Mary; Protestants only of Christ; Hindus have experiences of Brahman, and so on. Or, to put this point more accurately, religious experiences are experienced as manifestations of phenomena appropriate to the recipient's belief system. Thus, there is no pure, objective religious experience prior to its interpretation in terms of the adherent's presupposed categories.[11] To state the objection baldly, the subjective biases of the recipient affect the experiences through and through, and thus they cannot provide any independent confirmation for the presupposed systems of belief.

Part of the answer to these objections is to note that MacIntyre's circularity charge is based on a foundationalist understanding of knowledge and, furthermore, would apply equally well to much reasoning in science.

An example from science that would be entirely analogous to the situation regarding religious knowledge, as MacIntyre understands it, is the following. Suppose one puts a closed container of gas over a bunsen burner. The container has a constant volume gas thermometer and a pressure gauge affixed. The result of the experiment is that as the temperature goes up, the pressure goes up as well. This experiment provides confirmation of Boyle's law: the pressure of a gas multiplied by its volume is equal to some constant times its temperature.

However, this same law is involved as a theory of instrumentation to validate the use of thermometer readings as reliable and

---

11. See, for example, Steven T. Katz, "Language, epistemology, and mysticism," in *Mysticism and Philosophical Analysis*, Steven T. Katz, editor (New York: Oxford University Press, 1978) pp. 22-74.

useful data for such purposes. So MacIntyre could make the same objection to this bit of scientific reasoning as he did in the imagined dialogue with Catherine: "You are claiming that thermometer readings are reliable signs of the temperature of the gas, and you are using those readings as evidence for the gas laws. But you cannot know that thermometers provide reliable measures of temperature unless you already accept Boyle's law. So the reasoning is circular. The experiment with the gas cannot provide any evidence for the law."

MacIntyre's imagined objections to both Catherine and to our example from science show that he is operating with a foundationalist theory of knowledge. He is assuming two things: first, that we only argue *from* experience *to* theory, and second, that *one* experience supports *one* theory. Thus, one experiment supports one theory (or law) in science; one vision supports the one simple theory that God exists.[12]

However, we have just seen that reasoning in science is much more complicated: we argue from a variety of experimental results to support a network of scientific theories. Some of those theories, in turn, give us grounds for regarding the experimental data as sound. To illustrate this, consider a more complete account of the relation between experimental measurement and theory regarding the expansion of gases. First, there exist a variety of procedures by which to measure temperature: the familiar mercury and alcohol thermometers, procedures based on the thermo-electric effect, changes in electrical resistance of material such as platinum, and others. The confidence we can place in any of these measuring techniques is based in part on the consistency of results obtained by the various methods.[13]

Secondly, the operation of each of these instruments is explained by, and thus validated in part by, the scientific theory. For example, Boyle's law is now explained by means of the kinetic theory of heat,

---

12. In fairness to MacIntyre, it is important to mention that MacIntyre's own recent works are some of the most interesting and valuable contributions to the recent epistemological revolution. See especially his *Whose Justice? Which Rationality?* (University of Notre Dame Press, 1988).
13. I wish to thank Jack Dodd and Lyndon Rogers for assistance in clarifying this example.

according to which gas pressure may be defined as momentum change in molecular impact with the walls of the container, and temperature is defined as the average molecular kinetic energy. The kinetic theory also partially explains the expansion of liquids when heated, and so stands behind the use of ordinary thermometers.

Thus, an entire network of theory, laws and experimental results is accepted as a whole because of its consistency and its explanatory power. There is always a degree of circular reasoning involved, but it might be called virtuous rather than vicious circularity because it is part of what is involved in showing the consistency of the entire network.

Theories of instrumentation in theology

Let us see what happens to MacIntyre's position if we apply a holist account of knowledge to theological reasoning. I claim, on the basis of an analogy with science, that we ought to expect to find vast networks of theological theories, where no single theory is supported by any single religious experience; instead, a variety of experiences contribute support to the whole network. Furthermore, we ought to expect there to be something that plays a role equivalent to theories of instrumentation in science, or to the theories of interpretation that we have seen to be required to validate the use of Scripture in theology.

Let us return to the example from Catherine of Siena. Catherine did not have an experience of God speaking to her out of the blue. She had a whole network of background theories about God, about Jesus Christ, about God's will for human life, and so forth. She also had a long history of previous experiences relating to God, as well as knowledge of others' experiences.

Of particular interest here is the set of criteria described above for recognising when she was dealing with God, and when not. Recall that her criteria are gladness and hunger for virtue that remain after the experience, growth in humility, and being set ablaze with charity toward others.

To investigate the value of such criteria, let us compare them with a proposal made by Teresa of Avila in her sixteenth-century guide to the spiritual life, *The Interior Castle*.[14] The purpose of Teresa's book was to set out the stages her sisters should expect to go through in their relationship to God. Thus it was obviously necessary to explain how they were to tell if they were in communion with God, and if so, what God was doing "in their souls". Here is a passage in which Teresa is explaining how to recognise when one has reached the state of union with God in prayer:

> This union is above all earthly joys, above all delights, above all consolations, and still more than that... (p. 338).
> God so places himself in the interior of the soul that when it returns to itself it can in no way doubt that it was in God and God was in it. This truth remains with it so firmly that even though years go by without God's granting that favour again, the soul can neither forget nor doubt that it was in God and God was in it (p. 339).

If Teresa were familiar with modern theology, she might say that such an experience is self-authenticating — an experience such that the one who has it cannot doubt *that* the experience was and *what* it was. There have been assorted attempts to ground religious knowledge on self-authenticating experiences. Such moves are, rightly, I think, to be regarded with suspicion. The subjective certitude described here surely has value to the recipient, but has no *evidential* value, at least not for anyone else.

The difference between Teresa's and Catherine's criteria is that Catherine's judgment is based on the *connection* between the purported experience of God and other experiences — some at the same time and some later — and most important, to *observable* changes in the recipient's life. The one experience, taken to be an encounter with God, is validated by the way it fits into a network of other experiences or phenomena. Is it *accompanied* by gladness? Is it *followed* by greater humility? Is a felt increase in charity borne out in action in the days or weeks or years to come? Because of this last criterion, Catherine is not left to make a judgment alone; her

---

14. In *The Collected Works of St. Teresa of Avila* 2, Otilio Rodrigues and Kieran Kavanaugh, editors (Washington, DC: ICS Publications, 1980) pp. 261-499.

confessor and friends will be able to see the changes in her if the experience is valid, and will help her to judge its authenticity.

The significance of requiring an interconnected set of experiences and, especially, a publicly-observable criterion such as growth in charitable action, can be seen by considering the most prominent of the competing explanations for religious experiences. Catherine was most concerned that she not be misled by attributing to God experiences that were actually induced by the Devil. Teresa was apparently more worried by the possibility that the experiences were merely the product of the recipient's *imagination.* Modern investigators, similarly, will be most concerned by the possibility that religious experiences are merely psychological phenomena with no reference to a transcendent God. At first glance, such experiences can easily be explained psychologically. Religious people want to have experiences that affirm their beliefs. This desire is the cause of the experiences, whether directly and intentionally or, more likely, through a process of autosuggestion such that the experiences seem to come from an external source. Let us call this the self-inducement theory of religious experience.

Note that we are looking at a situation exactly parallel to one that arises in science. The value of empirical evidence for a research programme is called into question by showing that the same phenomena, if differently interpreted, serve equally to support a competing research programme. The self-inducement theory can be construed as an auxiliary hypothesis in a *functionalist* programme in the sociology or psychology of religion. In my judgment, one of the most important tasks for Christian apologists is to show that non-theistic programmes of this sort cannot do as good a job in accounting for religions experience as do theological programmes.

That Teresa was concerned about the self-inducement theory of religious experience is shown in the following passage, where she attempts to convey the reasons why some experiences seem as if they could not have been produced by the person's own imagination:

> Wonderful effects are left so that the soul may believe; at least there is assurance that the locution doesn't come from the imagination. Furthermore, if the soul is attentive, it can always have assurance for the following reasons: first, there is a difference because of the clarity of the locution. It is so clear that the soul remembers every syllable

and whether it is said in one style or another ... But in a locution
fancied by the imagination the words will not be so clear or distinct but
like something half-dreamed.

Second, in these locutions one often is not thinking about what is
heard (I mean that the locution comes unexpectedly and even
sometimes while one is in conversation) ... It often refers to things
about the future that never entered the mind, and so the imagination
couldn't have fabricated it.

Third, the one locution comes as in the case of a person who hears,
and that of the imagination comes as in the case of a person who
gradually composes what he himself wants to be told.[15]

So Teresa is arguing that the characteristics of the experience itself
can provide adequate evidence against the self-inducement theory.
However, it is easy enough to discount this claim. First, we simply
do not know how great are a person's powers to create such
experiences without realising it. Secondly, Ludwig Wittgenstein's
arguments against private language are relevant here. Without
external, public criteria there is no real difference between saying
something such as "this locution *is* clearer than that" and saying "this
locution *seems* clearer than that". Thus the first expression has no
real use, and is therefore meaningless.[16]

So let us consider whether any of Catherine's criteria are public in
the required sense, and whether they could possibly serve to
distinguish between the two explanatory theories: divine encounter
versus self-inducement. The criterion of gladness is public enough;
that is, we are often able to tell whether people we are close to are
happy. However, this criterion is likely to be met whichever of the
theories is true: if one is strongly motivated to have an experience in
conformity with one's religious beliefs, and the experience occurs,
then one ought to be happy as a result.

The criterion of increased humility begins to create problems for
the inducement theory. Greater smugness is the reaction more to be
expected from a person who has just had his or her desires met and
beliefs confirmed.

---

15. *Ibid.* p. 376.
16. See Ludwig Wittgenstein, *Philosophical Investigations,* G.E.M. Anscombe,
    translator (New York: Macmillan, 1953), especially sections 258-263.

Hunger for virtue is a noble sentiment, but does not mean much unless it is enacted. This leaves the criterion of increased charity. Can this be taken as a reliable sign of the working of God, or is it compatible with the inducement theory as well? It could certainly be argued that in a setting where good works count as validation of one's status as a spokesperson for God, one would have strong motivation for performing such acts.

Catherine's confessor and biographer Raymond of Capua states his intention to relate "the events which establish the credibility of Catherine's account of her inner life".[17] To this end he notes that she never confessed a serious sin. Furthermore, even if we take due account of tendencies to exaggerate and embellish the biographies of saints, Catherine can be said to have adopted a remarkable pattern of service to the poor and sick in her community. However, Raymond's intention is to show that Catherine's charity went so far beyond the ordinary as to warrant her claim to have been in direct contact with God.

This issue raises a theological question: is there a limit to the extent one can reform one's own character for the purpose of gaining a hearing for visionary experiences? This is an instance of the larger question: is moral perfection within the grasp of the human will? Christians have generally answered no, and no one has said it more elegantly than the Apostle Paul:

> Though the will to do good is there, the ability to effect it is not. The good which I want to do, I fail to do; but what I do is the wrong which is against my will ... I discover this principle, then: that when I want to do right, only wrong is within my reach. In my inmost self I delight in the law of God, but I perceive in my outward actions a different law, fighting against the law that my mind approves, and making me a prisoner under the law of sin which controls my conduct. Wretched creature that I am, who is there to rescue me from this state of death: Who but God? (Romans 7:14-25, *passim*, REB).

Here Paul is making a straightforward empirical claim about human capacities: we want to do good; we often do evil instead, no

---

17. Conleth Kearns, translator, *The Life of Catherine of Siena* (Wilmington: Michael Glazier Inc., 1980) p. 85.

matter how strong our motivation. I know that young people do not always believe this, but I suspect that everyone over forty does.

So it is possible to recognise lives that do not fit the pattern; lives that violate our expectations regarding the natural limits of virtue. This means, in turn, that the self-inducement theory has limits; exceptionally noble lives may justifiably call us to raise the question whether a higher power is not involved after all.

The criterion of increased charity, or as we might now express it the criterion of charity beyond the bounds, interacts with the criterion of humility. If the self-inducement theory is true, and its corollary, that good works are undertaken for the purpose of self-accreditation, then good works done in secret will be of no value. Hence it is common to find spiritual writers warning their readers to pay no attention to good works that are done in a highly visible manner.

So my claim is that Catherine's criteria have some interest for the religious epistemologist. Given the right circumstances, such as the opportunity to observe changes in the lives of those who claim to receive visions or teachings from God, these signs would have some value for distinguishing between experiences generated by the recipient's own imagination and others that could not be so easily explained away.

The Christian tradition contains a number of teachings similar to Catherine's on criteria for recognising the work of God in people's lives. There are some variations from one denomination to another, and some individual variation from one author to another, but over-all quite a bit of agreement. So we have here a theory, which I shall call the theory of discernment, which states that it is possible to recognise the activity of God in human life by means of signs or criteria, some of which are public and relatively objective. My claim is that the theory of discernment functions in Christian theology in exactly the same way as theories of instrumentation do in science.

The criteria for discernment can be grouped conveniently under two headings: consistency and fruit. 'Consistency' for Protestants means consistency with Scripture. For Catholics, it also includes consistency with church teaching. Use of the consistency criterion, of course, raises all the problems of interpretation that go along with use of the Bible for any purpose — a set of problems I shall not go into here, except to note that a wooden application of this criterion would mean that no religious experience could ever challenge traditional teaching, since such an experience would automatically be judged inauthentic. However, if this criterion is used in conjunction with others, there will be cases where an experience, attested on the grounds of other signs, conflicts with a traditional *interpretation* of Scripture, and the experience, together with critical reflection on the received interpretation, may result in that interpretation being overturned. So there is room for a dynamic interplay among texts, interpretations and religious experiences.

If this is the case, there is a clear parallel with science, where an observation or experimental result that conflicts with accepted theory will be regarded with suspicion. The decision either to ignore the datum or to revise the theory can go either way, and will only be made after re-evaluating the theory and performing additional experiments.

The criterion of "fruit" refers to various effects in the life of the recipient and her community. The term is appropriate in that Jesus declared that false prophets could be known by their fruits (Matthew 7:16). Paul listed the fruit of the Holy Spirit as love, joy, peace, patience, kindness, generosity, faithfulness, gentleness, and self-control (Galatians 5:22-23). Catherine, as well as many other spiritual writers, would add humility and contrition for sin.

The one significant difference in views of discernment from one branch of the Christian tradition to another has to do with *who* does the discerning. In both the Catholic and the Reformed traditions, the assumption is that discernment is exercised by the one receiving the experience, or at most by that person and his pastor or confessor. In a third major tradition — the Anabaptist or Radical-reformation tradition — discernment is a function exercised by the gathered community. That is, it is the job of the Church to decide who are the true and false prophets.

The communal nature of discernment among Mennonites, Quakers, and other Churches from this radical tradition allows for another kind of fruit to be added to the list, the agreement and unity of the congregation. This means in the first instance that all members need to agree that the other criteria are met — consistency with Scripture and production of love and virtue. But, in addition, the experience being judged must contribute to the building up of the body of believers, not to discord and dissension. It is important to note that this criterion presupposes a church community in which evidence of conversion is required for membership, since, as Jesus himself noted, the presence and activity of God produces conflict between true believers and the world.[18] Yet, even among "true believers" dissension is so common that the Church's being brought to unity of mind and heart can well be taken as a sign of the activity of God in their midst.

The circularity problem

We began with two objections to the use of religious experience as evidence for religious beliefs: the subjectivity problem and the circularity problem. I have described a theory of discernment, and have claimed that it functions in theology in the same way that a theory of instrumentation does in science. Now I want to show that circularity is not a problem after all — in fact, the modest degree of circularity involved in employing a theory of discernment is a virtue of the system rather than a vice.

Let us return to the example from science. Temperature readings are accepted as usable data because we have theories of instrumentation that connect the measurements to a conception of "kinetic energy". That is, the theory states that there is a regular relation between this observable sign (for example, changes in the column of mercury) and an invisible quantity (kinetic energy). Now, recall MacIntyre's claim that we can only infer the presence of the unseen from the visible sign if we have had *experience* of the connection between the sign and that which it signifies. But the example of the thermometer shows this claim to be false: no one has ever seen kinetic energy. How, then, is this particular theory of instrumentation confirmed? By the conjunction of two factors: one is the experienced reliability of the instrument — it produces similar or identical readings again and again under similar circumstances —

---

18. "But when you are arrested, do not worry about what you are to say, for when the time comes, the words you need will be given you; it will not be you speaking, but the Spirit of your Father speaking in you. Brother will hand over brother to death, and a father his child; children will turn against their parents and send them to their death. Everyone will hate you for your allegiance to me..." (Matthew 10:19-22; cf. Matthew 10:34-36).

and these results correlate with results produced by other measuring devices. The other is that the theory of instrumentation follows from theoretical beliefs that we have no good reason to call into question. In other words, the truth of the theory of instrumentation is supported by its consistency with a network of other statements, some rather directly from experience, others of a theoretical nature.

I claim that the Christian theory of discernment is likewise supported by its connections to a variety of other statements, some from experience, others of a theoretical (or theological) nature. For example, Jonathan Edwards, the theologian of the Great Awakening, presents a simple theoretical account of why the fruits of the Spirit should provide valid signs of God at work in a human life. The fruits of the Spirit jointly constitute a particular kind of character, what Edwards calls the "lamb-like, dove-like character" of Christ. In the light of Christian theology, this is exactly what is to be expected. The fruits are signs that the Holy Spirit is at work in a person's life; the Holy Spirit is otherwise known as the Spirit of Christ; Christ's spirit should manifest itself in a Christ-like character. How could it be otherwise?

The second kind of support for the theory of discernment needs to be experiential — does it work *reliably*, and is it connected in a consistent way with other experiences? As we saw above, the process of discernment is exactly the test of whether the inner experience, putatively of God, is correlated with the other sorts of experiences that our theories lead us to expect. Reliability means, simply, that a measurement or process results in roughly or exactly the same results under similar circumstances. Reliability is always a matter of degree; different degrees are required depending upon the complexity of the matter under study. Measurements with a ruler are highly reliable; measurement with an IQ test is only moderately reliable. We have no data on the reliability of believers' judgments regarding the presence or absence of God's agency in certain events. But it is significant that communities that exercise communal judgment do not readily abandon the practice. This fact suggests that the results tend to be somewhat consistent over time, since a practice that yielded erratic results would soon lose its appeal.

It might be objected that the variety of beliefs and practices found throughout the Christian movement across denominations and through time argues for the unreliability of discernment. I suggest, however, that it argues instead for the need to make more frequent and determined use of the practice. In fact, much of what goes on in the life of Churches has never been subjected to this sort of testing. Greater reliance on discernment would turn Churches into laboratories for testing theological formulations.

So the theory of discernment may not be as well-confirmed as many of the theories of instrumentation in the hard sciences, but some informal confirmation does exist; and the fact that it presupposes some aspects of Christian theology is a factor in its favour, not a detriment.

The subjectivity problem

Much of what is needed to address the subjectivity problem has already been said. It is clear that suspicions about our ability to delude ourselves calls for greater emphasis on discernment criteria that are public and intersubjective. "Gladness" could be as much a result of effective self-deception as of the presence of God. Humility can be feigned. But, I have suggested, there are limits to the degree to which growth in charity can be undertaken at will. So the criterion of greatest interest for the philosopher must be fruit of a publicly observable sort such as extraordinary growth in virtue. While we have no laboratory instruments to measure virtue, it is nonetheless a public phenomenon, there for anyone to see.

So the kind of experience that is relevant for confirming religious belief is not so much the immediate experiences of the mystics, but rather "experience" in a different sense: the accumulated observ-ations made by a discerning community regarding correlations between reports of private experiences such as visions and other, publicly observable phenomena such as acts of charity.

Here, as in science, observations and the conclusions drawn from them will interact with theory. For example, if Catherine's experience is judged genuine, then her teachings will be taken to be true by the community in which she lives. Their lives will be affected, and the next generation will be able to see the fruits (or lack of fruit) manifested in the lives of her followers, and so on. Theologian Peter Moore observes:

A mystic is, precisely, one who has tested through his own experience the claims made by earlier generations of mystics. Finally, there is in mystical writing much evidence for the epistemological stability and hence objective validity of mystical experience: concordance among the reports of different mystics, refinement of observations, development of theory, improvement of technique, and so on. In sum, it could be argued that most if not all of the conditions which are met in the case of experiences known to have objective validity appear, from the accounts given by mystics, to obtain in the case of mystical experience too.[19]

Moore's comment raises the issue of objectivity. "Objectivity" is a word used rather loosely in many circles — perhaps it is more of a commendation than a description. The most appropriate use of the word for present purposes is that of social scientists, whose difficulties in measurement are almost as great as those of the empirical theologian. Here "objectivity" can be equated with an observation's or measurement's reliability, validity, and inter-subjectivity.

We have already addressed the reliability of the results of discernment. The validity of a measurement refers to its genuine connection with the thing measured; for example, is IQ a valid measure of intelligence? The value of Edwards's theology, mentioned above, is that it provides a rationale for believing the fruits of the Spirit to be *valid* indicators of God's activity, not because of some accidental connection, but because they participate in the divine character they represent.

We have also addressed the issue of intersubjectivity: discernment criteria that involve publicly observable effects will be given greater weight by the philosopher just because they allow for, even demand, intersubjective agreement. So Catherine's experience of God in the depths of her soul, in the privacy of her room, is not a suitable datum for theology. But the fact that such experiences were coupled with extraordinary acts of charity, known throughout much of the Christian world at the time, may very well be an objective datum for confirming her claims to receive revelation from God, and thus also the belief system with which her revelations cohere.

---

19. "Mystical experience, mystical doctrine, mystical technique," in Steven T. Katz, editor, *op. cit.* p. 126.

Further problems

I now wish to address another epistemological worry that may have arisen during the presentation of this paper. I have been arguing that under proper circumstances some instances of some kinds of religious experiences might provide suitably objective empirical support to confirm religious theories. I have emphasised the consistency or coherence of beliefs drawn from experience with beliefs belonging to the theoretical or theological structure of the system. The new worry that is likely to have been raised by the foregoing arguments is that the system now appears too neat, too pat. A genuine empirical theory has to be falsifiable as well as confirmable; we need to be able to specify what experiences would call it into question.[20] If the data of religious experience are theory-laden — interpreted, even in a sense produced, in light of the theories they are taken to confirm — if one of the criteria for recognising a relevant experience is its conformity to Scripture or church teaching, then have we not described an essentially unfalsifiable system?

I have already mentioned the possibility that the consistency criterion could be used in such a way as to make the system unfalsifiable, but it need not. Consider another passage from Catherine's *Dialogue*:

> I have shown you, dearest daughter, that in this life guilt is not atoned for by any suffering simply as suffering, but rather by suffering borne with desire, love, and contrition of heart. The value is not in the suffering but in the soul's desire. Likewise, neither desire nor any other virtue has value or life except through my only-begotten Son, Christ crucified, since the soul has drawn love from him and in virtue follows his footsteps. In this way and in no other is suffering of value. It satisfies for sin, then, with gentle unitive love born from the sweet knowledge of my goodness and from the bitterness and contrition the heart finds in the knowledge of itself and its own sins. Such knowledge gives birth to hatred and contempt for sin and for the soul's selfish sensuality, whence she considers herself worthy of punishment and unworthy of reward. So you see, said gentle Truth, those who have heartfelt contrition, love for true patience, and that true

---

20. This is Karl Popper's claim. See Popper, *op. cit.*

humility which considers oneself worthy of punishment and unworthy
of reward suffer with patience and so make atonement.[21]

If it is the case that this locution comes from God, it has definite
theological implications. I selected this particular passage because it
touches upon a disputed point in Christian theology: does human
suffering atone for sin (as some Catholics have taught), or does
atonement come only through the suffering of Christ, mediated
to sinners by grace (as most Protestants maintain). On first glance,
this passage seems to confirm the Catholic view that human suffering is meritorious. But careful reading shows that the correct
understanding is more complicated than either Catholic "works" or
Protestant "grace alone". Suffering is of value, but only insofar as
one is united by love to Christ, which leads to true contrition and, it
can be presumed, opens the penitent to grace.

So here is the record of an experience that Catherine judged to be
a communication from God, that her Catholic superiors saw fit to
publish as such, and that modified the Catholic thinking of her day
in the direction of a not-yet-enunciated Protestant emphasis on grace.
(Recall that Catherine was writing nearly two hundred years before
the Protestant Reformation.) So it is, indeed, possible for religious
experience to clash with and thus correct theological theory.

A second problem that really ought to be addressed here is the
problem of the plurality of religions. David Hume recognised over
two hundred years ago that the claims of one religion, if taken
seriously, tend to cancel out the claims of the others. If Christian
experience confirms Christian beliefs, then is it not also the case that
Jewish experience confirms Jewish beliefs, and Hindu, Hindu, and
so on? The first step in addressing this problem would be to ask
whether each of these other religions has a criterion comparable to
the Christian theory of discernment to separate authentic encounters
with the divine from counterfeits, which are presumably as common
in other faiths as they are among Christians. If such procedures
exist, giving warrant for the claim that their members experience the
presence of God (as I presume they do), then we have a situation,
again, that is entirely analogous to science: competing research
programmes, each with its own supporting evidence. Lakatos has

---

21 Noffke, *op. cit.* p. 29.

provided a criterion for choosing among competing research programmes, which can be summarised briefly as a test of the amount
of *progress* each programme makes in explaining novel facts.[22]
This criterion needs to be used to arbitrate among competing
theologies within Christianity, as well.

Summary

I claimed earlier that what was needed to show theology to be like
science in terms of structure, reasoning and evidence is to consider
the core theories, auxiliary hypotheses, theories of instrumentation,
and data. The picture I have presented of systematic theology
construes the theologian's treatment of the theological loci as akin to
the scientist's elaboration of an interconnected network of auxiliary
hypotheses. The scientist's theorising is controlled by the central
vision of reality dictated by the hard core of the programme and
by the requirement of consistency with empirical data. Similarly,
the theologian's work is constrained by a central vision of what
Christianity is basically all about — some construal of God's
relation to the world.

The bulk of this paper was addressed to the question of a
theological analogue for scientists' empirical data. I have suggested
that the theologian's data come primarily from Scripture, history and
religious experience. I claimed that while some of these categories
of data may seem defective by scientific standards, they really are
not when we consider the role of theories of instrumentation in
science and the quite comparable theories of interpretation and
discernment in theology. Such data differ only in degree from those
of science: they are somewhat less reliable, less objective than those
of the hard sciences, but probably comparable to those of the human
sciences.

What is the significance of my conclusions? I mentioned above
that showing theology to be compatible with the epistemological
standards derived from science would have apologetic importance,
overcoming one of the most significant critiques of theology in the

---

22. See Lakatos, *op. cit.*; and my *Theology in the Age of Scientific Reasoning*
    for an application to theology.

modern period. I also believe that the account I have given here provides workable guidelines for how to do theology, and how to recognise whether or not one has succeeded at the task.

There is a third consequence, especially important for the discussion of the relations between theology and science. An account something like mine is needed in order to justify the supposition that theology and science could possibly have anything to say to one another. That is, it is necessary to show that the discipline of theology aims at *knowledge* of a reality independent of the human subject. If theology is really only about human values or meanings, then there is no more reason to think that theology and science can engage in dialogue than to think that science ought to dialogue with ethics or art or literary theory.

So the deeper agenda of my work is an attempt to reverse the turn taken by modern liberal theology — the "subjective turn" from discourse about God and the world to discourse about human religiosity. The great increase in conferences and publications, such as this one, wherein theology is treated as a fit dialogue partner for science, encourages one to think that such a reversal may indeed be possible.

Response by Grant Gillett

Before I embark on my substantive worries about Nancey Murphy's interesting paper there are one or two preliminary points of detail to which I should respond. The first concerns Wittgenstein's objection to private language. Wittgenstein famously and, in my opinion, cogently argued that the meaning of a term could not be given by an in-principle private or Cartesian object or criterion.[1] He did not conclude, however, that one could not talk about private experiences or aspects of mental life which are both important and private to the person who experiences them. He argued that the criteria by which these could be identified and described might derive from a public sphere of language and communication but, having learned the use of terms such as "gladness", "set ablaze", and so on in such a way that one feels confident in their meaning, one can apply them to experiences which are not shared or validated by anybody else, in the same way that one could observe or report a red and yellow butterfly as one walked alone in the woods and be in no doubt that one had correctly discerned the striking features of its appearance. Indeed if one could not generally be sure, without corroboration, about one's psychic experience one could conceivably say and mean "I think I am in pain but could you please check for me", which is patently absurd. Therefore, once we have established that a witness is generally reliable and confident in her grasp of the meaning of psychological predicates, there need not invariably be publicly accessible criteria available to validate her use of them.

This, in fact, is likely to be an important conclusion for Murphy because she will surely want to say that a subject who shows the requisite public criteria of godliness is then to be trusted when she goes on to use the disputed psychological or phenomenological predicates to locate her experience of God in a tradition of revelation. Now, if the said subject could be trusted only where the reported

---

1. I have discussed Wittgenstein's theory of meaning at length in my *Representation, Meaning and Thought* (Oxford: Clarendon, 1992).

experience was accompanied by some public manifestation, that would put impossible constraints on our corpus of revelation (for instance, large tracts of Ezekiel, Daniel, Isaiah and Revelation). This having been said, the overall point that the tradition of visions and revelations ought, if it is genuine, to be accompanied by the moral features of divine contact, seems to be sound (exceptions like Balaam notwithstanding).

I would next like to take issue with the suggestion that true beliefs are in some sense subject to confirmation, even if at a broad theory or paradigm level, by observation. This neglects an important point arising from the social sciences, which are mentioned by Murphy in connection with subjectivity. In the social sciences the claim that a true belief is subject to any kind of confirmation or disconfirmation by observation is not sound. Consider the following two examples:

- Henry Smith's bullet killed Pierre Gaston at Waterloo.
- Jane believes that men are not very good at theology.

Let us say of these propositions that they are true and believed by Henry Smith and Sebastian respectively. It is easy to envisage circumstances where the first belief cannot be confirmed by any possible observations whether present or contemporaneous with the events, and whether the observations were made at Waterloo or anywhere else. Imagine that Pierre Gaston's company was advancing and came under fire from Henry Smith's company. Now, even if it is objectively true that Henry Smith's bullet did kill Pierre Gaston, there is no observation which could establish its truth. Imagine that Smith was sighting along his barrel at the French soldier whom he later identified as Pierre Gaston and saw him fall as a result of the volley fired by Smith's company. This does not establish that Smith's bullet, rather than one of the hundred fired simultaneously, cut short Gaston's life. Thus for a whole class of historical beliefs there is a problem with the claim that observation may act as a gold-standard for objectivity or truth.

The second belief is also problematic in that it may never be betrayed. Jane may be civil and respectful to male theologians, she may criticise them as harshly but no more harshly than others do, and she may never express her opinion in public, and yet it might be a deep and firm conviction. Sebastian may have a hunch, or even a conviction, that Jane feels this way but he can never demonstrate that it is true by any observation. Such phenomena, where no evidence could confirm that a certain person at a certain time had a given thought, reflect the holism of the mental in the explanation of behaviour so that a desire, expectation, intention, hope, or belief may not be expressed or even manifested unless other (intentional) factors are right for its expression.[2]

Both examples are highly relevant to our present topic. They show that for historical and personal beliefs, the idea that objective truth issues from theory and observation may be seriously flawed, quite apart from the theory-ladenness of data about which I concur with Murphy. This runs somewhat counter to the tenor of her key claim about the relevance for theology of core theory, auxiliary hypothesis, data and instrumentation because it suggests that theology (which for the orthodox concerns beliefs about a person who acted in history) may, like the social sciences and humanities, have important points of epistemic difference from the modes of study appropriate to physical science. If that is true it leaves us with an important task in the location of, and the proper constraints on, theological knowledge.

To discharge our analytic debt in relation to theological knowledge and, in particular to the orthodox idea that God is personally active in redemptive history, we need to turn not only to the methodology of social science as traditionally conceived, but also to some radical reconceptualisations of the study of persons. These force us to reconsider the metaphysical and epistemological underpinnings of science in general. The reconceptualisations involved are particularly relevant as our knowledge seeks to embrace the actual, spontaneous and historically located actions of persons. The fundamental revision involves replacing the idea of an observer and theoriser contemplating certain phenomena with a conception of the knower and agent herself being known by the topic of her investigation. In this situation she is being formed and transformed by the one who knows her. This means that we cannot accept the idea of unilateral formulation and revision of the structures and content of knowledge according to traditional, or even post-Kuhnian philosophy of science; instead we must consider the dynamic

---

2.   Donald Davidson, *Essays on Actions and Events* (Oxford: Clarendon, 1980).

knower–known interaction as central to what can be known and what counts as truth. The view that the perspective and self-definition through communication of the one known should be significant constraints on the truth that is known is, of course, without parallel in the natural sciences and is an ontological fact which cannot help but change our epistemology at a very deep level.

To begin to appreciate this change in our epistemology we can focus on a preliminary confusion, the dispelling of which clarifies the task of the orthodox theologian. The confusion relates to our tendency to think of actions as events associated with physical objects that happen to be people. We identify certain events as actions because they are caused by human or animate individuals. The action is identified with the physical events and the person's body provides the appropriate physical object or substance to be credited with producing these events. (This substance can itself be studied as an object taking part in causal transactions and, *voilà*, a science of behaviour.) But the account is badly misconceived throughout.

The first level at which it is misconceived is a basic method-ological one but one with roots which take us a long way into the epistemology of science. Consider the case of Polly the poltergeist.[3] In this case a family comes to discern the presence of a benign disembodied agent in their house because they discern a pattern of activity which has the unmistakable mark of intentionality about it. Their detection of the agent is based on their recognition of the presence of intentionality — behaviour with meaning and purpose. This looks to be a hopelessly difficult task if we conceive it on the model of physical events emanating from a complex object and requiring to be explained by a theory.[4] However, the task becomes tractable if we drop the mantle of physical science and its presuppositions, and open ourselves to the possibility that primary perceptual information for human beings includes the (intentional) doings of other human beings and is highly dependent on communication or interpersonal interactions. If this were so, and it seems to be, then carrying things, smiling, looking at things, being

---

3.   Grant Gillett, "Disembodied persons" *Philosophy* 61 (1986) pp. 377-386.
4.   M. Morris, *The Good and the True* (Oxford: Clarendon, 1992) especially pp. 243ff.

addressed, discerning the feelings of others toward oneself and so on would be the ground on which our understanding of the world would be built.[5] On such a view, intentionality would form our knowing at a foundational level and we must contemplate a radical shift in epistemology from the model offered to us by scientifically oriented philosophy and psychology. The shift recommends an epistemology in which the interpersonal is primary and the objective-description-theory model is derived or secondary. In this case, the mode of understanding personal or human reality would be that of agent and subject among other agents and subjects, that is, the mode of knowledge as being-in-relation.

The problem of agency and the fixation on bodily events as the essence of behaviour introduces my overall and more fundamental problem with Murphy's paper. The model of knowledge to be found in the natural sciences (for example, physics, chemistry, astronomy and biology) investigates objects as things to be submitted to cognising. It rests on the epistemic duality of the subject and object, and applies a range of impersonal categories to the objects of study. Knowledge is defined and refined by assessing the adequacy of those categories and the theories from which they spring. Murphy rather nicely points out the limitations of the traditional theory–observation split and its implications for certain critiques of religious knowledge but she does not go a step further and ask whether this entire model of knowledge is appropriate to theology. God, according to orthodoxy, is not an object but a person and, furthermore, a person who is in a creative and sustaining relation to those who undertake theological inquiry. The recent radical reconceptualisations of sciences such as sociology, psychology and anthropology have occasioned a revolution in methodology and in the conceptions of truth and knowledge that operate there, but in theology one needs a more radical reconceptualisation still.

In the social sciences we no longer systematically downgrade persons to make them complex objects about which we can derive knowledge. I have already attacked the scientific reduction implicit in much of psychology by suggesting that behaviour cannot properly

---

5.   George Butterworth, "Origins of self-perception in infancy" *Psychological Inquiry* 3 (1992) pp. 103-111.

be understood in terms of physical events. That criticism is rein-
forced by two further strands of argument, one general to social and
interpersonal knowledge, and the other more particular to theology.
The first concerns the primacy of the two epistemic viewpoints in
any knower–known relationship. This is problematic in the social
sciences in general, and is of fundamental importance in theology.

Since the work of Winch, leaning rather heavily on the later
Wittgenstein, we have realised that if we want to understand the
behaviour of people we have to involve ourselves with the
discernment of meaning. This rests on the use of *verstehen* (Weber)
or *menschenkenntnis* (Wittgenstein).[6] These terms refer to a
technique in which our own nature as persons is part of the process
of coming to know. We use our intuitive empathy and awareness of
the feelings of others to recognise how it is with another person and
then interpret his actions by locating them amongst the meanings
which inform our lives. This way of knowing has two important
features. First, it is holistic and yields not exclusively propositional
knowledge, the contents of which are themselves imbued with the
significance being searched for. Secondly, its truth is radically
dependent on successfully glimpsing situations from the vantage of
the other, a fact which, Leibniz notwithstanding, is not appropriate
to the theory–observation model of knowledge about objects. For
instance, imagine that I see a man and a woman walking together but
apart; the woman is crying and the man expresses his inability to say
anything appropriate. Their situation is replete with meaning and is
subject to a range of possible interpretations. Someone may drop a
hint such as "they have been to the adoption agency" or I might
notice that they are leaving a lawyer's office. These meanings have
so tenuous a connection with the geometrical arrangement of light in
front of my eyes that a science or epistemology which begins from
that foundation has a task comparable to weeding a jungle with a
garden fork.[7] What is more, the criterion of success for my
interpretation is the occupation, however partial, of the standpoint of
those whom I am observing. Thus my knowledge of the situation is
not aiming at a synthesis which makes the evidence available

---

6. On Wittgenstein's term *menschenkenntnis* see his *Culture and Value:
    Beyond the Inner and the Outer* (Dordrecht: Kluer, 1990).

7. The problem here is not only technical but conceptual in that it is
    completely unclear what counts as a weed in the jungle.

coherent to me, but rather aims to capture or duplicate the synthesis actually made by the subjectivities or conscious subjects who are my topic. Once we begin human epistemology from such a relational and interpersonal foundation, we begin to see the model of knowledge implicit in scientific theory-data and critical refinement as one rather specialised and rarefied subsection of the whole. The categories within this part are adequate for the restricted task that natural science sets for itself but they should not be regarded as normative outside those bounds. If we wish to reduce our understanding of the world to the dimensions apt for the control of inanimate objects and the understanding of machines, then science is fine. As soon as we have aspirations beyond that restricted range of phenomena, our conception must adjust to essentially interactive and unfixed ways of relating and knowing which take seriously the viewpoint of those with whom we are engaged. And for these modes of knowing, the truth is fixed by the thoughts of the other who presents himself to me rather than by a workable theory of one's own.

Once theology is considered in this light we find ourselves necessarily working within the parameters of faith in order to be counted as gaining knowledge about the person God. Faith becomes the appropriate epistemic ground for knowledge of God because relating to the other, through one's own personhood, is the appropriate ground for understanding the meanings of the doings of any person (including God). Moreover, the presentation of that person and his own conception of himself is normative for my knowledge in a way that has no parallel in natural science or the detached scientific method. We therefore cannot escape the dependence of interpersonal epistemology on the relation between the subject being researched and the subject doing the research.

This task has its own key methodological concepts such as making sense, intentional content, interpretive distance, and perspective or phenomenological situation, but they are not concepts drawn from the relatively blunt methodology of the sciences. Even in their use within the social sciences, they still fall short of the categories of theology. In the task of understanding God, we should not only bring to bear our own conceptions of what makes sense for a person to do but should bring also a fundamental recognition of the moral significance and influence of the relation between the knower and the known in the discernment of theological truth. From within the perspective of repentance and faith, we discern that we are flawed in our ability to understand God because we do not naturally share the divine perspective or even the mind of Christ (God made human). What is more, we realise that the reason for our being flawed is not only constitutional but moral or evaluative because certain key aspects of the relatedness between knower and known will only emerge within a moral commitment of a certain type. Therefore, our making sense of God is likely to be incomplete and provisional. It is less so where we have a growing body of consistent hermeneutic content paying faithful attention to revelation but it still does not allow theory to have any life apart from a moral commitment which constrains one's conceptualisation of the one being known. Nevertheless, certain important points can still be drawn from the revised epistemology of post-modern social science.

The hermeneutic content at which one is aiming in theology is the "intentional content" ascribed to God who, on our model of human beings, will have an integrated subjectivity or character over time. (This claim might be attenuated for a human subject.) The discernment of character involves recognising that certain experiences and interpretations count for or against a given conceptualisation, but only in the context of a whole package of understanding and relationships in which one draws on praxis and intuition as much as on the formulation of propositional descriptions. In the attempt to discern God's intentionality we will be even more dependent than we normally are on the self-revelation of our subject. There are a number of reasons for the dependency which have to do with interpretive distance and phenomenological situation. Because the ideas of God have a unique and constitutive relationship to creation, there is a radical difference between theological epistemology and that of other enquiries. God's ideas which we are trying to discern are, at the moment of our investigating them, sustaining our own existence and cognition. We are, therefore, being constituted by the topic of our understanding in a way that is intentional rather than in the mode of Dawkins' famous blind watchmaker. There are, however, more accessible and less profoundly problematic features of theological knowing.

God is differently situated from us with respect to temporality and, therefore, causality or antecedent conditionality. This is an immensely important difference. It is almost impossible for us to imagine a perspective inhabiting no time and every time, no place and every place, and undistorted although fully informed by human acculturation, gender, vulnerability, historicity and physicality. These transcendencies which characterise the orthodox understanding of the mind of God imply that we ought to take this interpretive distance and perspective or situation in our theology seriously, because our understanding, as Kant so clearly noted, shows a fundamental dependence on time, space, and discursive formulations of the features of states of affairs. The stripping of these conditions of human existence from a conception of truth leaves us crucially dependent on God's self-revelation. We cannot profitably objectify God in the way we do the observed or posited entities of science because God's subjectivity must come to us and speak or breathe into us before we can begin our task of knowing. Thus, when we are looking for good theology, we may have to give a similar answer to that given by a famous jazzman to a visiting observer who asked, "How can you know if a piece of jazz is good?" He replied, "Man, if you gotta ask, you ain't never gonna know."

No interpretation of God's nature can escape the cultural and discursively located terms which pervade human knowledge but this does not mean that theology must inhabit a closed circle of constructions internal to a science-like paradigm with its core features and methodology. Interpersonal knowledge is singular and distinct from scientific knowledge in that the topic of knowledge has a contribution to make which is itself discursive and intentional. God, for the orthodox, speaks to us and takes us into his divine self. This grace transforms us as objects who are subjectivities. Theology must, therefore, be conducted in terms of a moral pilgrimage of self-transformation in the light of knowledge graciously induced and shared among the faithful. God is not an object about which we can formulate theories that can be tested for their adequacy against a rather flimsy and remarkably self-authenticating data base. God is a person who transcends, creates and inspires, and who imposes the divine personality on the process of gaining knowledge. In relating to God as a person, as in one's relation to any other person, there is no evidence which cannot be shaken and there is no interpretation which can be considered ultimate. We thus have an eschatological model of truth. In this model one's discernment of truth rests crucially on the place at which one is located, both personally and in terms of one's epoch in redemption history. From the post-modernists theology can accept the critique of the fact-value distinction and conclude that this knowledge will depend to some extent on one's prior moral commitments so that truth may have an essential relation to what Lacan calls "the purity of the soul of the operator".[8]

The idea of eschatological truth and the focus I have brought to bear on the interpersonal aspects of one's understanding of God imply that it is incorrect to see the theologian or seeker after religious knowledge as a theory-builder discovering and accommodating data. If the knower does not know herself as a knower-who-is-known and, in the light of that understanding, see theology as an exercise within a walk of faith, then there is little theological reason to see her as epistemically well-placed to discern the truth about her topic. This does not mean that the knower who counts as knowing is epistemically insulated from her culture or discursive situation, but it does at least mean that one, in the broadest sense, is not condemned forever to see in a succession of glasses darkly.

8.   Jacques Lacan, *The Four Fundamental Concepts of Psychoanalysis*, A. Sheridan, translator (Harmondsworth: Penguin, 1979).

Response by John Puddefoot

The bulk of my response to Nancey Murphy's paper will involve an attempt to interpret her own arguments slightly differently, mainly by suggesting a different way of thinking about the relationship between theory and evidence in the context of theology, because while I substantially agree that the problems theology has had to face as a result of the rise of science have been primarily epistemological, I am extremely uneasy about the path that Murphy chooses to take in response to those problems.

She begins by arguing that modern theological scholarship — that of the past 300 years — has been largely an attempt by Christian theology to recover from the rise of science. She regards science's challenge to our understanding of knowledge as more profound and threatening than any of its challenges to specific Christian doctrines. In particular, science's empirical emphasis is claimed to threaten Christian theology because of its claims about the nature of knowledge and the process of knowing.

There are basically three ways to respond to the empirical challenge. First, to accept a complete divorce between theology and science (a line I shall not pursue); secondly, to try to accommodate theology to empirical demands (which is substantially Murphy's line); and thirdly, to try to soften the emphasis on the empirical in science by showing that it involves a misunderstanding. This is the line I shall follow. Murphy and I do not really disagree about the tools, the levers and wedges that are needed to move beyond a foundationalist metaphysic; I think that she strikes an admirable balance between modern and post-modern thinking which largely avoids the traps in both. Where we differ is over the interpretation of the widespread shift in emphasis that follows from using these tools. In particular, I think that to argue that theology works with biblical and experiential data akin to scientific data is misleading in a way that exacerbates rather than dissipates the empirical discord between theology and science. Let me begin with our agreement.

I agree that foundationalism, that is, the view that knowledge must be based upon unquestionable premises to avoid an infinite regress, must be superseded, and I find the three criteria that Murphy proposes to assess modern theology helpful: its response to the empirical challenge; how it deals with the problems raised by those responses; and how it attempts to sidestep foundationalism and with it those problems. However, if foundationalism was and is mistaken (as she and I both believe), it is surely not right to say that it must be "sidestepped", since one scarcely needs to sidestep an illusion. I am less happy when she proceeds to identify three classes of modern theologian: biblical foundationalists, experiential foundationalists, and those who deny that theology belongs in the category of knowledge at all. Since I do not recognise myself in any of these classes it must follow either that I am not a theologian, or that this is an inadequate classification.

As she starts to defend theology against empiricist attacks, Murphy refers to Quine's "Two dogmas" and the views of Lakatos regarding the centrality of scientific research programmes with their heavy theoretical content to show that the empirical element in science, while powerful and important, is not all that it seems (pp. 103ff.). These two references seem to me to be pointing us in absolutely the right direction. I shall try to say, however, in what respect I would use the same general thrust to take a different line from her in what follows.

I do not start from a position in which religious experience seems likely to help to substantiate theology because I do not believe either that theology *can* be empirical or that science really *is* empirical, and I certainly do not believe that either of them *needs* to be. For me, the meeting-place of science and theology (which would better be called the point at which we realise that they have never really been apart) is the state of mind where we acknowledge that Quine was perhaps more right about webs of belief than even he realised at the time. Webs of belief are not, and cannot be, merely personal or individual. Webs of belief are only possible, as language is only possible, from a communal perspective. Private beliefs are no more intelligible than private languages, and the methods we must employ to resolve the difficulties that our private experiences occasion, religious or scientific, are for me the basis of the sociology of knowledge and hence the infrastructure of all webs of belief.

To give my response some substance, I have to retrace my steps a little. It is always of interest to ask of any account in philosophy of science (and in the theology–science debate) what status is being afforded to evidence and to rationality in that discussion. Evidence and rationality are usually taken as givens, inviolable bedrocks to which appeal can be made — the inviolable nature of rationality and evidence are effectively the foundations of science. Putnam has observed that Kuhn presupposes that the essences of rationality and justification are not themselves subject to paradigm changes.[1] But both rationality and the nature of justification change with paradigms. Christian theism, for example, may actually force us to revise our very notions of evidence and rationality, because the mode of God's self-communication must dictate the nature of rationality and of what is to count as evidence to be that rationality and that view of evidence which enable us to receive his communications.

Secondly, it is significant that two philosophers of science, Nancey Murphy and Wentzel van Huyssteen, Professor of Philosophy of Science at Princeton Theological Seminary, both seem to believe that the question which Murphy puts into her imaginary dialogue (p. 110) between Catherine and Alasdair MacIntyre — "How do you know that it was God who told you that?" — admits an answer governed by some criterion of demarcation.[2] It is exactly this which I would deny, despite her powerful defence of the thesis, as a vestige of the very foundationalism she seeks otherwise to supersede. It seems that

1. Hilary Putnam in his *Realism with a Human Face* (Cambridge: Harvard University Press, 1990) p. 126, where he discusses the "Principle of Charity".

2.. See Wentzel van Huyssteen, *Theology and the Justification of Faith* (Grand Rapids: Eerdmann's, 1989) p. 84: "[H]ow can the theologian be sure that his statements are in fact about God's Word, and not merely about a human expression of a supposedly divine Word?" To my mind the theologian can be given no such assurance, and the word "merely" indicates a yearning for a foundational certitude based upon a mode of speaking that is somehow *more than human.*. No such mode of speaking exists.

her defence replaces one foundationalism, MacIntyre's, with another (her own). I do agree, however, that replacing individual with communal (church) discernment offers us a better analogy with scientific self-regulation, although the balance between the rejected individual, such as the prophet, and the accepted individual will always introduce tensions into even this account. A theology which placed too much emphasis upon communal ratification would lead us to reject the prophets, St Paul and even Jesus himself.

I thoroughly approve of Murphy's emphasis upon webs of theological belief and theory where "no single theory is supported by any single religious experience" (p. 112), but I would go further and say that a whole web of theological theories may not be supported by any religious experiences at all — and that usually there are no such experiences. This, she will observe, all depends upon what you mean by an experience, so let us try to agree that "experience" here means some kind of phenomenon with an apparently external source, rather than just a "thought".   In that case I would repeat my remark: much, perhaps most religious conviction is not based upon experience in this sense. When Teresa of Avila speaks of the "self-authenticating" presence of God in the human soul, Murphy rightly objects. However, the basis for her objection, that self-authenticating inward experiences have no evidential value for anyone else, is to my mind quite the wrong reason for the objection.

The real reason for any objection to self-authentication is that it is vacuous. "This experience was self-authenticating" says nothing that "I believe this to be true" does not say, but it disingenuously *pretends* to say more. For example, "this is *self*-authenticating, so I am not responsible for asserting its authenticity", and as such it involves an insidious appeal to a kind of givenness. It still presupposes a fundamental object–subject dichotomy in which what goes on "in us" has somehow to be shown to correspond with something "out there". But what should really be thrown out is the object–subject dichotomy, the attempt to satisfy the correspondence criterion of truth, and the attempt to adopt and substantiate some strong (metaphysical) form of realism.

I would say, to put the matter with intolerable brevity, that Catherine's problem, Teresa's problem (at least as Murphy presents their cases), Murphy's problem and van Huyssteen's problem, are one and the same. They all want to find some quasi- or crypto-foundational way to guarantee to themselves that what they believe is true, and in this respect the latter two are not post-modern or post-foundational enough. They all want a set of criteria by which to determine when they should regard an explanation as an explanation. In other words, they all want a set of rules by which to determine when an argument is won and lost. From a critical standpoint I think that this is worthy and noble, but futile. There are no such guarantees, at least none which satisfy criteria borrowed from empiricist science, and this is because the criteria of empiricist science are themselves bogus. Scientists may think that they believe in science because of its empirical base; I think they believe in it because it articulates aspects of a conceptual web of such richness that it overpowers all resistance. They, like St Paul in Romans 8, "are persuaded". To have quantum theory explained is to be overpowered by it regardless of the evidence for it. The Cern and Stanford accelerators were not built to substantiate a theory that nobody would otherwise believe!

No — I rescind that. To have quantum theory explained is not to be overpowered, because that smacks of self-authentication and the persuasive power of the given. It is to be given something, something conceptual, which — if you are a certain kind of human being sensitive to certain kinds of input stimuli and able to make sense of them — will convince you that it is true. Exactly the same is true of Christian teaching.

Quantum theory, like Christianity, defines its own rationality. It redefines what constitutes evidence; it demarcates those who allow their minds to submit to its rigours and its initially counterintuitive aspects from those who insist on clinging to their prior notions of causality, reason and proof.

In the end, Cern and Stanford are so complex that they may actually embody some unrecognised guarantees that they will work, because like all scientific experiments, they have to embody the theory that they are testing. But that does not make them useless: it makes them aesthetic; it makes them beautiful; it makes them manifestations of a conceptual totality which we want to live by and to believe in because we have found nothing better and can, at the moment, conceive of nothing better. It makes them, so to speak, statements of faith which have more in common with cathedrals than those who worship in them might wish to acknowledge. Particle accelerators are places where we seek to encounter those entities which our pre-theoretic and theoretic commitments lead us to believe in. But we do not build them to resolve our doubts, we build them to affirm and confirm our faith. So much for empiricism.

Let me dwell on this point for a moment. It may seem trite to say it, but in the end we are all trying to find out how best to live our lives: what to believe, what to do, what to value, what and whom to love, and what to abhor. This search is undertaken despite painful awareness of our fallibility, so we look for ways to reduce the risk. Since personal whim and opinion strike us, and many of our forebears, as the least reliable and most misleading of our traits, we eschew them and seek impersonal criteria: rules and criteria for demarcation. I think that what happens in science is that we find the subject-matter of science particularly sympathetic to a certain kind of activity, and certain actions — experiments — particularly satisfying as means of demarcating and supporting our theories about the world. In fact, as has so often been pointed out (not least by Lakatos), we even allow ourselves to be persuaded when there are gaping holes in the data and unexplained rogue results. In other words, science is empirical because we think it helps us to make up our minds about the way the world is. Science helps us to set our doubts aside and to feel comfortable about doing so. Of course, sometimes we are wrong, but that is not to say that at the time we were not comfortable with the decision, as is illustrated all-too-clearly by the fiasco associated with the "discovery" of cold fusion. The fact that we feel comfortable with this encourages us to try to apply the same criteria in realms where it is really much less suited or, as with scientific positivism, to reject all such realms as beyond the pale.

It is here that I become self-consciously theological and say that all this amounts to, when applied to theology, is an attempt to know God without the involvement of God in the process. Murphy's objection, that this is an appeal to self-authentication, with which I generally have much sympathy, cannot be applied to overrule the event of existential persuasion which in Romans 8 inspired St Paul. At that point the problem ceases to be "How can I be sure that I am not deceiving myself?" and becomes "How can I help you to be persuaded?" Here one is tempted to draw another scientific parallel and say that a scientist who is not persuaded by your theory is unlikely to be persuaded by your evidence. To persuade you, I have to tell you a story that engages your mind and your imagination in such a way that you start to want it to be true and start to look at the evidence in a way that will allow the evidence to corroborate it. Without that prior conviction the evidence does not really have a chance. Teresa, for instance, in the examples that Murphy cites, was concerned lest her sisters should be misled. She was not concerned for herself.

I am a Christian because I find myself persuaded to look at existence through mental apparatus shot through with, and constructed out of, a Christian understanding of the world. I have never had a religious experience. I know that the Bible may be hoodwinking me right down the line. I know that the facts about what Jesus said and did are hopelessly questionable according to the criteria of empirical science. But out of this tradition something has been articulated. A conceptual system of such power has been formed that questions of truth as defined by those quasi-scientific criteria tumble into insignificance in comparison with the overpowering vision of what life is about that comes through the pages of this book and the life and death of this man. Who knows whether we are right, whether something better or someone wiser will not turn up tomorrow? What use is such speculation? In this event and in these stories we find ourselves presented with something that persuades us to redefine our rationality, to reconstruct what we will count as evidence and to reconsider how we will interpret it. These things define the kinds of persons we become. Others reject them: that rejection and what they put in its place, whether it be scientific empiricism, mysticism or scepticism, defines them just as much.

What is clear to me is that it is only when we accept the profound, literally earth-shattering changes in epistemology that follow from the work of philosophers such as Quine that we shall be able to see the true harmony between theology and science.

Only then shall we be able to see that what makes them true is our willingness to have not our individual but our collective lives shaped by the kind of rationality that they define. It is this that defines the being of the Church within which the being of each Christian is defined.

To the charge that this leaves us open to "demonic" influences, we must give a reply that centres upon the community, not the individual, because it is in the discernment of others that the true nature of our faith is made apparent. I am much less worried about the self-inducement problem than Catherine, Teresa, or Nancey Murphy, since it is just not clear to me that the distinction between "God-induced" and "self-induced" can, or should, be maintained except insofar as others measure our degree of godliness by the fruits of our faith. Whose words am I to speak, if not my words? Yet as a theologian I feel obliged to speak my own words out of a deep, and I hope humble, sense of ultimate obligation to the God by whose Word I endeavour to speak. To this extent I think the American pragmatists were right to emphasise the "true" as what it is best for us to believe, for it is difficult to see how else we could discern what is true. If I have a thought, I cannot — as the older theology maintained — expect to distinguish between a "God-induced" thought and a "self-induced" thought, but the difference is, in any case, just another yearning for guarantees and as such another form of foundationalism. In the end, I decide which of my thoughts to utter, and in their utterance I lay them before the world and, more narrowly, the scientific community and/or the Church. This sociological dimension in both science and theology is what Michael Polanyi made central to his thinking, and it is vital to any understanding of how humankind hopes to move towards the truth. We speak and we are heard, and in the response of the community to our hearing, its "yea" or its "nay", our words either find their resonant frequencies or they do not. Sometimes, as with Old Testament prophecy, the community rejected what the speaker believed and the speaker, like the modern dissident, accepted his rejection (and even exile and death) to retain the integrity of his message and vision. Sometimes a few listened and their influence spread long after their teacher was dead. No doubt many spoke whose words were neither heeded nor written down, for good and

ill. But there was never any guarantee either that we would listen
or that individuals blessed with valuable insights would choose to
speak, still less that when they spoke they would speak God's
Word.

I am advocating a strong modern version of community and self-
constituting choice which systematically eschews all searching for,
and belief in, guarantees. Somewhere along the line things like
historical and scientific evidence play their part, but if we
encounter something that strikes us as so important that we lay hold
upon it despite the absence of historical or scientific evidence, that
too is our right, and that is the basis for Christian faith. To the
extent that the scientific enterprise persuaded Christian theology to
place evidence at the centre of its apologetic concerns, Murphy is
correct to say that the last 300 years have been preoccupied with
redeeming theology from the clutches of science but, if I read her
correctly, I still believe that she is trying to place the emphasis for
theology and science upon yet another version of empiricist
foundationalism by attempting to respond to this false centrality of
evidence rather than to show that it involves a misconception of the
role of evidence not only in theology, but also in science.

I think that the real difference between Murphy and myself is
summarised at the end of her paper when she refers again to the
need for theology to aim for knowledge of a reality independent of
the human subject. That is obviously true, but it is one thing for it
to be true and quite another thing to suppose that we can ever be
sure or, by applying some method, assure ourselves that we have
succeeded in "climbing out of our minds" with all its attendant
distortions. So I would want to emphasise the acts of personal
judgment and communal affirmation and reaffirmation that
underpin all the knowledge we have of all things, not on the basis
of correspondences mysteriously discerned between theories and
their referents, but because we have looked at the world through
those theories and found what we saw to be as good a picture as we
could presently hope to find. The mystic, on this basis, plays a role
similar to that of the scientific dissident, whose vision "must
conquer or die",[3] and who as such seeks less to persuade by

---

3.   Michael Polanyi, *Personal Knowledge* (London: RKP, 1962) p. 150.

argument than to invite and induce others to share her visions so that they will find themselves affirming her answers, reports and insights. That, I think, makes the mystic's experiences less matters of evidence than contributions to a jig–saw of conversation. I retain a worry that the supposed externality of the source of the vision should make us more rather than less doubtful about its authenticity. Perhaps the real point is that genuine experiences of God must fight their own battles in the wilderness of human ideas.

We can never climb out of our minds and should, therefore, place more stress on, and devote more resources to, those checks and balances that enable us, trapped inside them, to decide which ideas are worth pursuing and how to make the kinds of self-constituting choices that we are all called upon to make during our lives. I think that this demands a revision of theology along lines dictated more by pneumatology than has been the case in the past, when theologians have tended to invoke the Holy Spirit to plug holes in their theories. All our writing and speaking must be guided by a fundamental sense of responsibility to that which is beyond, while accepting that in the end it will need to be ourselves, and not some impersonal criterion of demarcation, that decides whether we have been faithful to that end and to the one who is the beginning and end of all things. In a way that summarises my growing anxieties with Murphy's approach to the theology–science interface: her account is too impersonal, too free from risk, and too rooted in the dichotomies and foundations of the critical modern era.

For example, "it is necessary to show that the discipline of theology aims at *knowledge* of a reality independent of the human subject. If theology is really only about human values or meanings, then there is no more reason to think that theology and science can engage in dialogue than to think that science ought to dialogue with ethics or art or literary theory" (p. 126). There seems to me to be *every* reason to hope for a vast increase in the amount of conversation that takes place between science and "ethics or art or literary theory" precisely because ethics, art and literary theory are not and should not be conceived "only" to be about human values or meanings, but to be legitimate and important manifestations of the kind of deep sense of meaning and value that human beings are in touch with when they behave as *persons* rather than objects reducible to scientific analysis. To believe that science affords some especially privileged and reliable access to the truth of an independent world, as Murphy clearly believes, and to yearn for theology to share that privileged access is, as I observe in my opening remarks, to exacerbate an already deeply divisive element in critical epistemology that tears asunder the seamless garment of human knowledge and experience.

Finally, I would say that I cannot recognise in Murphy's paper the capacity to account for the free experience of the God who reaches down into my being and asks me questions about the nature of my soul.

4

The relationship of natural order to divine truth and will

John Puddefoot

There are at least four different strands of thought in this paper. The first and fundamental point is that the world as the work of God must embody his intentions, however hard they may be for us to discern. This gives rise to three related points.

- If the world does not seem to embody or point to divine authorship, that may be because the way that we are interpreting it is inappropriate.
- If the world appears to rule out one hermeneutic, it also points to the need for a different hermeneutic which may involve a different conception of rationality, explanation and evidence.
- In seeking to articulate a view of God that can do justice to this new rationality, we may need to move beyond the critical and pre-critical ways that have given us our presuppositions about the nature of reason, explanation and evidence without renouncing (as so many have done) our responsibilities to the external realities of God and the world. I mean this as a specific warning against the siren voices of the post-modernists.

The new sciences, particularly quantum mechanics and chaos theory, point us in the direction of a new conception of God that lies between the individual and the universal in the realm of what is best called the personal. This personal realm is both singular and plural, one and many, since each self and each community of selves is constructed out of the efforts of its forebears and its contemporaries in ways that render the notion of the individual, and a separatist

148

notion of the self, illegitimate. A personal God should not be conceived in terms of the kinds of absolute abstractions that were characteristic of much medieval theology, characteristics that because they were compatible with scientific universalism, generally survived into the critical era. Instead, to recover from metaphysics, we need to go back into prehistory to the God of the Bible, who is largely non-metaphysical, who must not be seen (just as those documents must not be read) from the perspective of a critical metaphysics, and who gives us clues to the kind of personal particularity that must be embodied in our new theology.

Lastly, and more concretely, I have included a simple model of divine action drawn from computer science which serves three purposes.

■ It illustrates the openness of a highly structured, scientifically comprehensible system to boundary conditions.
■ It illustrates the fundamental ambiguity of the material world if we decline to adopt high-level ordering-principles.
■ It illustrates one possible way to revive natural theology by concentrating upon the potentiality of the deep structure embodied in the universe.

This paper is an exercise in the *hermeneutic* rather than the *apologetic* aspects of theology and science. I make no attempt to argue *for* the reality of God on the basis of what we know of the natural order. My purpose is rather to say that *if* we begin from theistic presuppositions, certain things need to be said about the world as we know it.[1]

If "the Book of Nature" is a text through which an author expresses intentions, we would expect to find an order in nature which embodies those intentions. It need not be the order we see most readily or regard as most natural, nor need it be present

---

1. As will appear from subsequent remarks, I envisage this paper as a reflexive exercise which does what it advocates; that is, it constructs a theological edifice compatible with science and asks that it be understood in terms of its holistic intelligibility, rather than starting from a scientific understanding of the natural order and moving from that to infer the existence of God. The "theological conditional" that John Honner refers to in his response is therefore deliberate, but it is not the "if" of doubt; it is the "if" of faith, and the two could not be more different.

unambiguously, but belief in another who has created the world seems to require us to expect to find evidence for his intentions in that world, however hard they may be to discern. In particular, belief in God as a benevolent creator who acts with purpose seems to oblige us to affirm that we live in some sense in the best of all possible worlds, however difficult that may be to believe when we contemplate the widespread suffering endured by the creatures who inhabit it.

So Christian theism demands that the world be intelligible to God and that the existence of the world with all its difficulties at any particular time also be justifiable to God. We should therefore expect to find that the world exhibits two characteristics indicative of that intelligibility and justification: a deep structure which is as it is because it is the best possible way to achieve God's purposes, and an order which is rendered intelligible by an ordering principle which is known at least to God, even if it can never fully be known by anyone less than God.

The deep structure and the order in the world should not be confused with (or blamed for) the ways in which they have been used, as can be seen from the following story. Someone bought a very powerful computer with all the latest multimedia technology only to return it to the shop after a few weeks with the complaint that it was "useless". The shop tested it thoroughly and found nothing wrong with it. "Yes, I know it works," said the customer, "but it writes terrible novels."

In view of the openness of the structures of the universe to higher-level ordering principles (or the ambiguity of texts in the face of different readings), if the world's meaning seems ambiguous, its order unclear, its deep structure indiscernible, its intelligibility complex; if, in particular, its proper interpretation is not self-evident, and if despite all these problems we are to retain the conviction that a benevolent God created and sustains this universe, then those very difficulties may be symptoms and indicators of that deep structure and the kind of response which the creatures God has seen fit to create must embody if they are to fulfil his purpose. In other words, the very difficulties that give rise to doubt and unbelief may function to differentiate appropriate from inappropriate modes of intellectual life.

If this conjecture is correct and the supposed insufficiency of the evidence for God that so irritated Bertrand Russell is a manifestation of the deep structure of the world as God has seen fit to engineer it (and it is difficult to see how any other view is compatible with theism) then our response to that insufficiency should be to reconstruct our ideals and expectations of what constitutes a satisfactory argument and a satisfactory explanation. To reconstruct, that is, our whole concept of what it is to be rational, because it is obvious from the existence of sceptics and atheists that the world does not admit arguments and explanations of the existence of God that can be regarded as incontrovertible or self-evident according to the criteria of critical thought.

It is appropriate, however, to begin by considering a more fundamental question of obvious relevance to any attempt to infer something of divine truth and will from the natural order: how do we make sense of what we find?

When Alan Turing and his collaborators in the Second World War cracked the German code by developing the Enigma Machine they were helped by the fact that the deciphered code would probably be in German, the encryption would have been done by machines constructed by human beings, and the results would relate to the business of warfare. If we were faced in some future millennium with the task of deciphering the code of a completely alien race whose physical attributes we did not know, whose planetary environment we could not guess, and whose means of warfare we could only imagine,[2] an already difficult task would be rendered impossible because of the unrestricted ambiguity we faced.[3]

---

2. If such an alien race had evolved in a universe governed by the same natural laws this ambiguity might be reduced to some extent, of course, as emerges from the following remarks on evolution.

3. If we are to understand something, it seems that we must share some common conceptual framework with either the process or the person that produced it: with natural processes we have evolution as a common denominator (although the senses which evolved to enable us to manage in the macro-world need not necessarily be well-suited to knowledge of the micro-world); with man-made processes we share broadly similar objectives and modes of operation. But we only see a few of the world's faces, and a theist really has to argue that the universe is only fully intelligible at God's level, and that a merely human or, especially, scientific account of it cannot but be inadequate.

According to scientific principles, order must be a manifestation of a law and the law must be expressible as a general principle such as can be embodied in a formula. But why should this principle be correct? Why should not particularity be a manifestation of an order whose ordering principles lie at a higher level than we can understand, or at a level involving a particularity foreign to current mathematics? Mathematicians know that patterns can be deceptive. For example, most of us would say that what comes after 1, 2, 3, 4... is 5, and that anything else would be "unnatural". But any number of mathematical functions can be produced which will generate any number next in the sequence in a perfectly "natural" way if we are prepared to shift our notion of normality sufficiently to accommodate them. Patterns in themselves cannot dictate the nature of their own ordering-principles. The sequence 314159 may look like the first six digits in the expansion of π, but it may be a telephone number, or the number of people in a large town. The sequence i a i a o i e e e o u u o i o o i e i a a o o e e e i o a a o o a o e may seem to have no pattern unless we are told that it is the sequence of vowels in the first stanza of the Sayers translation of Dante's *Inferno*.[4] Order or disorder are not just matters of recognisable regularity or pattern; they rely upon the presence or absence of an ordering principle, on whether they can be set in an intelligible context, whether they can be explained.[5] Sometimes, as in the latter case, nothing less than the original instance in which the order occurs is adequate as such an explanation, and no general law or formula can be given to generate the sequence automatically; to understand anything we may need to understand everything.[6] As

---

4. I owe this illustration to Tito Arecchi of the University of Florence. See, for example, his "Why Science is an open system implying a meta-science" in *The Science and Theology of Information,* Wassermann, Kirby and Rordorff, editors (Geneva: Labor et Fides, 1992). The same volume contains my "Information and creation" which is of general relevance to the present essay.

5. The celebrated Aspect experiments investigating the EPR paradox set out a quantum world for which we yet have no explanation. In other words, we cannot set it within an overall context which will enable us to see separated yet connected events as somehow co-ordinated because we lack an ordering principle of sufficient power.

6. The point at issue here is discussed extensively by Gregory Chiatin in his various articles on Algorithmic Information Theory.

Michael Polanyi once put it, "deepest reality is possessed by higher things that are least tangible".[7] This has three important theological implications.

First, the epistemological parsimony exhibited by science, often stated in terms of Ockham's razor (*entia non sunt multiplicanda praeter necessitatem*),[8] which gives rise to natural laws of enormous generality, may be constitutionally incapable of knowing the universe in its enormous particularity and diversity. As I put it in *Logic and Affirmation*, we ask how many leaves there are on the tree, not what each leaf is like.[9]

Secondly, the only perspective capable of embracing this particularity (of recognising the order in the particularity of the world — see the letters from Dante's *Inferno*) may be that of God or of sentient creatures. But those creatures are part of the world, and may even be the part of the world responsible for discerning and articulating the meaning of the world, and if they, because of some philosophical prejudice or predilection, refuse to participate in giving the world meaning, it may for that very reason lack meaning for them.[10]

Thirdly, can we know the meaning of the world by knowing as God knows? Certainly not if we conceive of it in Stephen Hawking's terms as a "formula on a T-shirt". Within the structure of Christian incarnational theology, however, we are offered the hope and the reassurance that God does in a sense know as man knows, and that man can in some sense know as God knows — that is one of the most penetrating insights to follow from the person of Jesus Christ. What is more, such a perspective acts to affirm and

7.   Michael Polanyi, "On the modern mind" *Encounter* 140 (May 1965) p. 15.
8.   This common formulation of so-called Ockham's Razor is due to John Ponce de Cork, according to A. C. Crombie, *Grosseteste*, p. 167, n. 7. The original version, *quia pluralitas non est ponenda sine necessitate* (a plurality is not to be posited unnecessarily), is in Ockham's *Quodlibeta Septem* V. Q5, volume IX of the *Opera Theologica* p. 495. I owe these references to the late Harold Nebelsick.
9.   John C. Puddefoot, *Logic and Affirmation* (Edinburgh: Scottish Academic Press, 1987) p. 98.
10. I do not mean to suggest that human beings create the meaning of the universe, but that the meaning is inaccessible to them unless they employ imagination and eschew certain philosophical prejudices about what is and is not rationally justifiable.

underline the value and importance of human knowing in precisely the particularity eschewed by science.

The world may seem to lack intent (and may even seem to lack order) if we lack the imagination or the intellectual courage and equipment needed to perceive it otherwise.[11] So the ordering principles by which the world will be rendered fully (or at least more) intelligible are likely to be of a higher order than those allowed by scientific rationalism.[12] Discovering such ordering principles may depend upon the exercise of human powers stretching beyond those usually countenanced by science.[13]

The ordering principles known to God, which make sense even of the desperate suffering in the world that confounds our understanding, place suffering on an explanatory par with the disorder that appears to us as such because we lack explanatory systems of sufficient and appropriate power. But if it is at the level of personal, not subatomic or galactic existence, that the price is paid for this global, universal strategy intelligible only to God, so it is at the level of personal life that God's explanation of that strategy must be given and its price paid. To entertain a theology that falls short of being fully incarnational is to relinquish perhaps the highest-level ordering and explanatory principle of all, that "God was in Christ reconciling the world to himself".[14]

Christian theology strives to articulate the structure of such high-level ordering principles and so to forge such explanations. It ought to be, therefore, the highest level of description to which we aspire

---

11. I swiftly pass over a simply huge problem with this sentence: does order always indicate the presence of an ordering-principle (as Polanyi believed); what makes order "significant"; must significant order always reflect design and hence intention? I have made some preliminary observations on these matters in my forthcoming "Information Theory, Biology and Christology" in *Building Bridges Between Science and Theology,* Ed. Mark Richardson, CTNS, Berkley, 1994. (Projected title.)

12. That is, that all and only those things susceptible to scientific description and explanation are properly knowable or worth knowing.

13. See C. S. Peirce's concept of "Musement" and his emphasis on "pure play" as the means whereby we come to formulate hypotheses and to understand their validity. Compare with, for example, "A neglected argument for the reality of God" in *Charles S. Peirce: Selected Writings,* Philip P. Weiner, editor (Dover, 1966) pp. 358-379.

14. 2 Corinthians 5:19.

rather than the down–trodden poor relation of modern scholarship. It is a pity that the theology–science debate has been largely pre- occupied with defensive apologetics rather than with the task of drawing upon scientific insights to further this all-encompassing theological task. No considerations arising from science can con- strain what we should want to say about God, for if this is God's world, he must control the ways in which the laws of the world are made to serve his purpose.

Science deals with the structure of the world not because it is science, but because it is something that takes place within the world. It cannot, however, stipulate its boundary conditions (which can only be perceived and determined from beyond the world or by creatures capable of manipulating them), boundary conditions which work "all the way down". They should not, for example, be associated with the values of the four fundamental physical constants as is suggested by some versions of the anthropic principle.[15] There can be no contradiction between theological and scientific accounts of the world except for the scientific imperialism that insists that what science is capable of talking about is all that is worth talking about.[16] Science comes into conflict with theology when it believes itself able to specify the kinds of things that are possible in the world. But to do this science must be able to specify all possible boundary conditions that might be applied to the world as well as their mode of application, whereas in fact science can specify none of the boundary conditions and none of their possible points of application without invoking some form of scientific imperialism.

Another aspect of my computer analogy may make this clearer. The computer on which I type these words works on principles that

---

15. The term "boundary" does not imply "edge" in a spatial sense. God does not act on the fringes of the universe and is no more remote from where we are than from anywhere else. Just as we, being three-dimensional creatures, can write wherever we please on two-dimensional paper, so God, beyond all dimensionality, can act where he pleases in the universe.

16. This bold statement is intended to mean exactly what it says: a theology that finds itself in conflict with science is either bad theology (creationism) or theology that demands a retraction of some form of scientific imperialism, for example, when science claims to be able to do exactly what I subsequently claim it cannot do, that is, produce a self-explanatory system of the world that includes an account of its boundary conditions. (Although see what follows on the subject of "boundaries".)

are well understood by science. Yet the purpose of the computer is not discernible from within the framework of how it works. We must stand back and see the flexibility of its input and output devices, see that the keyboard represents a relatively crude set of boundary conditions (on only one level) capable of configuring its internal states, and that its screen displays shapes which are invisible and, even if visible, would be meaningless from a perspective originating within the conceptual field defined by the internal workings of the device. In fact, from a perspective inside the machine, the pressing of a particular key effects changes that constitute miracles within the framework of the device, since from the limitations of that framework no reasons can be given why one key was pressed rather than another and, worse, the concept of a key that can be pressed is at best speculative and at worst unintelligible. All that could be noticed is that one connection had been made rather than another, and being without rational cause or explanation, such a connection could only appear as a singular event. Now imagine that the universe has as many keys as there are events on every scale from the cosmic to the subatomic, and the notion of an uncaused change to the universe as a result of the imposition of certain boundary conditions through a procedure which is completely unintelligible, and indeed unthinkable, in one rational system, becomes intelligible in another.[17]

On the other hand, certain characteristics relevant to discerning the purpose of a device can be perceived from "inside", namely those that can be inferred from its deep structure. The internal workings of a computer can only achieve certain states and produce certain outputs, even if we cannot be certain how they would appear and what part they would play were we able to take a "longer" view. The universe, for example, can be seen to exhibit a capacity for complexification, and the earth exhibits a capacity for producing varied forms of life that rely upon such complexification, so what the universe can do (and what we can do to it) may be clues to the ultimate purpose that it serves and to the kind of rationality that it demands.

---

17. This has nothing to do with "gods of the gaps", for the natural processes involved are completely described by natural laws.

If an enlarged and altered system of explanation makes the inexplicable explicable and the unthinkable thinkable, then theology, if it is to be the highest or most comprehensive descriptive system available to us, must seek to make room for itself by enlarging the compass of imaginations that are restricted to, and by, a critical reading of scientific concepts. But theological interpretations that are unwelcome can be dismissed for many different reasons (many of them only thinly associated with science), and attempts to define a new rationality compatible with theology will be viewed with deep suspicion. Yet we can only have access to the intent manifested in perceived order if we allow ourselves to engage in intention-identifying imaginative hermeneutic endeavour. That is, by constructing new ways of looking at the world which render old ideas more intelligible, and by daring to interpret the order we discern as being evidence for intention. Otherwise we find ourselves in the worst of all possible worlds, believing that there is only one permitted interpretation of the natural order, and that the one provided by our current version of science is a reflection not of science but of the way the world supposedly interprets itself. The choice is, in a sense, between being the slave of biology and having something to set over against it that arises from the creativity of the human mind.

The success and progress of science, however, hinge upon a more fundamental assumption than just that the universe is rational: they presuppose that it is rational in a way that may transcend current understanding, and as such all our current "clear and distinct ideas". If belief in a benevolent, wise and intelligible God influenced the rise of science, it may be here that it did so, by making us feel confident about reaching beyond current thinking on the basis of faith in a rationality that transcends it: a confidence that in relinquishing faith in the comprehensiveness of our own rational systems we can nevertheless rely upon and be supported by the higher-level comprehensive rationality of God as the creator and sustainer of the world.

The questions of evidence and, as we shall see in a moment, of explanation, illustrate this dilemma particularly clearly. "This X is evidence for Y" does not possess the inescapable persuasive power attributed to it by pre-critical and critical thought. No item of data — indeed, no collection of data however large or exhaustive — has the power to substantiate a theory without the intermediate contribution of the scientist, historian or whoever grants it evidential status by deploying a fallible skill.

Similarly, it is essential to our notion of a rational being that one can give explanations of one's beliefs and actions, yet explanation is all too easily understood in a foundational sense to lead back to undeniable (and impersonal) premises. Since there are no such premises (except those we define as such, for example, the axioms of a mathematical structure), explanation only ends when it satisfies someone, that is, when it has gone far enough to link the framework of ideas requiring explanation with that person's existing web of beliefs. Determining what constitutes an adequate explanation involves as much an act of judgment as determining whether X is evidence for Y.

The history of the West from Cartesian scepticism through empiricism to positivism (and therefore of critical thought) can be seen as a search for objective grounds for truth that will relieve us of all responsibility for our knowing by locking us into a self-sufficient and self-authenticating system guaranteeing impersonal certainty.[18] The ultimate canon of perfect reasoning is often regarded as mathematical logic or, failing that, the scientific method, because both are supposed to remove completely all human fallibility and susceptibility to whim and opinion. But the rope by which mathematics and science are raised high is also that by which they are hung, because the price that mathematical logic pays for its certainty is vacuity, and the one thing that the natural order tells us with unerring and unnerving regularity is that it cannot be known by science unless we allow science to dictate the criteria by which it is to be known. The ubiquity of the scientific metaphor — the success of scientific method accompanied by the rigour of mathematical proof — has nevertheless so coloured our vision and our concepts that we now find it hard to remember or to imagine how the world, the natural order, might properly be known other than as it is known in science. Similarly we find it hard to imagine how truth might be conceived other than as it is demonstrated through mathematical proof. To reawaken the faculties that are rendered dormant by the

---

18. The godlessness of this objective seems seldom to have impressed itself upon theologians, who have resorted to God only when the programme fails them — that is, when they cannot satisfy its criteria — rather than as a matter of fundamental principle and conviction.

domination of science, theology desperately needs similar alliances with art, music, literature and poetry if it is to be able to appreciate afresh the wonder of the natural order.

What we think of as "the natural order" depends very much upon the intellectual apparatus we bring to bear upon it. We do not know as God knows: "And God saw everything that he had made...",[19] but what exactly did he see, upon which level from quarks to galaxy-clusters did his "eye" fall? How is the metaphor of seeing to be understood of God? We cannot conceive of the world as God conceives of it, but through an incarnational theology we can at least say that God has through his Son conceived of the world as we conceive of it. Without the doctrine of the incarnation God's knowledge of the world *in which we live* becomes highly prob-lematic, since lacking our sensory organs it is difficult to conceive how the world could appear to God as it appears to us. Most theistic statements overlook this difficulty with a broad appeal to divine omniscience, but in so doing they commit the heresy of "incarnating the Father", that is, making God the Father know the world as it is only knowable by his creatures.

Just as the development of critical thought challenged the medieval world-picture and its attendant assumptions about God, so the transition from a critical to a post-critical era will demand further revisions in theology which will render a metaphysical conception of God that embodies the medieval picture less and less tenable.[20] The

---

19. Genesis 1:31.
20. Every stage in the history of science has run the risk of smothering the offspring that would overthrow it. In my view, the responses to Galileo and to Darwin illustrate the contrast between conservative and progressive modes of thought far more than they illustrate the opposition between religion and science. One manifestation of the rebellion of science against its theological ancestry lay in its espousal of the impersonal ideals of pre-critical and critical thought which distorted the question of truth and led us to lose sight of the significance of the order in the world and our roles in perceiving that order. Truth became divorced from, and independent of, any and all self-constituting choice. But we are free to deny any truth, however basic (and so the Emperor has no clothes) if, as Quine saw, we are prepared to make sufficiently drastic revisions to other aspects of our system (rather like making a number other than 5 follow 1, 2, 3, 4). It is only because we habitually accept and hence reaffirm most of the assumptions built into our

pre-critical world had neither the mathematics, nor the concepts nor the instruments to develop science, and as a result the world seemed fragmented and unpredictable. Critical thought, arising during the sixteenth and seventeenth centuries, succeeded in replacing the piecemeal world of the Middle Ages with universal laws governed by mathematical equations of extraordinary gener-ality. The success of this programme led — paradoxically if seen as a product of an image of a personal and rational creator — to the ideal of impersonal generality and completely objective truth in which the medieval notions of God survived because their most general attributes (changelessness, almightiness, omniscience, ubiquity and so forth) were compatible with the love of generality in the prevailing intellectual climate.

The collapse of the critical era began in the middle of the nineteenth century, when we had to come to terms with new geometries and with different and sometimes incompatible axiom-atisations of mathematics. More recently the development of a new particularity in science, as it has rediscovered limitations to its predictive powers occasioned by supersensitive systems and the problems raised for realism by quantum mechanics, has further suggested the need for a reappraisal of the notions of absoluteness presupposed by medieval conceptions of God and critical philosophy.[21]

The combination of particularity in science and choice in mathematics — gleanings from the natural order that suggest reassessments of divine truth and will — suggest to me that renewed interest in individual and personal elements in science may lessen our sense of alienation from the world. It may enable us to face new challenges with new intellectual tools that are not rooted in an intellectual milieu which is still objectivist and impersonal. It is self-contradictory to attempt to solve a crisis in human self-understanding using methods that are inimical to those attributes which lie at the heart of that understanding and which have helped to precipitate that crisis. It is, in fact, to fall foul of the protection racket principle (by

---

culture and because we call them "normal" and "natural" that truth seems to be incapable of revision because of its self-evidence.

21. This is as true of the God whom critical philosophy rejects as of the God whom critical Christians accept.

which the source of a problem is greeted as a potential means of protecting oneself from it).

Christian theology looks to a God who is a source of renewal of unimaginable power, who requires a dynamic theology ready to embrace the complexity of a changing world with its ever-changing creator. In particular, we look to him for the new interpretative skills that we need to understand the world in the face of the new science.

Only a metaphysical medieval prejudice makes us draw back from the thought that if God's being is self-renewing he must therefore be changing in a way that makes him more every second, not less. Yet the space–time concepts of modern physics enable us to see that just as the universe is no longer conceived as expanding into space–time which already exists, but as generating its own space–time as an essential part of its expansion, so the being of God entails a growth that redefines the totality of all things by virtue of that growth. It is not that there is something other than God into which God changes, absorbing it and so becoming more; it is rather that, through changing, God generates that which is always more than there ever was hitherto: he grows without becoming more just as he gives without becoming less.

One way to see the power of this new way of thinking about God is to use it to address a problem that has troubled Christian thought for centuries, and which I touched on in my opening remarks: whether God foresaw all that would happen in the world when he created it, whether the incarnation was always inevitable and always going to be necessary, whether God really countenanced the colossal scale of human suffering from the beginning, and what it means for the omnipotence of God if "course corrections" to the development of the universe are necessary to produce the best of all possible worlds.

A radical, post-critical, personal answer to this question would deny that God did or could, or even wished to, foresee all that would happen in the universe in the finest detail. Such an answer would instead affirm that he gave it a deep structure sufficient to ensure that whatever it produced would be endlessly rich and incalculably worthwhile — a universe that he would think it worth dying for. Parents do not foresee how their children will grow up, neither can they foresee all the demands that their children will make of them as a result of their dependency. But they (like those women and men who engage in Christian marriage) accept such unspecified and unspecifiable constraints "for better, for worse". Such an open-ended commitment is typical of the Old Testament notion of the covenant. In fact, the Old and New Testaments contain remarkably little metaphysical speculation about the nature of life, the almightiness of God, and the predictability of the world. Instead they tell sometimes quite small-scale stories about the faithfulness of individuals, tribes and peoples living their lives under sometimes appalling provocation and hardship. This seems primitive only if we choose to read those documents through the filters of a critical second-millennium metaphysics.

Significantly, that same metaphysics was largely responsible for the rise of modern science, because it encouraged belief in the uniformity of the world, and gave rise to notions of law and of order conceived on a universal scale. Yet recently we have had to come to terms with particularity in science by recognising that super-sensitivity in systems can demand particularity and forbid generality. The abstractions that brought us so far, the broad brush-strokes that have given us such power, have now to be set against personal needs and the subtleties of such things as ecosystems (whose boundary conditions are so sensitive) in a way that seems to threaten the universality of the critical scientific method. It is not that there are no universal laws, but that the universal laws are so sensitive to their boundary conditions that they prove in many circumstances to be virtually useless as instruments of prediction and control. We may find ourselves understanding only that our understanding confers no predictive or controlling powers upon us as we seek to live our lives, that the world is just too complex for us to grasp unless we grasp it so tightly that we break it or ourselves in the process. To render the theological imperative permanent, God has ensured that the world is such that we shall never be able to predict its future course, nor detect his action in it, and he has done so in such a way that the garment of nature is utterly seamless, with no gaps where we might hope to locate his presence.

One reason why the present age is so exciting is that it is rediscovering the ambiguity and openness of the world manifested through the diverse ways we make sense of it. The natural order does not exist as a given objective reality possessing or implying —

still less insisting upon — a unique meaning or interpretation. It is a reality which is what it is only in the context of the minds which know it and the modes of their knowing; it is known as it resonates with the complementary aspects of itself it evokes in us.[22] Objectivism, born of the generalised impersonal metaphysics of critical science and philosophy, says that things are what they are quite independently of our knowing, but the "myth of the incarnate Father" (in which we project the structure of the world as it appears to human senses and intelligence back on to God) shows this to be a confusion.

Take, for example, our appreciation of art. Objectivism would have us believe that a painting is good or bad, great or poor, according to some set of absolute criteria. In contrast, post-critical thought will say that a given picture may resonate with you but not with me; that it is therefore great, powerful and profound for you, but not for me, just as a piece of music or a face or a poem may move one person but not another. *A fortiori* one aspect of the natural world may evoke a sense of God's purpose, truth and will in you but not in me: one may be moved to a sense of God by Scripture; another by the great dome of the starry heavens; another by the wonders of science; one may find God as a Jew, another as a Moslem, a third as a Hindu. Only an objectivist stance says that one route is genuine or legitimate and the others worthless, because only objectivism denies the uniqueness of the resonances which are evoked in different human beings by different circumstances. In theology that objectivism tends to try to monopolise the right to God, to make God its own by forbidding the very particularity which he has ordained through the plenitude of the world, and I read that monopolistic objectivism (with Foucault) as a means of making knowledge into power.[23]

---

22. I have recently discovered, thanks to Peter Ochs of Drew University, that something very close to this understanding is found in the works of C. S. Peirce. See, for example, Ochs' "Theosemiotics and Pragmatism" *Journal of Religion* 72:1 (January 1992).

23. Participants in the symposium seem to have understood this paragraph as an invitation to, and affirmation of, relativism. I was specifically challenged by a friendly critic with the question "What about truth?" But what I have said here does not involve relativism of *truth*; it involves removing the exclusivity of particular *paths* to truth; in Polanyi's terms, of the notion

Faced with all these difficulties, theology can take comfort from the fact that the success of science relies less on the cleverness of scientists, clever as they are, than upon the embodied cleverness of that which science undertakes to understand. Theology and science both presuppose the flexibility, reliability and faithfulness of that which they endeavour to know. Science works because it is applied to systems and by organisms which already know what they are doing. In other words, systems which survive, and organisms capable of making science work, have evolved and developed in ways which embody skills necessary to compensate for the inadequacies of the conceptual systems, tools and, more recently, the science they employ. It is rather like riding a bicycle: whatever the mechanical theory says, we know that we manage to stay upright in practice because we are capable of processing and being guided by a colossal amount of information that incessantly flows into us. We ride by being open to the environment; we know what we are doing;

---

that truth may only be ascertained focally if we employ specific and even unique subsidiaries by which to come to it. It is this problem that produces the intractable interfaith and inter-denominational disputes about *formal religion* as if the trappings of religion are the same as the truths of religion. Nothing could be further from the truth. Iconoclasm in all its forms involves a deep and pathological failure to appreciate that it is in the mode of interpretation, not in the icon itself, that problems arise. What makes an icon into an idol is precisely the mistake of regarding the subsidiary as the focal, the path as the goal, the means as the end. And what makes *knowledge* into *power* is the insidious suggestion that because the one path to truth is *the* truth and that "I know it", I somehow have the power to determine whether and to what extent "you" can travel down it too. Yet this is to suppose that God is *simple* in the utterly unworthy sense in which he becomes the same as the way we speak of him or conceive of him. The point of this paragraph, which underlies the whole of this paper, is that the "object" is not itself sufficient to determine its mode of signification, whether it be a statue, a religious symbol, or even the entire "natural order". Somewhere an additional component must be added that translates a mere object into a vehicle for God's self-revelation, and that additional component always and irreducibly involves *God* in the process, for "through God alone can God be known" as Emil Brunner put it in the opening sentence of *The Mediator*. All philosophical attempts to know God in a way that excludes God from the process are therefore to be rejected as *de facto* inadequate, as attempts at self-sanctification.

we embody a skill. Theology is no better or worse equipped than science, for its equipment is frail and imprecise human language, and its limitations are imposed as much by human imagination as by human reason. Theology is also applied to and used by organisms and systems which already know what they are doing, which are the living embodiment of the work of the divine Word (could they but see it) and for that reason if for no other, certainly not the cleverness of the theologian, the Church comes in the power of the Holy Spirit to enliven and to communicate the Word of God to every new generation for all its inadequacies.

The capacity to compensate for inadequacy is essential in any living system. Yet our mechanical and rational ideals are still those shaped by a Laplacean worldview in which, given sufficient initial information, ongoing compensations and human feelings and intuitions would be unnecessary. We project these ideals into the universe and suppose that it simply ought to work that way (as if being a good batsman consisted in being able to decide which stroke to play before the bowler had released the ball). God's universe not only need not, but actually does not, work that way because he has engendered in it the deep structures necessary to promote real freedom.

I began by drawing attention to two potentially contradictory aspects of my task: the binding generality of the intelligibility of the universe as it is known and sustained by God, and the rich particularity and diversity of the natural order as it is encountered and interpreted by humanity, particularly in its suffering. To reconcile these two views I have undertaken to sketch a new way of thinking not just about theology in a scientific age, but a new way of thinking about the kinds of things science can and cannot do in the context of a world of virtually unimaginable complexity, a complexity which we underestimate at our peril. At the heart of this reconstruction a deep harmony emerges with the concept of a God whose universal will is that women and men should grow in uniqueness and know and be known in their uniqueness. To sustain such a view of radical freedom, knowledge of God becomes as many-faceted as there are creatures to know him, but the relationship that emerges — not only between God and his conscious creatures, but between God and the universe itself — is of a God who is deeply and intimately involved at every stage and in every aspect of

radical particularity of human circumstances must force us to reconsider many of the absolutes traditionally associated with Christian
ethical thinking. In particular, the God who speaks to those with
ears to hear may once again be understood to address individuals
rather than nations, to act here without necessarily acting there, and
to have a kiss to offer not, as Schiller believed, to humankind in
general, but to a few, or even on occasion only to one.[24] He will be
the God of Abraham, Isaac and Jacob rather than the God of a metaphysics that makes him all things to all flesh.

Unlike the kind of gift which is given and forgotten, this freedom
demands an everlasting covenant between God and the universe.
God is with the universe and with humanity, establishing his order
and expressing his intentions through them. But his presence is not
there unambiguously. It is subtle and deep. It allows us to regard
the universe as a great machine devoid of a designer, as something
which runs automatically without a helmsman, although we are
starting to see the severe deficiencies of such a model even in
science. We shall never understand the intention manifested in the
world's order until we respond to that call by allowing ourselves to
imagine the possibilities which are there for those with eyes to see
and ears to hear, while also allowing that no two pairs of eyes or
ears may ever see or hear the same way or draw the same inference.
Not the mechanical monotony of a clockwork universe, but the rich
variety and unpredictability of life provide the best clues to the
higher-level ordering principles that disclose God's intentions for
those of his creatures prepared to engage upon the great and often
lonely adventure in imagination that will lead them from the natural
order to intimations of divine truth and will.

---

24. The reference is to Schiller's *Ode to Joy* as sung at the climax of
Beethoven's Ninth Symphony: "This kiss is for all the world" (*Diesen Kuss
der ganzen Welt*). See Hans Küng, *Does God Exist?* (Glasgow: Collins,
1978) p. 430n.

Response by John Honner

John Puddefoot's paper presents a core set of ideas — about intelligibility, ambiguity, deep structure, and the personal revelation of God culminating in the incarnation — with which I am in agreement and which I find original, admirable and fertile.

At the edges of this core, however, I find two sets of ideas which are somewhat, if not totally, contradictory. One of these sets concerns Puddefoot's primary stance in faith. I have no objection to that and, indeed, I applaud it. But in my view his certitude of faith spills over into a certitude about the contents or expression of that faith upon which the rest of his case seems to depend. For example, his opening line and initial strand of thought is based on the belief that "the world as the work of God must embody his intentions" (p. 148). Shortly after that he states that "belief in another who has created the world seems to require of us..." And then: "Christian theism demands that the world be intelligible to God and that the existence of the world ... be justifiable to God" (p. 150). Further on Puddefoot uses the conditional if: "If this is God's world, he must control the ways in which the laws of the world are made to serve his purpose" (p. 155).

These are examples which illustrate one aspect of Puddefoot's approach: if we believe in a God who has these properties, then this and this follows about the world. Let me call this the "Puddefoot theistic conditional". His confidence is placed not just in a belief in God, but in a God of certain specific characteristics. Now all our faith must have content. But, while the stance of faith may be clear and definite, can its specific contents be equally as certain?

You might think that Puddefoot would say "yes". But in fact he does not. Rather, time and again he argues that, in our new found post-critical adulthood, we must revise our medieval or more latterly objectivist language about God and shape a more subtle, humble, interpersonal language. Let me give some examples:

- The transition from a critical to a post-critical era will demand further revisions in theology which will render a metaphysical conception of God that embodies the medieval picture less and less tenable (p. 159).
- In theology ... objectivism tends to try to monopolise the right to God, to make God its own by forbidding the very particularity which he has ordained through the plenitude of the world (p. 163).

As a result of this critique, and out of a consideration of the elusive deep structure of nature, Puddefoot argues that in our post-critical adulthood:

- Knowledge of God becomes as many-faceted as there are creatures to know him, but the relationship that emerges ... is of a God who is deeply and intimately involved at every stage and in every aspect of the process of universal history (p. 165ff.).

Now this conclusion I certainly agree with. But my problem is this: Puddefoot does not appear to have arrived at his conclusion from his theistic conditional. Not only that, it seems to me that this conclusion, about the many-facetedness of God, conflicts with his theistic conditionals insofar as their prescriptive contents are seen as definite and unrevisable.

There is a second set of peripheral statements which I find equally in conflict, although I can see in this tension that Puddefoot is aware of the careful dialectic that he is setting up. I refer to the tension between his quite strong reservations about the helpfulness of science in broader areas of learning, and the lessons from science that, in the end, help establish his claims about the untameable presence of God in every person and every aspect of history. Let me give some examples. First, his reservations about science are found in expressions such as the following:

- Science ... cannot stipulate its boundary conditions ... Scientific imperialism ... insists that what science is capable of talking about is all that is worth talking about (p. 155).
- The one thing that the natural order tells us with unerring and unnerving regularity is that it cannot be known by science

unless we allow science to dictate the criteria by which it is to be known (p. 158).

These are comments with which I agree. On the other hand, however, Puddefoot draws a great deal from post-empirical science. In particular, he points out not only the order and complexity in nature that science manifests to us, but also science's discovery of its own limitations:

■ More recently the development of a new particularity in science, as it has rediscovered limitations to its predictive powers occasioned by supersensitive systems and the problems raised for realism by quantum mechanics, has further suggested the need for a reappraisal of the notions of absoluteness presupposed by medieval conceptions of God and critical philosophy (p. 160).

■ The new sciences, particularly quantum mechanics and chaos theory, point us in the direction of a new conception of God that lies between the individual ... and the personal (p. 148).

Thus it is from this basis, the findings of natural science, that Puddefoot moves to a new language about God — one which is more personal, more aesthetic, and more involved. So, despite his protestations about science, he obviously believes that good can come of it. Similarly, despite his theistic conditional, he also believes that the ways we understand God can and must change. Indeed, these two sets of tensions roughly parallel the four strands of thought that Puddefoot confesses at the start of his paper.

Which brings me to a more positive response. Puddefoot does a very neat and original reworking of the design argument when he talks about the ambiguous intelligibility of reality. In the design argument you find a watch and you know how it works and you know what it is for — the argument is simply whether there is a designer. Puddefoot's insight is quite different. Let me give an example.

I find a gadget on the workbench of an inventor friend. It looks something like a can-opener, something like blunt scissors, maybe a pair of pliers. I can see that this gadget is probably meant to be hand-held, but try as I might, I cannot work out what it really is for, although it makes quite a useful large paper clip. It is only partially intelligible. I do not have all the background. When my friend comes into the workshop and I ask her what the gadget is for, she waves a plastic bag in front of my face but I still do not get the point. Then she tells me: "When you want to put something in the deepfreeze, you can use this to seal your freezer bags." And she shows me how it works.

An even more elaborate and fertile model would be a piece of creative art and the artist's comments on that work. If this example gets at Puddefoot's idea, what we have is a model for the incarnation. The God of the design argument is a God of the Deists (Einstein's, Newton's and Paul Davies' distant God), but the God of the ambiguous intelligibility argument is either a God who is a tease and malicious, or a God who will display the full intelligibility of the universe in the total revelation of the incarnation. At this point, Puddefoot's theistic conditional makes sense. If God is benevolent, and if the world is only ambiguously intelligible with an elusive deep structure, then God can only show the true intelligibility (that is, order and intent) by telling us, showing us, or being among us.

There is an alternative argument which starts with the incarnation in order to assert the love of God, rather than starting with the love of God in order to assert the necessity of incarnation. Both are circular, and neither is a demonstration, but I find Puddefoot's approach illuminating.

In some ways what he says is not new. Heidegger, dragging himself through abandoned human existence, ultimately concluded that "only a God can save us".[1] Karl Rahner, at the time under some influence from Heidegger, wrote his first two books on the human condition with the evocative titles *Encounters with Silence* and *Hearers of the Word*.[2] Both books argue that we can know nothing of God, only wait in pathetic silence before the ineffable mystery of God, until God chooses to speak a saving word to us. And, for that word to be truly saving, it must be spoken in our human history, totally a part of human existence.

---

1. Martin Heidegger, "Only a God can save us: *Der Spiegel*'s interview with Martin Heidegger", Maria P. Alter and John D. Caputo, translators, *Philosophy Today* 20:4 (1976) pp. 267-284.
2. Karl Rahner, *Encounters with Silence* (London: Sands, 1960); *Hearers of the Word* (London: Sheed and Ward, 1969).

What is significantly different about Puddefoot's argument, however, is that it is not merely a philosophical argument, a transcendental claim, but one that draws strength from science. It also creatively modifies the old and ultimately atheistic alliance of philosophical theology with empirical science based on design.

However, instead of a theistic conditional, Puddefoot's arguments are equally well based on a humanist existential conditional: if human life is like this, and if nature is like this, then only this kind of a God can save us, and this kind of a God we find in Jesus Christ.

Which brings me to my final difficulty in coming to terms with Puddefoot's interesting paper, although it is also a difficulty that I have with many papers in this book. It has to do with the nature of revelation. I once again find a set of apparent contradictions in Puddefoot's paper about how we are to discern the traces of God. On the one hand he seems to opt for a biblicist stance. His third strand of thought is that "we need to go back into prehistory to the God of the Bible, who is largely non-metaphysical" (p. 149). The point he wishes to make, however, is that "the Old and New Testaments contain remarkably little metaphysical speculation about ... the almightiness of God and the predictability of the world" (p. 162). I partly agree with this, but I find that it strains both his theistic conditionals and our need to shape some content, however revisable, for our apprehension of God. As well as calling for a return to the God of the Bible, Puddefoot is aware that "the Holy Spirit" has the power "to enliven and to communicate the Word of God to every new generation for all its inadequacies" (p. 165). This awareness, however, could be considered to contradict Puddefoot's rejection of "monopolistic objectivism" which tends to make God its own and turn knowledge into power To be fair, these are not contradictions so much as tensions.

However, and here I show my own hand, if these are tensions that we must live with, they also raise the issue of the difficulty between the record of revelation that we find in Scripture and the traces of God that we may find unfolded by the Spirit outside of, or subsequent to, the biblical record.

It seems to me that before any dialogue with science can occur, we have to work out where we stand with respect to the order of grace and the order of nature. If these two realms are seen as exclusive of each other, I cannot see how any real or fruitful dialogue can begin.

Scripture is normative for my faith not so much because of what it says — though that is not unimportant — but because I choose to accept that here is a record which tells a credible and attractive story of God's self-disclosure to us. The fact and process of self-disclosure have precedence over the contents of the record of that revelation. In my view the contents are continuously being reshaped both within and beyond the biblical record. While Scripture is miraculously central, it does not exclude the work of the Spirit elsewhere, even in science. If, by going back to the God of the Bible, Puddefoot means going forward with the spirit of the God of the Bible, then I am in agreement with him. Sometimes I hear him offering us, however, a monopolar God of the Bible, and I am not so ready to accede to that rhetoric.

In conclusion, while I applaud Puddefoot's central thesis, I am confused by his highly dialectical approach. I do not understand why he begins with his strongly specified theistic conditional about the God who orders, controls and has intent. These seem to be the very metaphysical models that he later resiles from when he speaks about God as creator (a much more attractive term than designer) and personally involved. I prefer to let my faith in the mystery of God, a gift located at the very centre of the web of Scripture's record of beliefs, be continually alive as the universe unfolds. This is the way it is in a healthy relationship of love, surely, and a way that lets God be both ineffably God and present in nature. It lets the dialogue between science and theology be open and fruitful, for in science we can find richer metaphors that converge nature and God asymptotically.

Response by Owen Gingerich

For me to comment on a theological paper puts me in mind of a certain survivor of the Johnstown flood disaster that has gone down in American lore. Late in the last century a dam broke, sending torrents of water down through a narrow Pennsylvania valley, essentially wiping out Johnstown. By heroic exertions our hero managed to get free of the treacherous waters, and forever after was all too eager to tell of his exploits. Eventually everyone went out of their way to avoid him, and he died a lonely old man. When he finally reached the pearly gates, St Peter told him that he would be granted one wish. "In that case," said our survivor, "assemble the heavenly hosts so that I can tell them about the Johnstown flood." "As you like," replied St Peter, "but remember: Noah is in the audience."

John Puddefoot has used the concept of order as a springboard into a series of provocative ideas on the relationship of the Divine to the created world and the intelligent creatures within it. For him, order is, in a sense, the special domain of the scientist whose exertions would lead nowhere were it not for the orderly processes revealed by critical thought. Yet the scientist does not automatically find God as these orderly processes are analysed; this is at first puzzling, and calls for some explanation. Puddefoot suggests that the universe contains within it a deep structure that by its very nature prevents us from seeing all its faces, rendering both God and the universe itself ultimately unknowable, especially in its particularity, except through God's personal revelation.

In response to Puddefoot's paper I would like to focus on two issues, each of which is connected to a word, two different words, that Puddefoot never uses. The first issue and word is transcendence. I originally began to appreciate transcendence as a powerful codeword when I read Milton Munitz's book *Cosmic*

Understanding.[1] Munitz, a distinguished American philosopher, takes an agnostic theological position, but as he examines the insights from modern cosmology, particularly the idea of an evolving universe with an apparent beginning, he concludes that philosophically the universe is not all there is, or was, or ever shall be, to quote the opening lines from Carl Sagan's *Cosmos* television series. According to Munitz' reasoning, there must be something more, a transcendence that goes beyond the physical universe that we observe and analyse.

To those of us in the Christian tradition, such a transcendence is fundamental to our beliefs, an intrinsic part of our faith. A creator God transcends the created universe. Theology, says Puddefoot, strives to articulate the structure of high-level ordering principles and to forge explanations. This, I submit, is the attempt to grapple with the meaning of transcendence, and this is why I claim that the first part of Puddefoot's paper deals with various aspects of transcendence.

Munitz, in *Cosmic Understanding*, argues that the transcendence, because of its very nature, is deep, dark, and forever unknowable. In reviewing his book for the journal *Nature*, I remarked that such a conclusion was not sound logic, for if the transcendence was unknowable, we could not in fact know that it is unknowable. By chance I met Munitz soon after writing the review, and before I could mention it, he remarked that he had seen and appreciated the review, and indeed conceded the point. The transcendence could have chosen to reveal itself. Whether Munitz would agree with me that such a revelation has actually occurred is another matter. Puddefoot goes straight to the point here, referring near the outset to Christian incarnational theology. He admonishes us not to entertain any theology that falls short of being fully incarnational because to relinquish the incarnation is "to relinquish perhaps the highest-level ordering and explanatory principle of all, that 'God was in Christ reconciling the world to himself'" (p. 154). In other terms, the unknowable transcendence became knowable, the word became flesh.

1.   Milton K. Munitz, *Cosmic Understanding: Philosophy and Science of the Universe* (Princeton University Press, 1986).

The other word missing from the paper is deconstruction, and perhaps the author will be shocked to think that his paper has anything to do with that. Or maybe not. Repeatedly throughout the paper Puddefoot mentions pre-critical, critical, and post-critical thought. It is obvious from the context that pre-critical thought is ancient thought, including even biblical language. Critical thought is connected, for example, with the scientific revolution, with Descartes or Newton. But if, like me, you are unfamiliar with the term post-critical thought, there are no clues until near the end of the paper. There Puddefoot identifies objectivism with critical thought, whereas "post-critical thought will say that a given picture may resonate with you but not with me; that it is therefore great, powerful and profound for you but not for me..." (p. 163). I might be moved to a sense of God by the star-spangled Milky Way, as I saw it so impressively from the Mt Cook National Park, but this might do nothing for you. Deconstruction is a form of literary criticism that strips away objective meanings and searches for the particularity of a given receiver in a given situation.

Of course, independent of the present paper was Puddefoot's public lecture given earlier in this symposium which explicitly addressed the third millennium of faith, presumably the post-critical period. There he made clear that he believes that the patterns of scientific thinking in the critical period have locked us into a deterministic framework with the unfortunate consequence that science has been pitted against traditional religion. If I understood the nub of that lecture, he argued that changes in our understanding of science now leave a kind of openness that readily allows for miracles. I have often considered that, while science is uncannily good at predicting many physical phenomena, it only predicts what is highly likely, not what is inevitable. Science can never deny the possibility of the highly improbable event that qualifies as miraculous. To this end I recall the poetry of Robinson Jeffers:

The mathematicians and physics men
Have their mythology; they work alongside the truth,
Never touching it; their equations are false.
But the things work.[2]

---

2.   Robinson Jeffers, "The Great Wound" in *The Beginning and the End* (New York: Random House, 1963) p. 11.

So to an extent I agree with Puddefoot. But there is the rub: the things work. Will science in the third millennium of faith provide an openness that readily allows for miracles? I think not. I suspect that despite the fundamental changes in the philosophical underpinnings of science, a tension will remain simply because of the efficacy of so many scientific endeavours, whether it is the building of the bomb that so exercised Robinson Jeffers, or the accuracy of probing Neptune with our spaceships, or the precision with which biochemists will be able to pinpoint genes and replace missing segments of DNA in diseased persons. And when science says something is very improbable, it will be just as strongly tempting to doubt the likelihood of a miracle in the post-critical age as in our own.

Particularity versus generality is an ongoing theme in Puddefoot's paper. Science, he says, deals with the structure of the world, that is, its generalities. In computer terms, science concerns the internal workings of the machine. God's inputs are the particularities, like the external pressing of keys on the computer. I rather like this analogy, and I think it is helpful. Much of his paper has to do with the way that science, in the period of critical thought, developed the generalities that form the explanative mode that satisfies our desire to understand the universe. But then came developments in science to rock the belief that scientific explanations had the situation under control. Puddefoot alluded to them in a sentence. To the expert they were codewords for huge areas of scientific development: Gödel's theorem, chaos theory, quantum uncertainty. And then he is off to something very interesting but quite different — whether God even wished to foresee all the fine detail in the universe. It is almost as if he has thought and written extensively on these connections, and has here forgotten that not all his hearers will have covered the same ground, or can swiftly reconstruct the missing paragraphs. I will not take it as my task to fill in any of the missing technical apparatus, in what Puddefoot himself admits is something of a "tangled web". It is enough to point out that particularity versus generality, and their appreciation in the pre-critical, critical, and post-critical worlds of thought, is one of the key threads tying this paper together.

Now the reason I find these two notions, transcendence and deconstruction, of special interest lies in the circumstance that for a number of years I have been working with colleagues in the American Scientific Affiliation. This professional organisation of men and women who take both science and the Bible seriously are planning a six-part series for public television on the nature of science. We have seen one previous series after another founded on scientific reductionism, essentially the view that science can explain everything without recourse to transcendence or particularity. This frequently borders on scientism, "scientific imperialism" as Puddefoot so nicely expresses it. The philosophy implicit in much of science television tacitly implies that "what you see is what there is", in other words, transcendence is ruled out from the start.

In contrast, our plan would be to present what is basically sound educational science, but with a different philosophical spin: that historically modern science has developed uniquely out of a Judaeo-Christian tradition, that scientific understanding is not incompatible with religious belief, and that the universe is filled with wonderful constructions that can be seen as the deliberate design or intent of a superintelligence. All these points have to be made subtly and with sensitivity because English-speaking public television is not the stage for Christian evangelism. One cannot display the passion and enthusiasm demonstrated by John Puddefoot in his public lecture to which I referred earlier. How can one make the point that scientism is a particular philosophy and a particular set of choices, by no means the only, or the best, choice for an educated person to make? After much thought, we decided that the final episode had to raise the idea of transcendence although it is a word we would prefer not to use, at least not on American public television. So we shall cast it in another form and ask, as a deliberate challenge to Sagan's *Cosmos* television series, if the cosmos is all there is. In effect, we ask what it means to be human. In Genesis 1 we read that men and women were created in God's image. Does that mean anything that can be put into TV images? I argue that it has to do with creativity, consciousness and conscience. This is not the place to detail how we intend to package that question into the entertainment mode that television seems to require. But if we get the funding to make the series a reality, I think we can cope with it.

The second problem of focus in such an undertaking concerns the movement to post-critical thought, to the attitudes of the deconstructionist, or as Puddefoot perceptively put it: "objectivism tends to try to monopolise the right to God, to make God its own by forbidding the very particularity which he has ordained through the plenitude of the world..." (p. 163). The guardians of the gates of American public television will ask why they should hear about our God and our reading of the texts. There are many approaches or non-approaches to deity in modern America, so why should one view have any priority over the other? America now faces increasing religious plurality, as does Britain. America nominally has a Christian majority, although we have for many years been aware of the Jewish population that provides the so-called swing vote in some states. By the year 2000, if not already, there will be more Muslims than Jews in America. Already in Los Angeles there are more Buddhists than Jews.

In a public television programme in America one can without difficulty, I believe, maintain a clear theistic position. But arguments from design, and natural theology in general, do not say all that much about God. As Puddefoot has reminded us, it is an incarnational theology that makes a meaningful theology. In a television series I would certainly mention the incarnation in the historical context of why modern science arose in Christendom and not within Islam, that is, I would mention the argument that God took the reality of nature seriously in the act of incarnation, and thus it was within Christian theology that nature was taken seriously enough for scientific reasoning to develop.

I am charmed by John Polkinghorne's motto, "epistemology models ontology" (p. 235). It helps us understand how and why we understand the universe itself. John Puddefoot's view seems quite different; he proposes deep structures in whose existence we must as theists confidently believe but which may in fact lie beyond our scientific and even perhaps our theological understanding. What links both of the John Ps' theologies is the essential and critical role of the incarnation. The idea that God has directly entered the world and revealed Godself to the world gives us a hope and confidence that our human understanding can indeed encompass much of the construction of the natural world. But that is something that I can hardly argue on public television.

I hope that these reflections on Puddefoot's paper have under-scored some of the main themes within it, and I am sure they have made manifest the immense difference in discussion possible at a thought-provoking conference of this sort and what can be done on television. I would like to think that the particularities of the plenitude of this world will allow both to happen.

5

The principle of relativity as a conceptual tool in theology

Carver T. Yu

Introduction

The spectre of relativism is haunting the present age. The Protagorean dictum that "man is the measure of all things" seems to have been revived and recast into a dictum that "subjectivity and contextuality are the measure of all things". Formerly, as it was in Kant, universal subjectivity was the guarantee against relativism. But as soon as this is questioned, subjectivism leads naturally to relativism. And as soon as subjectivity is explained in terms of social reality, truth becomes truth merely for a particular world of collective consciousness. Even scientific truth formerly held to be the objective representation of nature has now become one of many equally valid paradigms emerging out of different world-constructions in different historico-sociocultural conditions. Accordingly, truth must be understood purely as a product of constructions under a certain set of sociocultural conditions. To apprehend truth is to apprehend those conditions which give rise to the construction of such truth. Sociology is, therefore, the Queen of the Sciences.

We would, however, like to be a little more sceptical about what is in vogue. It is true that pluralism is part of our modern social condition. Yet the affirmation of plurality does not necessarily require the abandonment of a faith in, and a quest for, some kind of unity. Any attempt to apprehend reality has to be done from a definite frame of reference, and there is no such thing as an absolute frame. Relativity of reference frames, however, does not entail relativism. On the contrary, the principle of relativity has been formulated by physical scientists as a principle affirming the invariant structure of physical reality to all frames of reference. At the same time, the subjectivist as well as the contextualist concept of reality are not as unquestionable as some would like to think.

The question about the validity of knowledge can be asked at different levels of epistemological reflection. And in each of these levels of reflection, relativism can arise. The present paper is concerned with the most basic level, where we must consider the extent to which our knowledge is determined and shaped by our perspective or our frame of reference. Can our particularity so colour our knowledge that it is impossible for different knowers to come to a common picture of reality? Must we satisfy ourselves with the picture of reality which is peculiar to us? At this basic level, a form of relativism arises which is widespread in modern culture. It is not uncommon to hear people say: "You see things from your frame of reference, I see things from mine — what is true to you is true only to you." In theological terms, the case remains that, despite the claim of absoluteness, doctrinal truth is formulated differently in different historical or sociocultural contexts. This problem has often been used to suggest that doctrines are ideological in essence, thus leading to a relativistic explanation of the nature of doctrine. This problem needs to be addressed if theological relativism is to be avoided.

George Lindbeck has addressed the problem impressively in his *The Nature of Doctrine,*[1] with the intention of resisting an outright relativistic position which treats doctrines as nothing but metaphors that may be created anew or discarded at will in accordance with the situation. Such an attempt is admirable, and the linguistic analogy of understanding religion as a language and its doctrines as grammatical rules is both highly suggestive and eminently defensible. However, in fortifying truth within an internally coherent system, can Lindbeck avoid making truth sectarian or parochial? Can he show us why a story, unique as it may be, cannot be told in different languages? Is it not true that different sects within the Christian tradition are telling the same story in different languages with

---

1. George A. Lindbeck, *The Nature Of Doctrine* (Philadelphia: The Westminster Press, 1984).

different sets of grammar? If internal coherence is used as the criterion, is it not true that each and every sect can be as valid as the other? Could they not then continue to tell their story differently, with their own grammar binding for their community? What then is the point of ecumenical dialogue? Can there be dialogue among those who speak different languages, and who happen to believe that the languages they use do not refer to any objective reality? Does it not also mean that the necessity or possibility for genuine dialogue among religious faiths becomes doubtful? From a more pragmatic perspective, when truth loses the character of objectivity and absoluteness, how can it expect to remain conceptually powerful and continue to have culture-forming power?[2] How effective will it remain in binding the faithful into a community? All this is very much in doubt.[3] Perhaps an analogy of a different kind, without the relativistic overtone, has to be found. We think, drawing an analogy from the principle of relativity, that we may come to understand the relation between invariant truth and changing contexts (variant frames of reference) without falling into the trap of relativism.

Principle of relativity versus relativism

Luigi Pirandello warns us most vividly in *Six Characters in Search of an Author* that once a character has been created, be it in a novel or a play, it takes on a life of its own, beyond the creative intent or will of the author, and is shaped by the imaginations of different actors, audiences and so on.[4] Such a fate can also befall an idea or a scientific discovery. This has happened to Einstein's theory of relativity. Seizing on the word relativity, with little understanding of the meaning of the theory and its philosophical implications, many turn the theory into a cliché or a licence in support of relativism of all sorts, claiming that "everything is relative", that truth can only be

2. *Ibid.* p. 134.
3. I agree totally with Polkinghorne when he asks, "Why should anything be 'conceptually powerful' and 'practically useful' unless it [bears] some relation to the way things are?" John Polkinghorne, *Reason and Reality* (London: SPCK, 1991) p. 14.
4. Luigi Pirandello, *Six Characters in Search of an Author,* John Linstrum, translator (London: Eyre Methuen, 1979).

truth for one's own frame of reference, and that there is no invariant truth which is true for all.[5]

Nothing can be farther from the reality described by the theory of relativity than such a popular rendering. Such a misconception is unfortunate and modern culture has paid a high price for it. Einstein wished that he had used the term "theory of invariance" rather than "theory of relativity". Ernst Cassirer warns that when the theory of relativity is seen as "a renewal of ancient sophistical doctrines, a confirmation of the Protagorean doctrine that man is the 'measure of all things', its essential achievement is mistaken".[6] It is worth quoting him as he seeks to clear the misconception:

> The physical theory of relativity teaches, not that what appears to each person is true to him but, on the contrary, it warns against taking appearances, which hold only from a particular system, as truth in the sense of science, i.e., as an expression of an inclusive and final law of experience. The latter is gained neither by the observations and measurement of a particular system nor by those of however many such systems, but only by the reciprocal coordination of the results of all possible systems. The general theory of relativity purports to show how we can gain assertions concerning all of these, how we can rise above the fragmentariness of the individual views to a total view of natural processes.[7]

---

5. McFague, for example, is all too ready to seize on the insight of the theory of relativity as she understands it to affirm that "all our knowledge is *our* knowledge and subject to the limitations of the human mind and body". According to her, "relativity informs us that there are no absolute measurements possible ... all attempts to measure their motions are relative, since there is no simultaneous time at different points in space ... What emerges is a picture, not of objective, material substances being described and measured by a neutral observer, but rather of a network of movements and relationships in which the scientist is a participant." With such a simplistic and truncated understanding it is quite evident that McFague is making relativism out of the theory of relativity. See Sallie McFague, *Metaphorical Theology—Models of God in Religious Language* (Philadelphia: Fortress Press, 1982) pp. 77-78.
6. Ernst Cassirer, *Substance and Function & Einstein's Theory of Relativity* W.C. & M.C. Swabey, translators (New York: Dover Publications, 1953) p. 393.
7. *Ibid.* Also refer to Yakov P. Terletskii, *Paradoxes in the Theory of Relativity* (New York, Plenum Press, 1968) pp. 3-5.

The concept of relativity was not new when Einstein formulated his theory. It was a fundamental concept implicit in the theoretical formulations of Galileo as well as Newton. It is a concept used to express the invariant and symmetrical structure of reality. There are aspects of nature which remain unchanged even as we change our perspective or our state of observation. To Newton, the laws of motion remain equally true for all inertial systems, irrespective of where, when or in what state of motion they are. No one system enjoys a special status in regard to physical reality, all inertial systems obey the same laws in the same way, whether we make observations here or there, from this direction or that direction (we thus say that physical laws are space-invariant), or whether we make observations now, tomorrow or in a century (we thus say that physical laws are time-invariant). It is in this sense that all inertial systems are relative to one another, that is, no one system is better placed or suited to unfold the structure of reality than any other. Reality may be perceived through all reference frames and it "reveals" itself as invariant regardless of the conditions of the frames. When Newton uses Galileo's transformation to arrive at a common description of motion in terms of a single formula taking into consideration the different states of motion of different systems, he is expressing the faith that no matter how diverse are the states of motion of systems under consideration, a common description is nevertheless possible.

If the concept of relativity has long been held by Galileo and Newton, what is so revolutionary about Einstein's theory of relativity? The theory of relativity, as Einstein himself sees it, is not really that revolutionary.[8] What is revolutionary, if we insist on using the term, is that Einstein is more insistent than Newton in taking the principle of relativity to its intuitively natural conclusion.

Newton was insistent not only on the invariance of physical laws, but also on the invariance of the standard of measurement through which the laws of motion reveal their true character. He held that not only are laws of motion invariant, so too are the yardsticks and clocks with which we measure motions of different reference

---

8.   Abraham Pais, *Subtle is the Lord: The Science and the Life of Albert Einstein* (Oxford University Press, 1982) p. 30.

systems. This is where Newton misplaced his insistence on invariance. With this misplaced invariance, Newtonians would have enormous difficulty in understanding and accepting the constancy of the velocity of light, irrespective of the velocity of its source. To them, the velocity of light should change in accordance with Galileo's principle of relativity, that is, the velocity of light is relative in respect to different reference systems. In insisting on this, Galileo and Newton fail to see the constancy of the velocity of light as something implicit in the invariance of electromagnetic laws in all inertial frames (explained below). In effect, they have sacrificed the invariance of a set of physical laws for the invariance of a set of standards of measurement.

For Einstein, the constancy of the velocity of light is an intuitively natural conclusion of the principle of invariance applied to the laws of electromagnetism.[9] In very simple terms, light as electromagnetic waves is produced when an electric field in a region of space changes in time. This produces in neighbouring space a magnetic field, the emergence of which means that the magnetic field in that region also changes in time, that is, from non-existence to existence. This in turn produces an electric field, which then produces another magnetic field, and so on. Here we may note that time and space are intricately correlated in the symmetrical structure of electromagnetic phenomena. Now if we imagine[10] an observer moving side by side with this electromagnetic wave at the same speed as its propagation, what is she expected to see? She is expected to see a still (frozen) electric field and a still magnetic field which remain adjacent to each other forever, and occupy the same region of space next to her. The

---

9. *Ibid.*
10. Einstein tells us in his "Autobiographical Notes" of his thought-experiment at the age of sixteen: "If I pursue a beam of light with a velocity c (velocity of light in a vacuum), I should observe such a beam of light as a spatially oscillatory electromagnetic field at rest. However, there seems to be no such thing, whether on the basis of experience or according to Maxwell's equations. From the very beginning it appeared to me intuitively clear that, judged from the standpoint of such an observer, everything would have to happen according to the same laws as for an observer who, relative to the earth, was at rest. For how, otherwise, should the first observer know, that is, determine, that he is in a state of fast uniform motion?" P.A. Schlipp, editor, *Albert Einstein: Philosopher-Scientist* (La Salle: Open Court, 1970) p. 53.

dynamic nature of the successive propagation of magnetic and electric fields can no longer be observed. If that were true, the observer is inevitably led to ask whether the laws governing the propagation of electromagnetic waves are still valid for a frame moving at the same speed as light propagation. If they are still valid, then our observer should still be able to see fields generating fields in a continuum of neighbouring space. Even if she is moving at the speed of light, she should still expect to see fields generating fields away from her. That is, she can never catch up with the propagation of light.

It is with this thought experiment that Einstein was led to accept the constant speed of light, not merely as a given fact from the Michelson-Morley experiment, but as a natural consequence of insisting upon the invariance of electromagnetic laws to all frames of reference. In this light, the meaning of relativity is quite clear in the two postulates on which the theory of special relativity is based. These two postulates are:

- The laws of physics take the same form in all inertial frames.
- In any given inertial frame, the velocity of light, c, is the same whether the light is emitted by a body at rest or by a body in uniform motion.

Quite clearly, the first postulate repeats what has been stated explicitly by Newton as the principle of relativity. The second postulate is another way of stating that in any given inertial frame, electromagnetic laws governing the emission of light remain invariant irrespective of the state of motion of that reference system. It is a particular case of the first postulate, which is more general. Taking the two postulates together, it becomes all the more obvious that the theory of special relativity is a theory of the invariance of physical laws.[11]

The postulate of the constant velocity of light goes against our intuition. This is because we are accustomed to misplacing

---

11. It may be noted that Minkowski, who developed the four-dimensional geometry for the exposition of the theory of relativity, would prefer to call the "relativity-postulate" the "postulate of the absolute world". See Yakov P. Terletskii, *op. cit.* p. 6.

invariance to our measuring rods or clocks. We are shocked to find that what we have consistently regarded as constant actually changes with the states of motion in which measuring instruments are carried. We are therefore led to the impression that if the standards with which we measure things change, then we are left with no universal standards. Perhaps it is here that many feel driven to relativism. Yet it is also here that a deeper invariant structure of nature is being revealed to us. Indeed, the measurement of space and time also change as the frame of reference changes. The scenario is such that the measuring rod and clock of the experimenter actually change as she is moving in respect to the events she is to measure. What is being negated here is the absoluteness of space-by-itself and the absoluteness of time-by-itself (both conceived as independent of each other and of events to be measured in correlation to the event of measurement). However, in such negation, the intrinsic relatedness between space and time in the structure of reality comes into the picture. And with this a new invariant emerges. In place of the misplaced invariance of absolute space and absolute time is the invariance of the space–time interval between events. No matter from which frame of reference we measure it, the space–time interval between events always remains invariant. Thus a truly invariant standard of measurement remains. Instead of a measuring rod or clock, light is used as the universal standard for measuring space–time interval.

The principle of relativity expounded thus far is still not general enough. The description of nature is still restricted to phenomena in inertial systems in uniform motion. Despite insistence on invariance of natural laws for all reference frames, there is still a hidden preference given to reference systems in uniform motion correlated to the ensemble of fixed stars (source of inertia).[12] To extend the principle of relativity to all reference systems, Einstein has to deal with reference systems in constant acceleration as well as those in gravitational fields. His task is to show that the same natural laws which are invariant in inertial systems are also invariant in these

---

12. Louis de Broglie, "A general survey of the scientific work of Albert Einstein" in *Albert Einstein: Philosopher-Scientist, op. cit.* p. 117.

systems. To achieve that, Einstein introduces first the principle of equivalence and then the principle of covariance.

The principle of equivalence asserts that things behave in a uniformly accelerating reference system in the same way that they would behave in a uniform gravitational field. An observer enclosed in her reference system would have no way to distinguish whether her reference system was accelerating or whether it was under the influence of a gravitational field. With this principle, Einstein is able to describe gravitation in terms of the accelerated motion of reference systems rather than in terms of gravitational force acting at a distance. And with this priniciple, relativity of a more general form can be achieved, since all reference systems may be regarded as equivalent, and general physical laws may be formulated as invariant in whatever reference system we choose. However, the principle of equivalence does have an operationalistic character. At least it is liable to operationalist interpretation.[13] Nevertheless, it is an important step toward the formulation of the general theory of relativity.

Applying this principle, one may ask how light would behave in a gravitational field? Would the constancy of its velocity be maintained as postulated in special relativity? As it turns out, in the presence of a gravitational field, the velocity of light is no longer constant. The postulate of special relativity no longer holds. A more general principle has to be formulated, and the deeper structure of reality begins to unfold through this general principle.

When the constancy of the velocity of light does not hold, the formerly perceived geometrical structure of the space–time world is in question. Here the principle of equivalence is useful. The different behavior of light in different reference systems (inertial as

---

13. We do not need to discuss the status of the principle of equivalence as a conceptual foundation for the development of the theory of general relativity and its relation to the principle of covariance. It is not our concern here. Those interested may refer to John C. Graves, *The Conceptual Foundations of Contemporary Relativity Theory* (Cambridge: MIT Press, 1971) pp. 130-145; Christopher Ray, *The Evolution of Relativity* (Philadelphia: Adam Hilger, 1987) pp. 55-81.

compared with accelerating systems, or systems under gravitation) can be explained in terms of the difference in space–time structure which different reference systems find in themselves. As we probe deeper, we are able to see that the space–time geometrical structure in which light maintains constant velocity is comparable to a two-dimensional structure, describable in terms of Euclidean geometry as a "flat" space–time structure. Our universe, however, is more complicated. It may be perceived as a three-dimensional structure describable in terms of non-Euclidean geometry. What makes the difference between the two structures is the presence of mass. A space–time structure "without" mass can be described in two-dimensional Euclidean geometry, while with the presence of mass, space–time structure is "gripped" by mass, warped and shaped "in its image" (metaphorically), and is thus only describable in terms of non-Euclidean geometry.[14]

Given the difference in space–time structures of different reference systems, the constant velocity of light in "flat" space–time structures (those without the presence of mass) can be perceived as equivalent to non-constant velocity of light in curved space–time structures, those with the presence of mass and thus a gravitational field. To put all these in more general terms, Einstein introduces the principle of general covariance: "The general laws of nature are to be expressed by equations which hold good for all systems of coordinates, that is, [they] are covariant with respect to any substitution whatsoever (generally covariant)."[15]

The general laws of nature should have the same form in all reference systems, and all reference systems are equally well suited for description of nature. The form in which general laws of nature are to be expressed is independent of the reference system in which

---

14. John Wheeler uses vivid imagery to explain space–time geometry within gravitational fields. With the imagery of "the grip of mass on space–time" and "the grip of space–time on mass", Wheeler unfolds before us the intrinsic relatedness between space–time and matter, and ways that we may understand gravity in terms of space–time curvature. See John Wheeler, *A Journey into Gravity and Space–time* (New York: Scientific American Library, 1990).

15. Albert Einstein, *The Principle of Relativity* (New York: Dover, 1923) p. 117. Cited in John C. Graves, *op. cit.* p. 134.

they are formulated. The principle of covariance expresses a deep conviction that our choice of reference systems may be arbitrary, but behaviours of nature are in no way determined by our choice of reference. Nature will always behave in the same way, being governed by the same laws.

The conviction that laws of nature are invariant despite the possible multiplicity of space–time representations of events has far-reaching implications not only for science but for humanity as a whole. It keeps alive the conviction that our reference systems, diverse and unique as they are, are nevertheless commensurable, and a common world of discourse can be maintained. Such conviction has been badly shaken by ill-conceived relativism which asserts each reference system as absolute in itself, thus making common discourse impossible and unnecessary.

The other side of invariance

The principle of covariance unfolds a beautifully symmetrical world. Whichever way we turn or whichever way we rotate the world, wherever we are located, and whatever angle of perception we take, there are fundamental features of the world which always look the same. However, we have to mark the phrase "fundamental features" carefully, lest we think that we live in a world of static uniformity. Indeed there are invariant fundamental features, but the world we live in is nevertheless a world with multifarious distinctions and dynamic variables. These distinctions and variables are part of reality conjoined to those fundamental features to make this world a dynamic and multifaceted world.

We should not fall into the dualistic trap of Plato who insisted on assigning the status of reality only to "the really real" as distinct from that which merely "appears to be". Reality is no abstraction, it is that which unfolds itself in the concrete. If we are to take a more integrative approach to reality, we may say, what "appears to be" can be as real as what does not "appear" but nevertheless "is". To emphasise our point, we may ask what may seem to be a naïve question: what would our world look like if reality is nothing but a set of simple and invariant laws?

If a bare set of invariant laws were all there was to reality, then the world would be like an ideal but empty geometrical form, a world with an ultimate form comprising generalities with no particulars and concretes. But what kind of a world would this be? This is something we cannot even begin to think about, for it is certainly not the world we know.

It is quite clear that our world is a world in which fundamental universal laws of nature unfold themselves in and through variables in conjunction with invariable quantities. Variable quantities pertaining to the description of a concrete particular event are "language" through which laws of nature "speak". Or better still, to use the analogy of language, if nature speaks, it speaks with a language in which grammatical rules indwell each particular combination of words with a particular syntax for a particular context. The words involved are variables, the syntax is also variable, while the indwelling grammatical rules are basically invariant. Each expression of meaning can be transformed into a different expression of dynamically equivalent meaning, with the same grammatical rules governing it.

For an understanding of physical events rather than nature in abstraction, the unique situations of reference systems determine the mode in which reality is to be unfolded. "Appearances" are certainly real, although they are on a different level of reality from the general laws of nature. Reality at this level has to be taken into account for a full picture of the reality of physical events. Appearances *as such* certainly would not directly tell us the objective structures of nature. But, in Polanyi's terms, those which are unique in appearances can be tacit pointers or clues, through which the objective structures of nature may be grasped.[16]

Taking the unique situations of the reference systems into account, the level of reality which we generally call "appearance" will certainly vary from one system to the other. For the same set of physical events, observers in different reference systems will see things differently, and their descriptions of the physical event in terms of variables unique to each of their reference systems will be different.

---

16. See Michael Polanyi, *The Tacit Dimension* (New York: Doubleday, 1966).

Relations between the absolute and the relative

Relativists often refer to different perceptions or appearances of the same physical event observed from different frames of reference as the justification for relativism. The theory of relativity shows us how all the differences in perception or appearance may be transcended.

It is true, however, that some quantities which we expect to be constant (those we regard as standards) in our daily situations do appear to be different for observers in different states of uniform motion when the velocity becomes considerable. The standards of measurement appear to change in accordance with the change of relative motion. Standardised measuring rods or synchronised clocks placed in different frames with relative motion will appear to be different when compared with one another. As relative motion affects the standards of measurement, descriptions of a pair of events from different reference frames in terms of their spatial relations and time intervals are bound to be different. There does not seem to be a standard description with absolute quantities good for all frames of reference. This again seems to point to relativism. However, the relativisation of what had once been regarded as invariant standards does not necessarily lead to relativism. What is at stake is merely the abstract philosophic notion of length and time interval in abstraction from the reality of relative motion and not, as is sometimes supposed, that there is no Archimedean point of absolute rest. Invariance has been misplaced on these apparent standards. The fact that these standards are no longer to be regarded as absolute does not mean that there is no absolute standard. On the contrary, a deeper invariant standard is being unfolded as these apparent standards recede into the background. The true invariant standard turns out to be the space–time interval of this pair of events.

In observing the same set of physical events from different frames of reference, different observers are bound to come up with different quantities in measurement. The geometrical shape of the same object would appear to be quite different to different observers moving at considerable high speed, depending on their speed as well as from what position the object is observed. Indeed, the difference in appearance of the same object perceived from different frames is so striking that it seems no longer possible to talk about the original or true geometrical form that belongs to the object itself, because it seems that the geometrical form of an object depends on the state of motion of the observer. When the geometrical form as well as the mass (both formerly held to be fundamental categories) of an object change with the changing state of motion of the frame of reference from which it is being observed, or they change with the change of reference frame, what then can be said to be permanent and unchanging, subsisting as "the really real" of the object? Has this state of affairs not given good grounds for relativism?

However, we should not be misled by such discrepancies in appearance or measurement into adopting a relativistic position. The principle of relativity points towards a transcendence of that which appears to be, thus enabling us to appreciate the invariant order underlying all the variables. First, there is definite geometrical form and definite mass to a reference frame in a certain state of motion. They cannot be arbitrary.

Secondly, all changes in form or mass are governed by definite laws of kinematics. The state or condition of the reference frame that comes into the picture in our perception of reality does not mean that the state or condition of the reference frame determines how reality is to be unfolded. Rather, the state or condition of the reference frame becomes part of the reality to be unfolded, together with a wider context of reality. The unfolding of the total picture is determined by invariant laws of nature which remain the same for all frames of reference. It is true that all frames of reference are equally good for the apprehension and manifestation of the invariant laws of nature, and no one frame is better suited than the other for the unfolding of reality. This does not mean, however, that each frame of reference can represent reality arbitrarily so long as the representation is internally coherent. Representation of reality is determined by that which is invariant, which *shines* through all different reference frames.

Thirdly, if representations of reality from different reference frames are equally faithful, they would discover, even though the variables in their descriptions of the same events are different, that the form of their equations is fundamentally the same. This is because the general laws of nature that they apply are expressed by equations which hold good for all frames. At the same time, as soon as they come to know the details of the physical conditions of each of the different frames of reference, they can identify one with the others through *transformation*. That is, the variables in each of the reference frames are *translatable* from one to another: with detailed knowledge of one's state of motion, an observer does not just perceive the form or mass (or whatever parameter) of an object from his frame of reference, he can actually perceive all possible geometrical forms, quantities of mass and other parameters from different frames. The object is thus perceived in a much wider horizon of manifestation. The observer can communicate with other observers about the object and be certain that they are describing *the same object* and not *objects of their own making,* and that all their descriptions are governed by the same laws.

Thus, we may say that each frame of reference attains an "absolute" status in apprehending reality, each is equally as valid as any other in comprehending all possible manifestations of reality in all possible situations. Reality is equally accessible to all. There is no absolute position from which reality is to be apprehended, but that does not mean that there is no "absolute" in regard to reality. Reality is absolute and its absoluteness shines through all possible situations of apprehension.

Each and every frame of reference can be absolute in its comprehension of reality only if it allows the invariant structure of reality to shine forth in it, rather than subduing it to fit some self-constructed coherent structure of misplaced invariance. The absolute status of each and every frame of reference for the comprehension of reality can only be attained through a faithful compliance to the invariant structure of reality. The different perceptions of reality, or to be more concrete, the different descriptions of the same set of physical events for different frames of reference, have to stand the test of mutual verification through transformation. This is the main thrust of the principle of relativity.

The absolute and the relative in theology

As we have pointed out, physicists start with the simple postulate that the fundamental structure of nature is invariant for all frames of reference. It remains unchanged even as the perspective of observation or the state of the observer is changed. This is a dogmatic standpoint without which scientific knowledge could hardly bear much fruit. This dogmatic standpoint, however, is not out of arbitrary conviction, it comes from our attentive dialogue with nature, in which we are impressed by the constancy of order in nature.

Likewise, those who seek to know God through attentive dialogue with him are bound to come to the same conviction that divine reality as it is revealed to us is invariant no matter from what frames of reference we perceive God. Thus theological formulation, like scientific formulation, starts with the dogmatic standpoint of the principle of invariance. Insofar as God reveals himself to humanity, the truth of his revelation is equally accessible to all and is the same for all despite the fact that those who come to receive his truth may be in totally different sociocultural situations. The God who revealed himself to the early Church in its Greco-Roman world is the same God who reveals himself to us in the modern world: the fundamental aspects of God's revelation transcend the diversity of our perspectives or states of reception. Despite the diversity of perceptions, there is unity and universality in the knowledge of God. The faith in the possibility and meaningfulness of the communion of the saints is grounded on this principle; the divine reality revealed to the early Church is the one and the same divine reality revealed to all generations of the saints.

This position has been severely questioned and is regarded by many as indefensible because one's perception of reality is determined by one's frame of reference, and all frames of reference are relative. This, however, is a misunderstanding. If a scientist, acknowledging the particularity of his frame of reference, accepting without question that he cannot expect to go out of his frame to see reality in its totality, insists nevertheless that the ruler and the clock in his frame are absolute standards for him because they are the only standards he knows and uses; and if, further, he then seeks to describe physical events and understand the order in them as faithfully and intelligently as he can, then he would indeed be condemned to the narrow confines of his frame, and the structure of the reality that he sees would be confined to what his frame allows him to see. He would never be able to rise above the fragmentary nature of his particular view to a total view of the natural process. He would not be able to see that the space his ruler measures and the time his clock records, relative as they may be, can be correlated in such a way as to arrive at a space–time interval which is the same for all observers in various frames for each and every event. And as he strives to get a broader picture of reality, he will bump into a wall of paradoxes.

Such a picture is absurd. No scientist thinks this way. Acknowledging the relativity of each frame in the description of physical events for the unravelling of order therein, scientists nevertheless seek to transcend the confines of each and every frame to get to a total picture of reality, thus enabling them to envisage what reality would be like in the particularity of each frame. In so doing, they acknowledge that the measuring standards (measuring rod and clock) good for measuring things within their own frames are not enough for a wider horizon of reality. Some "stubborn" invariant standard independent of their frames has to be found, such as the velocity of light.

The analogy of the principle of invariance that is drawn from physics for theology is not without difficulty. For God's revelation is not sheer manifestation of divine essence, rather, God reveals himself in response to humanity as his covenantal partner. His revelation is initiated and determined by his divine intent to love us and to bear covenantal responsibility to us. Thus the divine reality unfolded to us is not something objectively found to be the case or not the case. Rather it is something bound up with the state or condition in which we encounter God. As God reveals himself, he comes forth to meet us where we are. The divine reality revealed is intentionally directed to address our situation as we struggle to actualise ourselves as God's covenantal partners, and so the God who comes to be known by us is not God-in-himself but God-in-relation-to-us.

It seems reasonable to assume that the situation in which we struggle to become fully human must have a bearing on the way in which divine reality is to be revealed. It is, therefore, quite conceivable that our knowledge of God is conditioned by our human situation. It seems reasonable to ask, is it not true that the knowledge of God grasped by each community or generation of saints carries within it the unique character of the situation in which each finds itself? Is it not true to say that, if divine truth is to be alive and relevant to each and every community or generation of saints, then each is to understand divine truth anew in terms of the unique existential questions that they encounter? Because God is willing to meet us where we are, is it not conceivable that God would unfold himself in different ways in response to our different existential states? If that is the case, what then is the meaning of invariant truth concerning divine reality? These questions serve to indicate that the analogy cannot be taken simplistically as an analogy of one-to-one correspondence. Yet at the same time, these questions also serve to bring out the meaning of relativity more clearly.

It is true that God reveals himself to us by entering into dialogue with us, and dialogue is always lively and dynamic, for in genuine dialogue there is always mutuality and reciprocity. In our dialogue with God, we can no longer stand apart as observers. We are drawn into the process of unfolding, and our being becomes part of the content of the dialogue. Thus it seems that the particularity of our situation stands out as a significant factor in determining the way divine reality is unfolded, unlike that of neutral observers of physical reality. Indeed, the significance of human context can hardly be emphasised enough, particularly when it has been ignored for centuries by theologians obsessed with timeless theological formulations.

My continual harping on invariance may give the impression that I wish to downplay the significance of context. This is not my intention. What I wish to affirm is the absolute status of each and every context for receiving revealed truth while avoiding the trap of relativism. There is another side to the principle of relativity other than invariance; the unique state of the observer has to be taken into account and expressed in terms of the variables for the description of reality observed. To avoid the trap of relativism, however, the relevance of context has to be put in proper perspective, lest it is absolutised. Yet it must be reiterated that our existential condition is central to God's dialogue with us, even though God cannot be reduced to a mere answer to our existential questions. The principle of relativity acknowledges the validity of each and every frame of reference in their unique state of being. And as the frame of reference changes, it is expected that the variables for the description of the physical reality perceived from that frame will change as well. Likewise, in our encounter with God and in our attempts to express the reality of the encounter, the state or condition of our being enters into the descriptive order. The variables in the description of reality within a certain state or condition will change as the state or condition changes.

In different sociocultural contexts, theological formulations will contain different sets of variables for expressing the divine reality in these contexts, and we have to remind ourselves that we should never misplace invariance onto these changeable variables. Perhaps unnecessary theological conflicts have too often been due to absolutising misplaced invariants. So, in theological conflicts, each of the communities of the saints involved should examine what has been regarded as absolute to see whether absoluteness has been misplaced.

At the same time, God's revelation is not merely revelation about divine reality. It is also revelation about human reality. Here the modes of human existence which humanity creates for itself come into the picture. Different sociocultural contexts are different expressions of human creativity. The contrast between humanity as it is and as it should be is bound to be different in different contexts. Thus different existential questions are to be asked and different answers are to be expected. No theological formulation should expect to be able to provide once and for all a set of definite answers derived from a set of universal principles for all human situations although, cutting across changing sociocultural contexts, there are fundamental aspects of the human condition which remain unchanged, and there are fundamental conditions determining whether divine–human encounters may take place which also remain constant. Those fundamental aspects of the human condition are too general for the understanding of the divine–human encounter. It is in concrete and unique contexts that such encounters actually take place, providing the occasion in which both divine and human reality may be unfolded. For example, we may talk about sin as a fundamental aspect of the human condition, but sin has many manifestations in different sociocultural contexts. Sin has to be identified as sin in its concrete manifestations. Even as we understand sin in terms of humanity's revolt against God, we immediately come to realise that, out of our creativity, there are many ways to revolt against God, and some of the ways are so subtle that they may not easily be identified as such. It is only in concrete encounters with God, standing under the judgment of God, that such revolts may be unveiled. And so the concrete human context is highly significant in understanding divine–human encounters through which both divine and human reality are unfolded.

The invariant in the knowledge of God

In a way comparable to our scientists' attentive dialogue with nature, in which they perceive the invariant structure of nature, those who are attentive to the way God acts and communicates the intention of his acts in concrete human situations are led to perceive the invariant in the unfolding of divine reality. The two are, however, comparable only in the way that both are compelled by the "stubbornness" of what is there to affirm what they have to affirm. Those in dialogue with God, however, do not come to the conclusion of the invariant structure of divine unfolding as a scientific discovery after observation. Rather, as in the dialogue between friends who are drawn into an understanding of mutual rapport, in which that which one friend unfolds is received and confirmed through an active involvement in understanding, so also with our attentiveness to God. Nature may be assumed to be "inactive" in making itself known to us, yet in our experience of God and our attempt to know him, such an assumption precludes *a priori* the real possibility of knowing God. In Christian experience, as well as in that of many other religions, God is not mute and dumb, but actively makes himself known in and through nature and historical events. And those who are attentive are led to confront the irreducible invariant in the unfolding of divine reality and to confess him accordingly.

The transcendent creator God

No matter which way we wish to interpret the Christian faith, it is inconceivable that we can take away the understanding of God as the creator. Such an understanding concerns not merely God, but the world. I agree with Thomas Morris when he says: "For centuries, theists have held that the single most important truth about our world is that it is a created world. And it is no exaggeration to add that it is one of the most important truths about God that he is the creator of this world."[17] Even Maurice Wiles, who purports to remake Christian doctrine in order to pave the way for interreligious dialogue, says: "However much it might seem to ease the intransigent problem of evil, there is no possibility of going back on the Christian conviction of *creatio ex nihilo*."[18] The conviction, according to him, contains two significant insights: first it appeals to "an underlying sense of wonder that there should be anything at all", and secondly, it implies the ultimate purposiveness of things.[19]

The doctrine of the Creator God is particularly important because it shows us that the God we experience is not a God-in-himself but a God who is gracious in giving reality to that which is other than himself. It is a doctrine which gives rise to our understanding of the fatherhood of God by which God is recognised as the ground and source of our being.

Equally significant is the fact that the doctrine of creation undergirds the Christian understanding of the transcendence of God. Transcendence can be understood in various ways. We may talk about transcendence in a relative sense where one level of being in nature transcends another level. We may talk about transcendence in a teleological sense, by which one stage of being transcends the previous stage. The doctrine of creation gives transcendence a truly ontological sense in that the uncreated Creator, who is unconditioned by anything other than his own being, stands in relation to the created order which is contingent upon the very act of creation. The doctrine of *creatio ex nihilo* serves to underline the absolute freedom

---

17. Thomas V. Morris, *Our Idea of God* (University of Notre Dame Press, 1991) p. 139.
18. Maurice Wiles, *The Remaking of Christian Doctrine* (London: SCM Press, 1974) p. 33.
19. *Ibid.* p. 34.

of God as well as the fact that there is no codetermining principle alongside God. The implication is: God is the sole reality and is absolutely unconditioned until he limits himself in a relation with the created order. The grace of God is all the more revealed. The true beauty of the creation story in Genesis lies in its picture of God as a creator who is involved in the created order and invites us to be his partner in such involvement. The creation story understood in the light of God's redemptive acts precludes any deistic understanding of God.

Faith in God as our Creator also commits us to a certain attitude in our attempt to know him. Confronted with the creator God who is the source of our being, we are confronted with the one whose unconditioned freedom determines the foundation of our being. It would not, therefore, be too difficult to understand and accept the fact that he has the freedom to determine the way we may come to know him.

God as the God who reveals himself

In our attempt to know, we are immediately confronted with the reality of our own limitations — the limit of our capability to know. In probing into the depth of the physical world, we are often impressed with the fact that what has been apprehended by us is merely the tip of the unfathomable immensity of nature. And as soon as we think we have grasped all there is to be grasped, something radically new is unveiled before us, opening up a new horizon of reality never anticipated. In our attempt to understand human persons, the human subject seems all the more indeterminate and impenetrable. Even with all these constraints, both the physical world and human subjects are ontologically akin to us and therefore accessible to us. They are, by the very nature of their being, present to us as objects of our knowledge. And so, limited as our capability may be, there is always the possibility for us to know them in a limited way. Their unfathomableness or unpredictability may be merely a relative concealment, which may one day be overcome. That is, so long as we have them as objects of knowledge, the possibility of knowing is open to us.

In our attempt to know God, however, we are confronted with something much more fundamental for ourselves and for God. We are confronted with the invisibility of God (Romans 1:20). God is not by nature of his being necessarily present to us as an object for our knowledge. Unless God objectifies himself for us, the possibility of knowing does not even exist. It is true that God is the ground (*hypostasis*) and power (*dynamis*) of our being, and "in him, we live and move and have our being" (Acts 17:28). It is no wonder that the depth of our being consistently points to a ground that is beyond our being. Yet the ground of being is nothing but a horizon of that which we should know but do not know.

Despite our ontological relatedness to God as the Image of God and as the manifestation of his divine act, our existence is nevertheless completely contingent; the reality of nothingness is always there in the very depths of our being. Without the creative act stemming from God's unfathomable love and incomprehensible freedom, the ground of our being is nothingness. Left to ourselves, the reality of nothingness is as real as God's creative act in our being. That is why nihilism is as powerful as religion in human history. In alienation from God, our being may be oriented towards non-reality rather than towards the reality of God's creative act. And while our being does "speak" of the divine reality in us, it nevertheless also speaks out of the very depths of its rebellion against God, that is, out of the depths of godlessness. Unless God makes our creaturely reality transparent to his divine reality and relates to it as an inseparable part of the totality of being, the contingent world will reflect nothing more than the contingency of its being.

At the same time, God is absolutely self-determining in all his acts as the Absolute Subject. He cannot be circumscribed by anything other than himself. Thus in confronting God, we confront the incomprehensibility or the hiddenness of God. We are also confronted with the reality that, because of our sinfulness, we are averse to any true knowledge of God, and we stand under the wrath of God even if we seek to know him. In Calvin's terms, God is hidden and humans are blind.

The hiddenness of God is thus the most primordial feature of our knowledge of God. As we seek to know God, we encounter first and foremost his incomprehensibility. And all knowledge of God beyond this hiddenness is grounded on his revelation. God's knowability thus consists in his readiness in revealing himself.[20] This has a far-reaching epistemological implication: since revelation can only be revelation when it takes place as an actual event, then all knowledge of God begins with the actuality of God's being known.[21] Before we know God as anything else, we know him primarily as the God who reveals himself. Either we do not know God at all or we know him as God who reveals himself. This is a precondition of the knowledge of God which applies to humanity in all generations and all cultures. It is invariant to all who come to know God as God, irrespective of their historical or sociocultural contexts. No matter in what different ways or from what different perspectives we attempt to perceive God, we cannot bypass the reality of divine self-revelation, and we cannot reduce it to anything else. Theological formulations of all ages in diverse situations must have their starting point in the actuality of revelation: they have to start with where God has acted and what he has spoken.

God as the God Incarnate

In its actuality, revelation is no sheer manifestation of divine power and sovereignty, nor is it the mere unfolding of divine essence and attributes. Rather, in the most astonishing way, in a way that marks the God confessed by the church apart from any other human understanding about God, revelation is an act of self-giving. God reveals himself right in the very act of creation as a self-giving God.

---

20. That "God's revelation is His knowability" is, according to Karl Barth, the answer to the questions "how far is God knowable?" and "how far is He actually known?" As such it is "the presupposition, continually to be renewed, of all Christian doctrine, of Church Dogmatics and therefore of the preaching of the Church." *Church Dogmatics* II/1 (Edinburgh: T & T Clark, 1956) p. 179.

21. T. F. Torrance would argue that even from the perspective of epistemological reflection, we cannot but be compelled to such a position. "It is because the nature of what is known, as well as the nature of the knower, determines how it can be known, that only when it actually is known are we in a position to inquire how it can be known." Modern science, as Torrance rightly points out, is likewise forced to recognise "the impossibility of separating out the way in which knowledge arises from the actual knowledge that it attains". See his *Theological Science* (London: Oxford University Press, 1969) p. 10.

In creating the world, not as anything else but as his covenantal partner, God has chosen to be bound by covenantal love and responsibility. In determining the mode of relation between himself and the world as a relation of reciprocity and mutuality, thus affirming the distinctive reality of the world, God reveals his sovereignty and freedom in a way completely different from what philosophers would expect of the Absolute — the Sole Reality with *potentia absoluta.*[22]

Grounded on the foundation of covenantal relations, the very act of creation is an act of self-limitation in which God affirms absolutely the integrity of the created order and does not violate it despite his absolute freedom and his remaining the ground and dynamic of all things created. By virtue of the fact that the world is created as a covenantal partner, the act of creation is also an act of commitment to participation and involvement with his creation. At the same time, the very same act also puts the world in a definite mode of being, being in communion with God.

Revelation as an act of self-giving is most clearly manifested in the reality of the incarnation. The incarnation is the actuality of God's revelation as God reveals himself as nothing other than God who became human. In the face of incarnation, we encounter at once God's utter incomprehensibility and his clearest self-disclosure. All the philosophical conceptions and explications of the absolute break down here. That "the word became flesh and dwelt among us" is the most unfathomable mystery of all mysteries. In the face of this "reason is driven beyond itself to its 'ground and abyss'..."[23] Unless reason is driven to its ground in God the Incarnate in whom and through whom all come to be and come to realise their own reality, it will be driven to the abyss of God's hiddenness.

As the most unfathomable mystery of all mysteries, the incarnation is the place where God discloses himself most unreservedly. It is the ultimate way in the sense that it is the way in which God may reveal himself in the clearest possible way, and also in this sense, it is the final way. And so, unless we are ready to

---

22. See E. Brunner, *Christian Doctrine of God,* Olive Wyon, translator (Philadelphia: Westminster Press, 1949) p. 249.
23. Paul Tillich, *Systematic Theology* (University of Chicago Press, 1967) p. 110.

meet God in the mystery of the incarnation, we may not encounter God as he reveals himself at all. All attempts to meet God in ways through which God has not prepared to meet us are nothing but "reason playing at blind man's bluff with God", as Luther points out.[24]

With full knowledge of God's revelation in the Old Testament, it would be preposterous for John to proclaim, "No one has ever seen God; the only son, who is in the bosom of the Father, he has made him known" (John 1:18) if John had not meant to proclaim that it is only through Jesus Christ that God may be seen most fully as he truly is. "The Law was given through Moses; grace and truth came through Jesus Christ" (John 1:17). In the same vein, Matthew also testifies to the necessary relation between true knowledge of God and Jesus Christ in Jesus' saying, "No one knows the Son except the Father, and no one knows the Father except the Son and those to whom the Son chooses to reveal him" (Matthew 11:27; also Luke 10:22).

Biblical witness to the truth of the incarnation in the New Testament is clear and unequivocal. The proclamation of John is forceful and unapologetic: "the Word was God, all things were made through him, and without him was not anything made that was made ... And the Word became flesh and dwelt among us..." (John 1:1-14). Knowing that to proclaim a "man" as God is a scandal to the Jews, John nevertheless underlines the scandal as he testifies to Jesus saying, "I and the Father are one", for which he was stoned (John 10:30).

The implication is unmistakable: Jesus Christ is to be understood as God, even if it is offensive to people's piety. Thomas also confesses him as "my Lord and my God" (John 20:28). Jesus Christ is represented a speaking with the authority of God himself when he promises to send the Holy Spirit to his disciples (John 16:7-15). In the christological hymn in the Epistle to the Philippians, Christ is proclaimed as being in the form of God, and his equality with God as something that may be "grasped", though Christ refrains from doing so (Philippians 2:6-7). Paul refers to Jesus Christ as "the Lord of Glory" (1 Corinthians 2:8). And the

---

24. See Karl Heim, *Jesus the Lord* (Edinburgh: Oliver and Boyd, 1959) p. 29.

confession that "Jesus is Lord"[25] is not a capricious confession of human origin, but is inspired by the Holy Spirit (1 Corinthians 12:3). It is a confession with spiritual gravity. His confession of Christ's sovereignty in Colossians is most astounding. It is the sovereignty of the Creator and of the Lord of history: "He is the image of the invisible God, the firstborn over all creation. For by him all things were created: things in heaven and earth, visible and invisible, whether thrones or powers or rulers or authorities..." (Colossians 1:15 ff.). Again in Titus 2:11, Paul refers to Jesus Christ as "God and Saviour".

New Testament Christians understood very well that for God to be "manifested in the flesh is the great mystery of (their) religion" (1 Timothy 3:16). Yet they also knew that they were completely grasped by this mystery, a mystery which set their faith apart from any other faith. Indeed, if we merely assert that all knowledge of God has to come from God himself through revelation, Christian faith would be no different from any other religious faith, as all religions in their own ways affirm the indispensability of revelation. Yet, no matter what form revelation takes, it is only when revelation takes place as an actual event that it becomes real; it cannot be received as a general truth derived from some general principle comprehensible to the human mind. No matter how difficult it may be to derive general truths from general principles, that which can be derived from what has already been comprehended has no need of revelation. Revelation is not reason coming to itself. Rather it is an event in and through which that which has been hitherto incomprehensible is comprehended.

To receive revelation is to accept it in the way it actually happens, and comprehension of it comes in the actual process of being revealed to. To try to prove or make revelation comprehensible in terms of some general truth established outside revelation is to turn revelation into something other than itself, and in so doing constitutes "a gross misunderstanding of the real meaning of revelation".[26] "The very fact that (revelation) arose this way"

---

25. For an insightful discussion on the meaning of the term, refer to Karl Heim, *ibid.* pp. 51-63.
26. E. Brunner, *The Mediator*, Olive Wyon, translator (Philadelphia: Westminster Press, 1947) p. 201. In this light, we can see how futile it can

and not the other way "constitutes the revelation" as it actually is.[27] The fact that God chose to reveal himself unreservedly in the incarnation reveals precisely what "kind" of God he is.

When Athanasius seeks to defend the doctrine of the incarnation, he repeatedly asks the question: "What was God to do in the face of the dehumanisation of mankind? What then was God to do?"[28] With these questions Athanasius seeks to highlight the fact that at the centre of the incarnation is God's compassionate concern for humanity. The God who reveals himself as God Incarnate reveals himself as God with humanity and for humanity, not merely with an act of coming to us, but in and through his actually being human.[29] In so being, the being of God himself as God is involved. It is as if God allows his being to undergo a change. Here, the unity of God's act and his being is most completely unfolded. It is an act of self-giving. And in this act of self-giving, God reveals the nature of his freedom through his self-limitation in being identified and unified with humanity. The glory of God coincides with his utmost humiliation for humanity's sake.

At the same time, it is not so much that God "allows his being to undergo a change" as that in the very being of God there is the openness for a union with humanity. By the fact that God actually became human, the ontological proximity between divinity and humanity is revealed. The act of incarnation is God's absolute affirmation of our being, for it is an affirmation with God's own being. In this sense, the Christian religion is most profoundly humanistic and anthropocentric. If transcendence and reconciliation are the two fundamental elements in all religions, then the incarnation opens the ultimate horizon of transcendence and reconciliation. It opens the horizon of the "divinisation" (*theopoiesis*) of

---

be for those who try to fit Jesus Christ into the straitjacket of human reason. The end result can only be obvious.

27. *Ibid.*
28. Athanasius, *The Incarnation of the Word of God* 13, A Religious of CSMV, translator (New York: Macmillan Co., 1946) pp. 40-41.
29. Athanasius emphatically points out that "the Lord became man and did not just come into man". Contra Arianos 3.30 ff., see T. F. Torrance, *The Trinitarian Faith* (Edinburgh: T&T Clark, 1988) p. 150.

humanity through participation and union with God.[30] With this in mind, the horizon of reconciliation set before us is our reconciliation with our true humanity. Reconciliation occurs as the return to our true nature of being with God and for God. It is a reconciliation with life.

If we take the incarnation away from the Christian faith, then we remove the most profound and distinctive element of faith. When incarnation is affirmed, the doctrine of the Trinity will also fall into its place.

The relative in the knowledge of God

Theology is a highly risky business. The risk is not that we will say too little, rather it is that we attempt to say too much and affirm too much as absolute. Are there not many misplaced invariants in the history of theology? Is it not true that in affirming a certain doctrine, theologians too often marginalise what is supposed to be central and irreducible and become obsessed with defending and clarifying a philosophical system because certain conceptual tools developed from that system are being deployed?

Take the doctrine of the Trinity as an example. The main thrust of the doctrine is to affirm that Jesus Christ, as well as the Holy Spirit, is fully and distinctly God together with God the Father, and that they are unified in such a way that God is One. The formula seeks to express both the distinction and the unity of the divine being. The formula of "three persons in one substance" may have been a very effective expression in the West, but do we have to regard it as definitive and absolute? Are there no categories outside the western tradition which may give a more imaginative and insightful expression? Are "person" and "substance" the best possible expressions, so that the Church is bound to express the substance of the doctrine in no other way?

Younger Churches such as those in China, Korea or Japan simply have no room for theological contributions of their own if

---

30. Athanasius says, "He, indeed, assumed humanity that we might become God. He manifested Himself by means of a body in order that we might perceive the Mind of the unseen Father." *Op. cit.* 54, p. 93.

certain doctrinal expressions are regarded as coeternal with the being of God. Chinese Christians, for example, may have no problem with accepting and even understanding the mystery of three-in-oneness and one-in-threeness with their dynamic concept of being as being in communion or as "being in interdependence and interpenetration". But should they develop conceptual tools from their Chinese context for the expression of what is central to the doctrine of Trinity? As the Chinese do not have an equivalent word for "person" (for them person can never be abstract, it has to be a human person who is not an individual entity but a person-in-communion) or for "substance" (the idea is simply too static for ontological use), what should they do to affirm the doctrine of Trinity affirmed by Christians in the West? Many in Asia have such misgivings. Because it appears that all the doctrines are so neatly formulated within western philosophical categories, there is little room for creative contributions drawn from Asian cultural contexts. As a result, some of my colleagues simply disown some of the traditional doctrines as western and embark on uncharted courses in creating new theological categories, sometimes quite arbitrarily as, for example, in the Theology of the Land in Taiwan.

Not only does the Asian Church need to face the problem of theological categories, the Church in the West has to reflect again and again on whether certain theological categories which have been held dear for centuries ought to be reviewed. Each generation of the Church has to explain anew the substance of a doctrine to a new generation, and there will come a time when old categories may obscure rather than enlighten.

Some of the theological categories in the past, true as they may be in reflecting divine revelation, may nevertheless have been cast in such a way as to be true merely for a certain generation. The doctrine of justification, for example, has certainly been a significant doctrine, which in a particular period of time served to convey a vital truth. But is the doctrine absolute in such a way that it has to be confessed in every generation in a certain way so as to ensure Christian identity? Is the doctrine of justification not more a reflection of social relations in a certain period of time than part of God's eternal scheme of salvation? Do we dare to say that some doctrinal formulations, significant as they may have been in the past, may now have outlived their potency, and whatever elements of truth that were expressed in them now have to be recast? Those in other cultural contexts, with a less judicial outlook, may find it difficult to understand God as a judge exacting justice. The Chinese, for example, have difficulty with such judicial language and more readily understand the salvation offered in Christ in terms of the contrast between humanisation and dehumanisation.

Some of the theological categories, important and true in themselves, might have been emphasised at the expense, and even at the exclusion, of other equally significant categories, due to certain mental attitudes in a particular cultural milieu. For centuries categories such as might, eternity, ineffability and infinity were predicated of God and repeated over and over again. Yet what about the humiliation of God, the pain of God, and the powerlessness of God?

What we have suggested above is tentative. It merely serves to underline the possibility of misplaced invariance in theological categories and the need for a posture of openness for variant representations of theological truths in different cultural contexts. However, it must also be emphasised that in order to avoid arbitrariness, principles of transformation must be established for mutual confirmation, thus assuring true communion of the saints.

Response by Lloyd Geering

If I had been able to foresee how Carver Yu's paper fitted into the context of those papers already presented, I might have shaped this response a little differently.

I have found the scientific contributions to this symposium more comprehensive and convincing than the theological papers. I am left feeling that the theological responses to the challenging nature of the rise of modern science have not adequately met the problems raised, and I further suggest that the size of the task faced by theology has been greatly underestimated. What is called for is not a set of adjustments or fine tuning, but a radical rethinking. John Puddefoot's paper has moved in this direction, even though I am not convinced in the end by his solutions. Yu also demonstrates an awareness of the problems but his positive responses are somewhat muted. Because they *are* there, I believe I should have made more of them than I have done and been a little less critical.

Let me illustrate, rather simplistically, what I mean by a "radical re-thinking" by making Galileo the starting point in the discussion. Galileo opened the door to a movement of thought which was to undermine the Christian scheme of things so seriously that my sympathies are with the Vatican. Yet I suppose that neither the Pope nor Galileo were aware at the time how serious it was.

It was not just a matter of the movement of the earth. It was the shock that Galileo received when he looked at the moon through his telescope and found craters — craters on a heavenly body! Impossible. Whether that story is apocryphal is beside the point. It is symbolic of what followed. There was a slow dawning in western consciousness that the moon, the planets, the sun and the stars were of the same fundamental stuff as the earth. The heavens operated according to the same laws as the earth. Galileo's discovery led to the desacralisation of the heavens. Heaven and earth became one universe. Previously humanity lived, as it were, in a two-dimensional world and the vertical dimension represented

the earth's relation to God. Galileo effectively secularised space and
dispossessed God of the spatial imagery which previously had been
divine.

We are all post-Copernican. We have made some theological
adjustments. It is said elsewhere in this book that liberal theology
claims to have taken the scientific revolution into account but actually
very little has changed. We pray to a Father in heaven. We speak of
a saviour who came down to be incarnate, who descended into hell,
who rose from among the dead and who ascended into heaven. We
live in the space-age but we use language which belongs to the pre-
Copernican world and has become obsolete. It will be said, of
course, that we now use these words figuratively. But, why is it
that we have not been able to create terms relevant to the world
which, as a result of the scientific revolution, we now see ourselves
living in?

It is this question which makes Yu's paper on the question of
relativity so appropriate. Yu explores how the principle of relativity,
as now used in physics, may be used positively as a tool by
theology without falling into what he calls "the trap of relativism".
He first expounds the principle of relativity in its scientific setting
and then he seeks to apply that understanding to a theological
setting.

I agree that the principle of relativity, construed quite generally,
must be taken more seriously by the theological discipline than it has
been in the past. When this is done, however, I am not as hopeful
as Yu that relativism can be avoided. It partly depends on how
relativism is defined. At one point, for example, he refers to an "ill-
conceived relativism which asserts each reference system as absolute
in itself". I would say that such a form of relativism is more than ill-
conceived; it is self-contradictory. Relativism, to be consistent,
must acknowledge the relative character of all reference systems,
including itself. It is true that a relativist may temporarily treat a
particular reference system as absolute because it is useful for
practical purposes within some finite area of interest; the test of
whether it is truly regarded as an absolute is shown by the readiness
to drop it in favour of another frame of reference which proves to be
even more useful. That I see as a somewhat different matter.

Yu acknowledges that "our knowledge is determined and shaped
by our perspective or our frame of reference" but asks whether "it is

impossible for different knowers to come to a common picture of reality" (p. 181).

To investigate this question he turns to physics. I shall make only brief comments on this section of the paper. I agree with much that is said, yet even in this area I feel some unease about the paper. Yu sets out to illustrate how behind the various frames of reference which physicists have used, there is an invariant reality to which they refer. As he puts it, "there are aspects of nature which remain unchanged even as we change our perspective or our state of observation" (p. 184). Following the lead of Einstein he is looking for "the general laws of nature [which] should have the same form in all reference systems" (p. 189). The conviction that we shall eventually find such laws, hopefully to be finally expressed in what has been called a "theory of everything", underlies the whole enterprise of physics.

This is an *a priori* conviction which not only has not been demonstrated, but may never be possible to demonstrate. Some philosophers of science such as Carl von Weizsäcker have held that the reason why empirical science developed in the Christian West, rather than elsewhere, is that there is an intrinsic connection between the axioms of monotheism and those of modern science. The concept of constantly valid laws of nature, he said, could hardly have arisen without the Christian concept of creation.[1]

So there are unproved and *a priori* convictions in the scientific enterprise as there are in theology. Yu rightly points to this when he says that "physicists start with the *simple postulate* that the fundamental structure of nature is invariant for all frames of reference" (p. 195, italics added). But having said this, he oversteps the mark when he asserts that "it is *quite clear* that our world is a world in which fundamental universal laws of nature unfold themselves in and through variables in conjunction with invariable quantities" (p. 191, italics added). It is rather the case, I believe, that we humans in our scientific endeavour devise ever more useful ways of expressing the invariables we expect to find in the natural world. Because of our empirical research we may even become more convinced than before that they are really there, waiting to be discovered. But while it is our hope to find a final and absolute way

1.   Carl von Weizsäcker, *The Relevance of Science* (London: Collins, 1964).

of enunciating laws of nature, it remains a goal, and we may never know if we have actually achieved the goal. I find that some scientists now prefer to speak of their findings as probabilities rather than as laws, and to regard their enunciation of so-called "natural laws" as useful approximations. For such reasons I believe it is also going too far to say that "the theory of relativity shows us how all the differences in perception or appearance may be transcended" (p. 192).

But these simple criticisms of the first half of the paper pale into insignificance compared with my thoughts on the second half. I agree with Yu that the standpoint of the scientist, while it does proceed on an *a priori* act of faith, is nevertheless continually having that faith confirmed by what appears to be the constancy of the order in nature.

But is it really possible to say that "Likewise, those who seek to know God through attentive dialogue with him are bound to come to the same conviction that divine reality as it is revealed to us is invariant no matter from what frames of reference we perceive God" (p. 167)?

In the light of what we are now being forced to acknowledge about the relative character of culture and religion, this seems to me to beg the question. Conviction about God as the divine reality is itself a frame of reference, and it is not analogous to the physical world being investigated by empirical science. The divine reality, if one chooses to speak about it, is analogous not to the world but to scientific theories about the world, such as Newton's laws of gravity and Darwin's theory of evolution. This is why the traditional Christian understanding of the divine reality came into direct conflict with Darwinism.

If we agree that physicists are dealing with an objective reality which displays a degree of constancy, namely, the physical universe which is open to empirical examination, and agree that it is to this objective reality that the various frames of reference relate, then the analogue in religious thought is not God but something which is universal to the human species.

All religious thought and practice emanates from the internal, and largely subjective, experience of the human species. The great variety of religious traditions, including the theistic traditions which arose in the Middle East, were all attempts by humans to express how they understood the external context in which they found themselves and how they came to respond to it in ways which brought the deepest satisfaction. Religious concepts such as God are all part of the (largely) symbolic language which humans devised to explain what they observed and to enable them to find meaning in their existence.

Scientists, however much they are increasingly impressed by the constancy of nature, have nevertheless found it necessary to keep reshaping their enunciation of natural laws. Similarly we may say that, if there is some constancy underlying all religious frames of reference, it is to be found in the basic human condition. The frames of reference, including even such basic symbols and concepts as God, are of human origin and are relative to the culture where they have arisen and continue to be used.

Consequently one cannot say that "there is unity and universality in the knowledge of God" (p. 195) underlying the diversity of the perceptions of God, for the term "God" is one which takes its meaning from particular cultures. The most one can say is that there is some sort of universality in the human condition, a universality of experience which could roughly be called "the quest for meaning", and that it is this universality which has led to the variety of religious traditions, each with its own concepts and frames of reference. In some of these cultures the word "God" has been used as the symbolic answer to that quest.

What I find difficult about the second half of Yu's paper is that, although he conceded that the various theologies of the past are no more than approximations, the discussion assumes that there is an absolute reality called God, who is culture-free, to whom these past theologies have referred. For example it is stated that "It is true that God reveals himself to us by entering into dialogue with us..." (p. 197). But is this statement true in any absolute or final sense? Is it not simply a statement that is relative to a particular religious community such as Christian theists who have, by their culture, been conditioned to experience and interpret human existence in certain ways?

The kind of theological discourse which we find in this paper may be meaningful and helpful among Christians who share a common commitment and language, but in a context intended to be an encounter of science and theology, where we should be using a form of discourse and the kind of argument which is publicly and religiously neutral, it constitutes a private language which is not appropriate because it is not universally understood. Genuine dialogue between theology and science is thus prevented from taking place.

In such ways as this it seems to me that the argument of the paper begs the question; it assumes the absolute being of God in order to be free to acknowledge the relative character of the formulations. For example, it states that "those who are attentive to the way God acts and communicates ... are led to perceive the invariant in the unfolding of divine reality" (p. 199). Even the concept of God as the divine Creator and the doctrine of *creatio ex nihilo* are not nearly such self-evident starting points for the construction of an adequate frame of reference for the understanding the world and our place within it, as they were once thought to be in the pre-modern western world.

Yet the kind of traditional theological converse, that marks the second half of Yu's paper and to which I am expressing some objection, is also punctuated by certain queries. I find myself in total agreement with Yu when he says that "the significance of human context can hardly be emphasised enough, particularly when it has been ignored for centuries by theologians obsessed with timeless theological formulations" (p. 197). I also agree with him when he says: "Theology is a highly risky business. The risk is not that we will say too little, rather it is that we attempt to say too much and affirm too much as absolute" (p. 208).

Yu goes on from this to raise the issue of whether certain Christian doctrines, such as the doctrine of the Trinity, have been wrongly treated as invariants, that is, unchangeable absolutes. He suggests that doctrinal formulae hammered out in ancient Hellenistic terminology may not be at all appropriate in the young Asian Churches. I thoroughly agree and if this were the sole object of his paper I would applaud it warmly. But I contend that there is a great deal more than that in the Christian tradition which is in danger of being treated as absolute and unchangeable. The principle of relativity is not to be confined to the Trinitarian formula.

We have been finding again and again in the last 200 years that so much that was long assumed by Christians to be absolute has turned out to be relative after all. This experience has come about as we humans have found ourselves entering a world with horizons greatly more extensive than those previously known. It has made us realise that however much we may treat new truths as absolute at any particular time, including the present, they may in the future turn out to be just as relative, relative to the finite cultural or epistemological horizon in which we now live.

Relativism is the polar opposite of absolutism. I am not convinced that relativism is quite the menace for religious thought that it is often made out to be. I do not see it as a dangerous trap we must avoid falling into. I see absolutism as more dangerous than relativism, for it can easily lead one to treat as absolute what will later turn out to be relative. I would venture to go even further and suggest that the Judaeo-Christian tradition is, in a strange way, committed to relativism. It abandoned commitment to absolutism when it took such a strong stand against the worship of graven images, a stand quite unusual in the ancient religious world. It is because we humans have to live our lives in the absence of any known absolutes that it becomes necessary to live by faith. Any kind of empirical knowledge of absolutes is actually a hindrance to the path of faith. It is this insight, I believe, which lies behind Kant's famous dictum: "I have therefore found it necessary to deny knowledge in order to make room for faith."[2]

It is very natural for us humans to be searching for absolutes because, believing that we have found them, we tend to feel more confident and secure. We like to feel we are standing on firm ground, both literally, epistemologically and metaphorically. That is why earthquakes unsettle us so much and why religious dogmatists are so afraid of heresy. That is also why scientific dogmatists so often irrationally resist the emergence of what Thomas Kuhn called new paradigms which threaten to undermine and replace the orthodox ones.[3]

Let us take this simple analogy. We feel much more confident on *terra firma* than we do in and on the ocean, or than we would if we were free-falling in space. The earth seems to us an absolute and we have long treated it as one. But we now know that the earth is itself

2. Immanuel Kant, *Critique of Pure Reason,* Norman Kemp Smith, translator (London: Macmillan, 1929) p. 29.
3. Thomas Kuhn, *The Structure of Scientific Revolutions,* second edition (University of Chicago Press, 1970).

in space, spinning around at quite a remarkable speed, relative to its own centre and to the sun. When the theory was first mooted that the earth was not the fixed stable and absolute centre it had long been thought to be, people found it very unsettling. But it no longer unsettles us. We continue to live as if we were on firm ground. We treat the earth as an absolute. We are happy to enjoy what stability we have, even though we know theoretically that it is only a relative kind of stability. Should some heavenly body come out of space and make straight for the earth, that confidence would quickly evaporate.

And so it is with religious faith. The belief that one possesses certain absolutes can bring a sense of security, but it is not necessarily the boon it has been thought to be. It may in fact be a hindrance to faith. I believe the principle of relativity *can* be a positive tool for theology. But, unless I have misunderstood Yu completely, I appeal to it for reasons rather different from those advanced by him. Or perhaps it is just that I wish to take the principle to its logical conclusion. The principle of relativity leads me to the acknowledgement that everything I do and say and think is relative to something else and that I must learn how to live in the absence of all absolutes. It is this principle of relativity which brings home to me, almost more than anything else, the real significance of what it means to live by faith.

1.
219

Response by Norma Emerton

Carver T. Yu's illuminating paper on relativity and doctrine raises a number of important points. On the lowest level, it is useful to be reminded of the common popular error that equates relativity with relativism and claims scientific support for some unwarranted theological inferences. We are reminded of the comparable misuse of the uncertainty principle to support the doctrine of free will. On a higher level, it is good to explore the ways in which our understanding relates to, and tries to grasp, a reality greater than itself. Theologians might well adopt Einstein's words: "Nature shows us only the tail of the lion. But I do not doubt that the lion belongs to it, even though he cannot at once reveal himself because of his enormous size."[1] The world is greater than us to a limited though enormous extent, for as fellow created beings, we differ from it in degree rather than in kind. But God is greater than us to an infinite extent, for as Creator he differs absolutely in kind from created beings. Yet our effort to understand the nature of the world from those phenomena that we observe and measure can give us insights into the ways that we can reason from phenomenological experience to the hidden ontological reality of God.

Einstein knew that "science without epistemology is ... primitive and muddled", though he also warned scientists not to be too closely tied to any one system of epistemology. He saw the scientific attitude to knowledge as an eclectic one:

> The scientist appears as a realist in so far as he seeks to describe a world independent of the acts of perception; as an idealist in so far as he looks upon concepts and theories as free inventions of the human spirit...; as positivist in so far as he considers his concepts and theories justified only to the extent that they furnish a logical representation of relations among sensory experiences ... even as a Platonist or

---

1. Abraham Pais, *Subtle is the Lord: The Science and the Life of Albert Einstein* (Oxford University Press, 1982) p. 235.

Pythagorean in so far as he considers ... logical simplicity as an indispensable and effective tool of his research.[2]

Do theologians enjoy the same eclectic freedom? Einstein's biographer Abraham Pais speaks of a distinction which Einstein liked to make between two kinds of physical theories:

> Most theories, Einstein said, are constructive; they interpret complex phenomena in terms of relatively simple propositions. An example is the kinetic theory of gases, in which mechanical, thermal and diffusional properties of gases are reduced to molecular interactions and motions. The merit of constructive theories is their comprehensiveness, adaptability and clarity. Then there are theories of principle, which use the analytic rather than the synthetic method. An example is the impossibility of a *perpetuum mobile* in thermodynamics. Their starting points are not hypothetical constituents but empirically observed general properties of phenomena. ... [The merit of] theories of principle is their logical perfection and the security of their foundation ... The theory of relativity is a theory of principle.[3]

Thomas Torrance has drawn attention to the significance of Einstein's contribution to epistemology:

> It was with Einstein himself that the really decisive advance, affecting the first principles of knowledge, came in his establishment of mathematical invariances in nature irrespective of [the] observer, enabling us to grasp reality in its depth ... General relativity ... carries with it the ontological indivisibility of matter and structure in the space–time metrical field and thus the epistemic unity of being and form in our scientific understanding of the universe. These advances established the objective intelligibility of the universe ... Theologians, like scientists, pursue their inquiry within the contingent intelligibilities of space and time ... Theological knowledge is bound to be related to the knowledge of the universe as the created medium of space and time through which God makes himself known to us.[4]

---

2. *Ibid.* p. 13.
3. *Ibid.* p. 27.
4. Thomas F. Torrance, "Christian theology in the context of scientific change" (1976) in *Transformation and Convergence in the Frame of*

Torrance goes on to examine three of Einstein's well-known sayings: God does not play dice, God does not wear his heart on his sleeve, and God is deep but not devious:

> "God does not play dice" imports a concept of order ... The universe is so inherently orderly that it is accessible to our rational investigation ... [This] is now discerned by the scientist not only to be essential to pure science but to human rationality as such ... "God does not wear his heart on his sleeve" stands for the ... conviction that the real secrets of nature, the reasons for that order, cannot be read off the patterns of its phenomenal surface ... A scientific theological approach ... does not operate with picturing models built up from observational phenomena, but with disclosure models ... which are correlative to the self-disclosure of God ... "God is deep but not devious" expresses the complexity and subtlety yet ultimate simplicity and reliability of the universe ... In spite of all that might appear to the contrary ... God does not play tricks with us ... God does not let us down.[5]

It is one thing to say that Einstein's relativity theory has implications for epistemology, or that it is compatible with Christian doctrine, or that it offers insights that are valuable to theology. It is quite another thing to suggest that its method could be imitated or even appropriated by theology. To what extent might that be the case? And if so, to what extent would that rule out other scientific paradigms? To give one example, Einstein insisted that strict causality was essential to his relativity theory. To the end of his life he never reconciled himself to the implications of quantum mechanics indicating indeterminacy — Heisenberg's uncertainty principle or Bohr's complementarity principle. Strict causality and indeterminacy both pose problems for theology. The first can be understood in terms of determinism, which has always been deemed a challenge to Christian doctrine; the second implies randomness, which seems to cast doubt on the Creator's will. So both relativity and quantum mechanics present problems with regard to theology

---

Knowledge, T. F. Torrance, editor (Grand Rapids: Eerdmans, 1984) pp. 247-248.

5.   *Ibid.* pp. 251-253, 255-257.

and if we adopt Einstein's viewpoint, each would seem to rule out the other.

Einstein and Niels Bohr never ceased to dispute the question of causality and quantum mechanics. Bohr said that:

> An independent reality in the ordinary [classical] physical sense can ... neither be ascribed to the phenomena nor to the agencies of observation ... The very nature of the quantum theory ... forces us to regard the space–time coordination and the claims of causality, the union of which characterises the classical theories, as complementary but [mutually] exclusive features of the description.[6]

He further claimed that:

> We find ourselves on the very path taken by Einstein of adapting our modes of perception borrowed from the sensations to the gradually deepening knowledge of the laws of nature.

But Einstein retorted sarcastically: "The soothing philosophy of Heisenberg and Bohr ... offers believers [in it] a soft resting pillow ... Let them rest! ... It does little for me."[7] He preferred to speak of objective reality and he rejected the indeterminacy of quantum mechanics. This was one of several occasions when he said that God does not play dice:

> Every element of the physical [objective] reality must have a counterpart in the physical theory. We shall call this the condition of completeness ... But quantum mechanics tells us that [the momentum and the position of particles] cannot simultaneously be elements of reality because of the non-commutativity of the momentum and position operators of a given particle. Therefore quantum mechanics is incomplete ... No reasonable definition of reality could be expected to permit this.[8]

Einstein once said that the incomprehensible thing about the world is that it is comprehensible. We believe that its compre-

---

6. Abraham Pais, *Neil Bohr's Times, in Physics, Philosophy, and Polity* (Oxford: Clarendon Press, 1991) pp. 314-315.
7. *Ibid.* pp. 320, 425.
8. *Ibid.* pp. 429-430.

hensibility derives from its rational structure because it has a rational Creator, and that we comprehend it because we are rational creatures made in the image of the Creator. The second half of Yu's paper concerns the theological covenant relationship between God, the world, and human beings. In earlier times this was expressed by calling humanity the microcosm, the little world, in comparison with the macrocosm, or great world. The two were seen as linked through Christ, by whom the world was created and in whose image human beings were formed. God revealed himself supremely in the incarnation of Jesus Christ, but it is all of a piece with the indirect way that he reveals himself as Creator through the world that he has made. The unity of creation and revelation is central to our faith, and likewise the unity of creation and salvation.

It is striking that the Bible nearly always mentions God's act of creation along with his saving acts for his people, thus showing creation and salvation as aspects of one activity. In the Psalms, verses referring to God as the author and ruler of nature are closely mingled with verses that speak of him as the protector of his people, as in Psalm 33:

> By the word of the Lord were the heavens made; and all the host of them by the breath of his mouth ... For he spake, and it was done; he commanded, and it stood fast. The Lord bringeth the counsel of the heathen to nought; he maketh the devices of the people of none effect ... Blessed is the nation whose god is the Lord; and the people whom he hath chosen for his own inheritance.

Similarly, Isaiah 40 repeatedly mixes praise of God as Creator with praise of him as his people's Deliverer from the heathen:

> Have ye not understood from the foundations of the earth? It is he that sitteth upon the circle of the earth, and the inhabitants are as grasshoppers; that stretches out the heavens as a curtain and spreadeth them out as a tent to dwell in; that bringeth the princes to nothing; he maketh the judges of the earth as vanity.

Judgment is the obverse of salvation, and it is depicted in the Bible as the opposite of creation. The descriptions of Noah's flood, the Old Testament prophecies of the day of the Lord, the visions of the end of the world in the Gospels and the Book of Revelation, all reverse the work of creation by confounding land and sea, shaking the solid earth, darkening the sky, casting down sun, moon and stars, withering plant life and killing living creatures including human beings. The New Testament has not much to say about creation, but the Epistles refer to creation in two contexts: to point out the primal sin of Adam and Eve which necessitates salvation by Christ, and (as at the start of John's Gospel) to identify Jesus the Saviour with the pre-existent Word of God by whom the world was made. So in the Bible creation and salvation are proclaimed to be one — not by philosophical statements but by a choice of literary context and imagery.

Yu ends with the question of contextualisation — the problem of making sense of Trinitarian and christological doctrines in an Asian culture to which their philosophical presuppositions are alien. In western culture these presuppositions are Platonic, and in spite of their inadequacy (for any human philosophy is inadequate to express deity), no better formulation has yet been found, for reinterpretations in modern times have met with no more success. Perhaps Chinese theologians will succeed better than western ones, though it seems to me inherently unlikely. It is more likely that there may be a pluralistic situation, with more than one formulation in existence, each seen as complementary to the others rather than as contradictory. Perhaps this will be the occasion for theology to enjoy the eclectic freedom that Einstein claimed for scientists who, he said, can appear as realists, idealists, positivists, or Platonists according to the context in which they are operating.

6

Theological notions of creation and divine causality

John Polkinghorne

A scientist is wary of any attempt to assess intelligibility on the basis of what is open *a priori* to a ready understanding. We have to be prepared for a testing engagement with the reality that we are trying to comprehend, allowing its idiosyncratic nature to instruct and inform our minds and to open them to rational possibilities of a wholly novel kind. In a phrase that I like very much, David Park speaks of science making use of "universe-assisted logic".[1] We need the nudge of the way things are in order to understand how it is that they are so. One has only to think of quantum theory to get the point. Who would have supposed in 1900 that the possibility of an entity sometimes exhibiting properties like a wave (spread out and flapping) and sometimes exhibiting properties like particles (little bullets) was an intelligible notion? Yet that is the nature of quantum entities and, under the pressure of actual circumstance, physicists were led to discover quantum field theory and thereby make this counter-intuitive behaviour comprehensible.

My approach to the theological issues of creation and divine action will, therefore, be that of a bottom-up thinker, starting with the particularity of experience and seeking to ascend from that to a general understanding, rather than attempting a top-down discussion stemming from first principles. I am concerned with theistic rather than deistic belief, so that the act of creation is very much more than the initiation of cosmic process — God is as much Creator today as

---

1. David Park, *The How and the Why* (Princeton University Press, 1988) p. 281.

he was fifteen billion years ago — and divine action is not to be confined to the single great act of maintaining the universe in being.[2]

Creation and providence are theological concepts and so their experiential anchorage lies primarily in religious life. The doctrine of creation asserts that there is a mind and purpose behind the flux of cosmic history. What is going on in the universe is not a random concatenation of events, but neither is it the unfolding of an inexorable history patterned according to an unchangeable divine blueprint. Christian theology has striven to maintain a distinction between the Creator and his creation, and to acknowledge that the gift of a loving God has been some due measure of independence for his creatures.[3] The universe is not God's puppet theatre, but neither is its history a tale told by an idiot, because the cosmos lies within his fatherly care. I think that the basis in experience for this claim is the deep-seated human intuition of hope. Despite the strange bitterness of so much that happens, we do not believe that it is the acting of a loving lie when a mother comforts a frightened child with the reassurance that "it's all right". Peter Berger[4] is correct to call this "a signal of transcendence". It is the unconscious discernment that we live in a world which is a creation.

The experimental anchorage of the theological idea of God's providential action lies in human recourse to petitionary prayer. Here is another deep-seated intuition of the divine. Many more people in Britain claim to say their prayers regularly than ever come to church, and there must be few indeed who have never felt it natural in a time of need to seek the help of an Other. I do not think that this is a desperate technique for keeping one's spirits up, but rather that it is another signal of transcendence.

There are some who would say that these are merely subjective experiences. They might wish to be respectful of their value for you and me, but they would see them as simply opinions, useful no doubt for some in making their way through life, but options to be taken or left as taste dictates. The contrast would be held to be with

2.   Contra M. Wiles, *God's Action in the World* (London: SCM Press, 1986).
3.   J. Moltmann, *The Trinity and the Kingdom of God* (London: SCM Press, 1981); *God in Creation* (London: SCM Press, 1985); J. C. Polkinghorne, *Science and Creation* (London: SPCK, 1988) chapter 4.
4.   Peter Berger, *A Rumour of Angels* (Harmondsworth: Penguin, 1969) chapter 3.

the indisputable "facts" of science, the only serious source of public truth. I have elsewhere[5] rejected this foolish dichotomy between public fact and private opinion, which both neglects the element of personal judgment indispensable to the practice of science and also devalues the religious quest for motivated belief. Yet I would want to acknowledge that the insights of science are to be taken absolutely seriously and that the way we think theologically about creation and providence must be consonant with what we know about the history and process of the physical world. Given this standpoint, I would like to address these questions of consonance to illuminate the interface between science and theology.

A popular perception is that scientific discovery has disposed of religious beliefs about creation and providence. Our ancestors believed that the world sprang into being ready-made at God's command a few thousand years ago. We now know that it has had a long history, of which life in general and humanity in particular are only a small part. Our ancestors believed that rain came when God opened the heavenly sluicegates; we know that the weather arises from the complex working of the great heat engine of the earth's seas and atmosphere. Evolution has made the divine designer redundant. The unrelenting laws of nature afford no room for divine manoeuvre within their network of causality. That is how the argument runs.

Such caricature accounts pay scant attention to the subtlety and variety of the theological thinking of the past. They also make no serious engagement with the science of the present. I wish to maintain that a doctrine of creation greatly enhances the intelligibility of the physical world and that the world's nature is sufficiently supple for us to begin to gain a glimmer of understanding of how human agency is accommodated within it. This then leads to recognising its openness to divine agency also, albeit hidden within the flexibility of unpredictable process.

If we are not willing to regard the physical world as the expression of the divine creative will, then we must follow David Hume and treat it as a given brute fact. The nature of that fact is most concisely expressed in the laws of physics. The question

---

5.   John C. Polkinghorne, *Reason and Reality* (London: SPCK, 1991) chapter 4.

then is, are those laws a comfortable intellectual resting place, a satisfying ground on which to rest the totality of our explanation? Or is their character such as to raise further questions pointing beyond themselves? I assume the consistency and empirical adequacy of those laws for the regimes in which they have been tested. Sorting that out is internal to science, which is very successful in such matters and, in its own domain, does not need the assistance of any other discipline. My questions are addressed to the deeper level where explanation gives way to understanding. Can we rest content with only what science has to tell us?

I do not think we can. One reason is that science purchases its success by narrowing its vision and thus leaving so much out of its account. We live in a moral world as well as a physical world. I do not think that my belief that abusing children is wrong is simply the result of a social stance adopted in my culture. It is a form of knowledge of what is the case. Sociobiological attempts to reduce moral imperatives simply to genetic necessities seem to me to be most implausible. But if the universe is a creation, then our ethical insights are intimations of God's just will, as our experiences of beauty are sharings in his joy in creation and our experiences of worship are responses to his veiled presence. The multivalent reality of our experience becomes intelligible if the world is a creation.

Even in the account of its own domain of knowledge, science fails to slake that thirst for an understanding through and through which is the natural desire of the scientist. Its laws are not sufficiently self-explanatory to be treated as self-contained; they raise questions which point beyond their own power to answer.[6]

The first of these arises from what Eugene Wigner called "the unreasonable effectiveness of mathematics".[7] Not only is the physical world rationally transparent to our inquiry, but the form of its basic laws has proved, over three centuries of exploration, to be always expressible in mathematical terms which have about them the unmistakable character of mathematical beauty. Time and again, it

6.   Polkinghorne, *Science and Creation, op. cit* chapter 3; *Reason and Reality, op. cit.* chapter 6.
7.   Eugene Wigner, "The unreasonable effectiveness of mathematics in the natural world" *Communications on Pure and Applied Mathematics* 13 (1960) pp. 1-14.

has been the search for beautiful equations that has been the heuristic guide to physical understanding. Einstein was led to the theory of general relativity in this way, as was Dirac to his relativistic equation of the electron — two of the most beautiful and most illuminating discoveries of twentieth-century physical science. There is a truly remarkable conformity between the patterns of our mathematical thought and the patterns of the physical world. This conformity goes far beyond that necessary, but relatively banal, matching of everyday thought and everyday experience which must have come about through the evolutionary selection process. For example, it is impossible to believe that our ability to make sense of the strange and unpicturable quantum world is just a spin-off from our ancestors having had to protect themselves against the attacks of sabre-toothed tigers.

Science does not itself explain why mathematics is the key to its strategy of understanding. It is part of scientific founding faith to believe that the world will be found to be intelligible, and the discipline is happy to exploit the heuristic power that mathematics affords it. Yet I cannot feel content to shrug my shoulders and say "That's just the way it is — fortunately for those of us who are at home with maths." The explanatory power of mathematics is something which in its turn calls for an explanation.

The unreasonable effectiveness of mathematics becomes intelligible if the universe is a creation. You could summarise what I have said by saying that physics discerns a cosmos which in its rational mathematical beauty is shot through with signs of mind, and for the religious believer it is the mind of the creator which is thus revealed. Unbelieving scientists are groping after this idea with their somewhat grandiloquent claims that physics reveals "the mind of God"[8] — though they fail to acknowledge that there is much more to the divine mind than science could ever encompass. There is no logical entailment from a mathematically structured universe to the doctrine of creation, but there is a deep and intellectually satisfying consonance between the two.

Interesting metaquestions also arise from science when we consider the history of the universe. It all started incredibly simply:

---

8.   S. W. Hawking, *A Brief History of Time* (London: Bantam Press, 1988) p. 175. The idea is at least as old as Johannes Kepler.

the very early universe was an almost uniform expanding ball of energy. One of the reasons why cosmologists talk about it with a certain degree of justified boldness is that it is such an easy system to think about. Yet after long aeons of cosmic history, the world has become rich and variegated to an astonishing degree — the quark soup of a universe 10^{-10} second old has humanity among its consequences fifteen billion years later. The simple recognition of that immense fruitfulness might itself encourage the thought that more is going on than just one damn thing after another, and prompt the question as to whether the process of the universe might not be the unfolding of a purpose. The intimation of something happening in what is going on is considerably strengthened by the insight of the anthropic principle[9] that such fertility is only possible in a very special kind of universe. For a quark soup to be able to turn into the home of humanity, the very fabric of the physical universe has to take a very precise and particular form, requiring that the laws of nature conform to patterns and strengths which lie within very narrow limits. It is not any old world which can produce such interesting consequences as you and me.

There are many cosmological considerations which lead to this remarkable conclusion that an anthropic universe is one which is very finely tuned in its given laws and circumstances. My concern here is to ask the question, "What we are to make of it?" It does not seem sufficient just to say that "we're here because we're here, and that's that". Yet science cannot explain the laws which are the foundation of its own explanatory endeavour. They are its givens, but once again there does not seem to be full intellectual satisfaction in resting on that alone.

Very helpful discussion of these issues has been given by John Leslie, who does his philosophy by telling parables.[10] To illustrate the rational laziness of not asking a metaquestion about why our universe is so finely tuned that it enables us to be among its consequences, he tells the story of an execution. You are tied to the stake. A body of trained marksmen have their rifles pointing at your

9. J. Barrow and F. Tipler, *The Anthropic Cosmological Principle* (Oxford University Press, 1986); John Leslie, *Universes* (London: Routledge, 1989).
10. John Leslie, *ibid.*

chest. The shots ring out and, lo and behold, you have survived! No reasonable person would simply shrug their shoulders and say: "That's it; a close one that time." They would want to know the origin of their remarkable escape. Leslie suggests that there are only two rational explanations: either many, many executions are taking place today and yours is the one in which they all happen to miss, or more is happening than you realised; the marksmen are on your side.

One sees how that translates into cosmology. One possibility is that there are many different disjoint universes with many different laws and circumstances. If the cosmic portfolio is big enough, by chance, in one universe the anthropic conditions will be fulfilled — and that is the one in which we live because we could not appear in any other. Those who espouse this many-universes interpretation acknowledge that anthropic fruitfulness is not by itself intelligible but requires a further explanation. It is important to note that the kind of explanation that they offer is essentially metaphysical. Physics has only adequate motivation to speak of the one universe of our actual experience.

An alternative metaphysical explanation of equal coherence and, in my view, greater economy is that there is but one universe which is a creation endowed by its creator with just those finely tuned laws and circumstances that will enable it to have a fruitful history (more is happening than we first realised). The idea of creation is a way of making the anthropic principle intelligible. Again there is no entailment, but satisfactory consonance.

So far, so good, but does not the theistic picture cloud over when we come to consider the processes by which that fruitfulness has been realised? At every stage we discern that novelty comes about through the offerings of chance, the happenstance that this configuration rather than that actually occurs. These offerings are then sifted and preserved by the necessary workings of a lawful universe. A matter fluctuation in the early universe is the seed from which a galaxy grows under the snowballing consequences of gravitational attraction; a genetic mutation just happens to produce a favourable new form of life, transmitted through the relative regularity of DNA and selected through competition in an orderly environment. Here is the celebrated interplay of chance and necessity, which a succession of biologists from Monod to Dawkins[11] are anxious to proclaim as the destruction of any claim for a purpose at work, because of the "blindness" of chance's random explorations of possibility.

Several responses might be made to this threat to the intelligibility of the idea of creation. One is to remind the biologists of the subtle role of necessity in an anthropically fruitful world. The underlying physical processes involved in the structure of replicating molecules such as DNA are controlled by simple laws (the Schrödinger equation and Maxwell's equations) whose mathematical expression I could literally write down on the back of an envelope. Biologists often seem to exhibit no recognition, let alone wonder, that such precise and compact characterisations of the fabric of the world can have as their consequences the possibility of you and me. It is not all chance. For sure, there are all sorts of fortuitous details about the way conscious life has actually come to be, but that it has come to be does not seem fortuitous. Rather, it was written into cosmic structure from the beginning. The well-known theoretical physicist, Freeman Dyson, once said that "the more I examine the universe and the details of its architecture, the more evidence I find that the universe in some sense must have known we were coming".[12]

Secondly, as I have already emphasised, the notion of creation does not require us to consider the universe's history as having been laid down by God in detail for all eternity. Rather than his being the cosmic tyrant, he is, in Arthur Peacocke's striking phrase, the Great Improviser. Peacocke presents, from his Christian biologist's standpoint, a very positive account of an evolutionary universe as one in which the shufflings of chance are the explorations of creation's potentialities.[13] The interplay of chance and necessity is a *creatio continua*. I personally believe that the God who is both loving and faithful has given to his creation the twin gifts of due independence and due regularity, which find their appropriate

11. J. Monod, *Chance and Necessity* (London: Collins, 1972); R. Dawkins, *The Blind Watchmaker* (Harlow: Longman, 1986).

12. Freeman J. Dyson, *Disturbing the Universe* (San Francisco: Harper and Row, 1979) p. 256.

13. Arthur R. Peacocke, *Creation and the World of Science* (Oxford University Press, 1979); *God and the New Biology* (London: Dent, 1986).

reflections in the fruitful interplay of chance (realising possibility) and necessity (enabling possibility).[14]

A universe able to explore its own God-given potentiality in this way will inevitably be a universe with ragged edges and painful malfunctions. The same biochemical process which allow cells to mutate and produce new forms of life will allow other cells to mutate and become cancerous. Claims that it is better to have a world of freely-choosing persons even if their choices are often disastrous, rather than perfectly programmed automata, are an attempt to make such a reply to the problem of moral evil. I have suggested that there is a parallel free-process defence in relation to physical evil.[15] God does not will that tectonic plates should slip and kill people in an earthquake, but he allows it to happen in a physical world which is given the gift of being itself. One might respond by querying the value of such freedom, suggesting that it improperly imports ideas from the personal domain into the impersonal sphere of general physical process. I would reply that we are intimately connected with the physical world that gave us birth and I believe it is unlikely that a universe to which the free-process defence did not apply could give rise to persons for whom the free-will defence was applicable. Its openness and our freedom are closely connected.

Ideas of this kind deliver us from the temptation to think of disease and disaster as being acts of divine punishment or even divine cruelty. A world allowed to make itself cannot be a world free from pain and suffering. We all tend to think that if we had been in charge of creation we would have done it better — kept the gold and removed the black threads from the tapestry of life. The more we understand the way the world works, the less this seems to be a coherent possibility. To this degree science helps theodicy to make physical evil intelligible. Of course, the problem of suffering is much too profound an issue to find adequate answers at this intellectual level alone. It engages us in all that we are and the ultimate Christian response looks to the cross of Christ as the enacted symbol of the God who is a fellow-participant in, and with, his suffering creation.

---

14. Polkinghorne, *Science and Creation, op. cit.* chapter 4.
15. John C. Polkinghorne, *Science and Providence* (London: SPCK, 1988) chapter 5.

A strong doctrine of providence such as is implied by the Christian tradition's usage of personal language for God (father, not force), requires that it is conceivable that God interacts with his creation in such a way as to bring about particular outcomes on particular occasions, whilst still respecting those gifts of otherness and independence that he has conferred upon his creation. Such thought as it is possible for us to make upon the mystery of divine action, will have to have recourse to analogy. Two broad strategies have been pursued. One is to exploit the notion that God interacts with human beings in the depths of their psyches by encouraging them in certain directions, and that he interacts with the rest of the created order in a similar way. This is process theology's idea of divine action through persuasion. I do not find it convincing, both because I cannot accept the implied panpsychic view of reality and also because I think it evacuates God of too much power, as he stands pleading on the margins of the world.

The second strategy supposes that God acts in the world in a way analogous to that in which we act in our bodies. At its bluntest, this approach talks of divine embodiment in the universe, but I find this an unacceptable concept when one considers the traumatic transformations of cosmic history, which would then appear to imprison the eternal God in a world subject to radical temporal change.[16] Instead, I think one must seek a more subtle and nuanced account of this analogy. How that might be developed is necessarily highly speculative, since we are very ignorant of how mind and brain, human intention and human action, actually relate to each other. However, there are certain moderately promising directions in which to look for insight.

Let me nail my philosophical colours to the mast and state that I regard the belief that we have experience of freely-chosen action, as being both true and basic to any account of human nature. I also believe that we are psychosomatic beings who fully participate in the process of the physical world. These two foundational beliefs together imply that the bottom-up causal network of that physical world, described by the energetic transactions of constituent parts and the concern of a methodologically reductionist physics, cannot

---

16. *Ibid.* pp. 18-23.

be drawn so tightly as to exclude the further working of holistic, top-down causal agencies, of which human-willed intention would be the one most clearly known to us. Our basic experience that we are not automata has always told us that this must be so.

It seems to me that twentieth-century physics has afforded a glimmer of understanding of how this might be the case. Our century has seen the death of a merely mechanical view of the world. In bringing about this demise I believe that it is likely that the insights of non-linear chaotic dynamics concerning the intrinsically unpredictable behaviour of many (indeed most) systems of everyday size are more significant than the corresponding uncertainties of quantum theory, located at the level of atomic process.[17]

The exquisitely sensitive systems of chaotic dynamics are so dependent upon precise details of circumstance that they exhibit an intrinsic unpredictability in their behaviour. That is a conclusion that no one questions. In my (necessarily speculative) approach to these matters I have suggested that we ought to go beyond the epistemological property of unpredictability, and conjecture that this indicates to us the ontological property that such systems, in terms of their bottom-up description, are open to the future. By that I mean that their nature provides scope for the operation of further causal principles of a top-down, holistic kind whose character, on investigation, is seen to be that of "active information": there are causally effective overall pattern-forming principles at work as well as transactions of energy among constituent parts. The deterministic equations, describing the behaviour of the classical systems studied in chaos theory, are then conceived of as being downward emergent approximations to a more supple and subtle physical reality.

The motivation for this construction is two-fold. One is to gain for science the ability to begin to describe a world of which we can conceive ourselves as inhabitants. The other is the basic realist conviction of a scientist, that what we can know is a guide to what is the case. "Epistemology models ontology" is our motto.

---

17. Polkinghorne, *Science and Creation, op. cit.* chapter 5; *Science and Providence, op. cit.* chapter 2; *Reason and Reality, op. cit.* chapter 3. For an account of chaos theory, see J. Gleick, *Chaos* (London: Heinmann, 1988).

(Heisenberg's uncertainty principle[18] is concerned with intrinsic indeterminacy and not mere ignorance; similarly chaotic dynamics are concerned with openness to the future, not mere unpredictability.)

If these bold conjectures make any sense, they offer us a glimmer of understanding as to how it may be that our willed intentions (information) are executed in the material world (energy). But cloudy chaotic process is everywhere present. There are "clocks" but most of the world is "clouds", and it seems to me that agency through "active information" may well be the way that God providentially interacts with the world as well as the way in which we ourselves are agents. I have said of these ideas:

> The metaphysical scheme [thus] espoused ... succeeds, in my opinion, in retaining some of the more attractive features of process thought without its defects. It is a kind of demythologisation of that panpsychic worldview.[19]

Such a view of God's action has several consequences for our ideas about divine providence. First, divine action will always be hidden, contained within the cloudiness of unpredictable process. It may be discernible by faith but it will not be demonstrable by experiment.

Secondly, the balance between active information given away by the Creator to his creation (either in the form of allowing willed intentionality or in the form of holistic laws of nature driving the universe to evolve greater degrees of complexity), and that retained by him for his own providential interaction with the world, is the problem of grace and free will written cosmically large. All the classical problems of prayer, of theodicy and of not trivialising providence, remain for discussion.[20] Such discussion is simply enabled to proceed with integrity, whilst taking seriously what modern science tells us about the process of the world.

Thirdly, the picture presented is of a world of true *becoming*, released from the dead hand of Laplace and his calculator for whom

18. See, for example, John C. Polkinghorne, *The Quantum World* (Harlow: Longman, 1984) chapter 5.
19. Polkinghorne, *Reason and Reality, op. cit.* p. 147.
20. Polkinghorne, *Science and Providence, op. cit.* chapters 3, 5 and 6.

there was no real distinction between past, present and future. God must know such a world *as it is*. I believe that this implies that God knows the universe of becoming in the temporal sequence of its becoming. This leads me to seek an understanding of a temporal pole within the divine nature as well as an eternal pole. (Here I gladly acknowledge a debt to process theology.) I also believe that in such a world even God does not know the unformed future, for it is not yet there to be known. Involved in the kenosis of creation is a kenosis of divine omniscience as well as the kenosis of omnipotence involved in allowing the other to be.[21]

The scheme proposed is not an unacceptable return to the God of the gaps, in the pejorative sense of that word, where the gaps were mere lacunae resulting from current ignorance. If the bottom-up description is not to preclude top-down causality, it must have *intrinsic* gaps in its description. We are "people of the gaps" in this acceptable sense and there is nothing improper in attributing analogous properties to God.

---

21. *Ibid.* chapter 7.

Response by Jack Dodd

Right from the outset of reading John Polkinghorne's paper I find myself in difficulty. For reasons that will become apparent I had expected to disagree about certain theological attitudes. Yet I find that I disagree with him in some *scientific* interpretations right at the start. He speaks of us needing "the nudge of the way things are in order to understand how it is that they are so" and quotes the creation of the quantum theory as an illustration of the point. "Who would have supposed," he says, "that the possibility of an entity sometimes exhibiting properties like a wave ... and sometimes exhibiting particles ... was an intelligible notion?" (p. 225). He implies that the entities that quantum theory deals with — atoms and light, or fundamental particles and radiation — are like this. This is not my view. The wave description and the particle description are only *models* of certain aspects of their behaviour, not descriptions of what they *actually are*. Again I do not think of mathematics as the key to their nature, but only as the language which scientists have constructed as appropriate for describing the properties that we observe. For example, I do not think of light as being sometimes a wave and sometimes a particle, nor an entity that has the nature of both. Light is the sum of its properties such as the way it is created in the decay of excited atomic states, the way it spreads through space, the way it passes by obstacles and through materials, the way it excites other atoms. These properties are, with some success, described by certain models of behaviour that can be placed in mathematical terms. The most successful, in all circumstances as far as we yet know, is the theory of quantum electrodynamics. But, whatever the description, *light is light*.

I am not here, however, to argue philosophical interpretations of physics; but you see, even when Polkinghorne and I talk about things that we *both* purport to know something of, we use different words and thereby create different pictures for others. I must turn to a subject I am rather less qualified to talk about. Like everyone who has wondered about the universe and our place in it, I have formed certain ideas — but can I express them adequately?

Polkinghorne speaks of there being a mind and purpose behind cosmic history; of there being a personal God who does particular things in particular circumstances, and that the experiential anchorage of these beliefs has some consonant relationship with what science tells us of the nature and history of the universe. I find that I differ with him in a number of ways. Before responding, I should lay before you my personal position regarding religious belief. I regard myself as an atheist — personally, I find no reason for believing in a God. I am also a scientist, however, and a true scientist knows that there are no absolute scientific truths — I should therefore describe myself, in proper sceptical scientific spirit, as an agnostic.

In my reading and thinking, and indeed in Polkinghorne's paper, I distinguish four different ways in which the concept of God is used. Perhaps not all of them are entirely separate.

First is *God the Creator:* "In the beginning was the Word and the Word was with God and the Word was God". A God who created fundamental particles and radiation from which he built atoms and molecules and the interactions between them, then perhaps things and beings and mankind, and later maybe mind and ideas; loves, hates and passions? In the beginning, however, there was the original stuff of nature and, presumably, the rules which govern its behaviour.

The second concept involves the *God of Providence*: who moves things this way and that, guiding the flow of events the better to fulfil his purpose.

The third concept is of a God, because he is a God of providence, who hears our prayers and intercedes on our behalf — *God the Interceder*. We pray for rain or for shine, for an end to conflicts, to cure and comfort those who are afflicted or suffering, to help us achieve our goals, to punish those who threaten us or make us suffer. We ask God through prayer to use his powers to change the course of events.

Fourthly there is *God the Father* who, in response to our prayers for *personal* guidance, helps us to make right decisions, to be better people and to lead us in the paths of righteousness; to lead us to salvation.

Now to many, and to Polkinghorne I suspect, these are all aspects of the same "entity", "being", "person" (if he made us in his own image), or "force" if you wish to depersonalise the description. To me, much of this is meaningless. I shall go through the different aspects, using some of Polkinghorne's illustrations, and try to explain my own views. Let me start with number four, *God the Father,* to whom people pray for personal guidance.

What many people call prayer, I call *trying to think things out carefully.* People who pray to God are seeking divine guidance in order to decide a correct course of action. I believe I rely on my experience, on the teaching I have received, on the examples that have been set by others, on the observation of the consequences of certain actions, and on a rational balancing of the consequences of different actions. Sometimes the "thinking out" by me does not turn out for the best, and in hindsight I consider that I have made a wrong decision but I have no doubt that this is much the same for those who pray. Let me consider an example. There is no doubt that, on the whole, we have a dislike of personal pain and take joy in pleasure and we believe that others have the same feelings. We therefore wish our actions to give pleasure rather than pain to those near to us, and hopefully to everyone. We pray, or think carefully, in order to come to a decision on an issue where we believe that pain *and/or* pleasure will be the consequence. We do not always succeed, nor should we expect to. We must not forget that pain is a natural characteristic developed as part of the evolutionary process for the survival of the species. The experience of pain warns us of the consequences of certain threatening actions — the burnt child dreads the fire. It is even the case that the inflicting of pain (perhaps by an occasional smack, or scolding, or banishment to the bedroom) is part of the teaching process for our children, before they can reason things for themselves; it strengthens their future decision-making. The punishment of criminals has the same logic. It also must be said that the suffering of pain heightens our joy of pleasure. Using Polkinghorne's metaphor, the black threads are necessary if you want to appreciate the gold; if everything was just gold threads, where would the joy be?

I dare say that if Polkinghorne and I sat down and talked together we would agree on many things, but he couches his arguments in words that do not have a meaning for me — I do not see the logic of

them. For example, quoting Peter Berger, he says that the loving lie
by which a mother comforts a frightened child with the assurance
"it's all right" is a signal of transcendence, by which he means
a behaviour beyond experience (p. 226). That seems to me a
completely illogical step. She does not *want* to see her child
worrying or suffering; she *knows* that comforts and cuddles soothe
the child; and she *knows*, or at least hopes, that the cause of fright
will pass. To me, "it's all right" is the natural behaviour of a
mother, part of a long history of loving care. It is a characteristic
trait of the evolutionary process and natural selection — people with
such characters and who pass them on are the survivors, the fittest.

Nothing that I have experienced leads me to believe that prayer
and its consequences are anything more than mankind's evolutionary
ability to observe, to analyse and to spend time thinking things out.
That we sometimes do not appear to have succeeded is no different
from the feeling that God has sometimes not heeded our prayer or
has, for some mysterious reason, decided to take no action that we
can see. The process is often a very humbling experience, and we
add it to our store of knowledge for the future.

Next I come to the idea of God who responds to prayers that he
may intervene in the course of events of the world, sometimes
remote from our own personal comfort — for wars, famine, that our
loved ones shall return safely, and even for the right numbers in the
Lotto draws. This, of course, is related to the matter we have just
discussed and to the second of the definitions — that, through our
prayer, we expect that God can alter the course of nature as a
consequence of our pleas. We may believe that the more grace we
have achieved in our person by the guidance of God the Father the
more chance we have that he will hear our prayer. Now I know that
there are many people who feel strongly that prayer *has* changed the
course of events, but surely there are as many (even more) cases
where people of goodwill have failed. I cannot accept this idea.
Those who believe in this have strong faith (perhaps I might say
blind faith) and tend to reject the cases that did not seem to work,
using excuses such as "the ways of God are mysterious" and "there
are more things on heaven and earth than we know of" or "God is
inscrutable". If *we* want to intervene in the natural flow of events
and to correct something that seems to be going wrong, then *we*
must either know something of the forces and energy processes of

what is going on, or of the social and political beliefs that are causing the situation.   Then the actions of the scientist or the statesman, insofar as actions are within the limits of their available technologies or political powers, may have some chance of success. I have no evidence for the intervention of any other knowledge, power or force.

The second case was the *God of providence.* This involves the concept that God, having once created the universe and set it in motion with physical laws which determine its future course, can from time to time interfere and alter the natural course of events. Now although we humans, scientists, everyone, have only been around for a very short time in the life of the universe, it *seems* that "the laws" are constant. I should point out that it is not just the few hundreds of years of local observation on the earth I am talking about. Astronomers and astrophysicists observe the remote parts of the universe as it existed millions of years ago. Using the same laws of physics that have been formulated recently, they seem to be able to explain what was going on in those far remote days. I want to say more about the laws of nature, but let us for a moment accept that there are such laws — not that we know all about them yet.

Of course, we do know that there are occasions in which the course of events does not seem to agree with what we have predicted. This is readily understood by the scientist: the inadequacy of our prior knowledge, of the initial conditions, experimental error (we twitched our muscles, something joggled the table), our senses are limited in resolution — the inherent noise in the system, the second law of thermodynamics, the indeterminacy of quantum mechanics, fundamental chaotic behaviour... These all add up to a fuzziness in our experiments and in the interpretation of what is going on. All we can say is that, within the limits of fuzziness, a particular law seems to be an underlying principle. As far as I am aware, all the accepted laws of nature plus the fuzziness of nature seem to work. I see no hand of God there.

What about *God the Creator*? It is only when I come to this that I find some reasons for accepting the concept of a God. Scientists have been very successful at explaining or inventing models for *how* things behave, but they are not successful at explaining *why* things go along as they do. Every question "why" provokes a further question "why" and so on in infinite regression:

Why is grass green?
Because it contains chlorophyll.
Why does chlorophyll make it green?
Because molecular bond frequencies...
Why are the bond frequencies...?
Because the strength of interactions... and so forth.

All the exhausted scientists can say in the end is something like "I don't know" or "because God made it so". Could they not have just said that at the beginning and saved all the investigation? But if we have any unique characteristic that distinguishes us from other forms of life it is the ability to inquire, to work out the nature of things, to adapt nature to our use — a divine gift if you like. If we did not use this creativity, a cultural consequence of our evolution as I see it, we would be as the vegetables. We would exist in a very different world or, should I say, exist in a very different way in the world. So that to say "God made it so", and do nothing because we think we have answered the question, would not be human.

I now want to say something about the "laws of nature" from a scientist's point of view — from my point of view. There may well be laws of nature. It is certainly the case that our observations of the world and universe around us lead us to believe that there are some underlying principles behind the structure and behaviour of the things that we observe. It is beyond the powers of mankind, however, ever to be sure that we have found out what they are. What we *know* about are *facts* and *observations*, some we experience personally and some which we believe because others, whom we regard to be reliable, have made and recorded them. Next, we have an analytic ability to categorise them, to recognise similarities, and to see patterns of cause and effect between them. The scientist, and here I include everyone who has ever thought about the nature of things and not just those who have had some sort of training in scientific thought and method, then constructs a hypothesis which encompasses those observations, facts, causes and effects which seem to have some common behaviour. If that hypothesis is nothing more than a summary statement of those facts it is not of much *scientific* use to anyone — it is nothing more than a summary or a listing, perhaps useful in itself but not of any scientific use — it is an *ad hoc* hypothesis. No! The real scientific hypothesis must incorporate the possibility of deducing from it something which has not previously been observed *so that that hypothesis can be tested.* This testability is an essential feature of a *scientific hypothesis.* In this sense the formulation of a scientific hypothesis *must* contain a leap of imagination, an act of creation, an inductive process; there must now be therein a new idea which was not there before. This hypothesis, before it can be regarded as having any scientific respectability, must survive an experimental test of this new deduction. If any such test should fail, then the hypothesis must be regarded as untrue; it must be rejected, or modified in some way to encompass the new observation, or it must be held in abeyance until the methodology or technology can overcome the doubts and fuzziness of the experiment. If the test confirms the hypothesis, and repeated tests done in different circumstances continue to confirm it, the hypothesis may be raised to the state of a *scientific theory.* Indeed, if the hypothesis–theory continues to be sustained for considerable time and under rigid experimental observation under all kinds of conditions, people may eventually start calling it a *scientific law.* But note that, although our confidence in the hypothesis–theory–law may increase, there is no sense in which we can ever say "the law is proved". *There is no such thing as scientific truth.* We never know for certain when, at some time in the future, a situation will be found, a new deduction will be made, or an experiment performed which show that a long-held hypothesis is false. The history of science is full of such failures. Scientists, at least proper sceptical scientists, are quite humble beings — they cannot honestly maintain fundamental *truths,* there is always doubt in their minds. Proclamations of absolute truth should be left to politicians, or to advertising agencies. Nevertheless, scientists do have *faith* in the sense that they believe that their tested hypotheses have a reliability on which they can build the activities and decisions of their lives with an acceptable degree of certainty — this is only common sense; to behave otherwise would be stupid.

I have said that the formulation of a scientific hypothesis must contain a leap of imagination or an act of creation, some idea which consciously or unconsciously was not known beforehand. To many people this may mean the hand of God — one of his acts of continuous creation, the gradual unfolding of his master plan to his creatures. As I have described it, it is not a changing of the course of nature but only of our ability to comprehend nature. It may seem that I am backtracking a bit and now almost accepting the second definition of the God of providence. However, that is not my interpretation of what is happening. I still see the process of evolutionary change and natural selection, accelerated by survival of the fittest, as having produced a species which has the ability to carry out the functions I have described.

In the course of his paper Polkinghorne has mentioned his rejection of the foolish dichotomy between *public fact* and *private opinion*, which he says "neglects the element of personal judgment indispensable to the practice of science and also devalues the religious quest for motivated belief" (p. 227). I agree that a dichotomy may exist in many people's minds but, I firmly say, not in the mind of the truly sceptical scientist. The truly sceptical scientist would admit privately that you can hold any view you like — you can quite conscientiously believe that the earth is flat (I could point out that it isn't around where I live) — but if you do I doubt that you can make many deductions from that hypothesis that could be supported by experiment. In parenthesis at this point I should admit that you could devise a flat-earth theory which *would* describe all observations about the motion of the stars, the sun and the moon, that would describe the direction of gravity and so on. It would simply be a mathematical transformation from spherical to planar geometry. But the price you would pay is simplicity and, *if there is one "faith" I have* it lies in the dictum of William of Ockham, nearly 700 years ago:

Entia non sunt multiplicanda praeter necessitatem
Entities should not be multiplied beyond necessity, or,
Try the simplest first

Belief is always based on some "faith". And I, as a sceptical scientist, am not going to quarrel with any person's right to belief under that faith. It is their own business and, provided they do not oppress me, they have a perfect right. And, if that makes them a better person, I shall respect them for it.

In accepting Ockham's razor, as I do, maybe many of you will say that the simplest explanation of how the universe works, and why it is the way it is, is to admit the "finger of God" and say "because God made it so". I believe, however, that that is just stepping aside. It solves nothing and gives me no personal joy as a creative scientist and thinker. As a sceptical atheistic scientist, I too am at a loss to explain why it is all so. But here we are with a mind to think, a life to lead, forefathers to respect, children to nurture and teach, and friends to love. We seem to have acquired a sense of wonder, an ability to question why and how it works, the skills to change the course of nature within the laws of physics for our own betterment, pleasure, and destruction. Because of the results of evolution it would seem that we are rather better endowed for this than other animals, insects, grubs and plants, all of which live in our world. Given a beginning and some laws of nature (neither of which we can be sure of) it is all evolution.

In his paper, Polkinghorne quotes the well-known theoretical physicist Freeman Dyson who said that "the more I examine the universe and the details of its architecture, the more evidence I find that the universe in some sense must have known we were coming" (p. 232). This is a very thought provoking remark, but what does it mean? If we had not come, then Freeman Dyson would not be examining the universe, and finding evidence, and making that remark! If we, mankind, or perhaps I should enlarge that to include any thinking species, had not evolved somewhere in the universe there would be no concept of God. And, to me, that sums it up: God (or the idea of God) is a creation of humanity, not the other way round.

Response by Carver T. Yu

John Polkinghorne's essay takes a modest approach, speaking persuasively to our common sense. It is nevertheless full of insights which provide clues for deeper reflection and hold promise for more profound understanding. I shall list just three of them.

First, Polkinghorne points to the "multivalent reality of our experience..." (p. 228). We experience the universe not as a mere arrangement of inert masses governed by physical laws, but a universe in which the physical and personal realms of being form a unified whole. To understand the universe in its wholeness, one cannot see the physical in abstraction from the personal. Rather, one has to take the personal into consideration as something holding part of the key to unlock the secret of the nature of the physical. The rational thinking with which we come to the formulation of the most profound scientific theories in our understanding of the physical universe cannot be severed from the rational thinking which leads us to affirm the moral principle that abusing children is wrong. Scientific rationality is not a rationality all by itself, a category all of its own, completely distinct from that by which we seek to understand the rational order intrinsic to the personal world. Rather, there seems to be continuity, convergence and consonance between the two. The consonance between the physical and the personal is manifested in the fact that "the world [is] rationally transparent to our inquiry" and that there seems to be a "remarkable conformity between the patterns of our mathematical thought and the patterns of the physical world" (pp. 228f.). It is the very act of rational inquiry of the human person that brings the rational order of universe to light, unveiling it. At the same time, what is more amazing is that this rational order finds expression in the structure of human thought.

When one see the physical universe as part of the larger whole in which humans form a significant part, then one cannot avoid understanding the physical universe in light of our grasping the nature of the human person in general, and the human experience in particular. The experience of, and the relentless quest for, purpose and meaning thus become an integral part of the totality of experiences through which we come to a holistic understanding of the true nature of the physical universe. Any attempt to brush these aside can only lead to a truncated universe that is full of holes and cannot yield complete intellectual satisfaction. The human quest for meaning and purpose is the starting point from which we may begin to see the intelligibility of the notion of creation and its relevance to the understanding of physical order.

Consonance is the key word in Polkinghorne's essay. He declares himself to be a bottom-up thinker, and his starting point is the multivalent experience of the human person. When the scientist is open to the "idiosyncratic nature" of the universe and uses "universe-assisted logic" to understand the way things are (p. 225), he is led to a much deeper level of experience and understanding. It is here that the universe is experienced to point beyond itself to something more profound. Where some theologians would supply God or creation as the answer whenever there is a gap in scientific explanation, Polkinghorne would listen carefully to nature, not only that it may serve as a pointer to a greater horizon of meaning, but also that it may serve to inform or confirm theology as to what creation or God as a loving father to the whole universe may be like. Scientists, together with theologians, would confirm that "What is going on in the universe is not a random concatenation of events, but neither is it the unfolding of an inexorable history patterned according to an unchangeable divine blueprint" (p. 226). Scientists, as much as theologians, have a deep sense of wonder about the contingency and order of the universe, about the subtlety of the structure and process within which human agency is accommodated. The universe, in unfolding itself, raises questions whose answers cannot be found in the universe itself, and thus it compels scientists to move beyond the regime of the physical laws for a more thorough explanation of things. Here the notion of creation becomes intelligible and relevant, not as something filling a gap left by the inadequacy of scientific explanation, but as something in consonance with what the universe itself is pointing to or something which scientists feel compelled to appreciate. Not only do the pointers in science suggest creation and thus make the notion of creation intelligible, the notion of creation in turn makes certain puzzling things in the universe, such as the anthropic principle, intelligible.

Thirdly, Polkinghorne attempts to apply the same principle for sound scientific judgment to the intelligibility of the notion of creation, that is, the principle of the economy of thought. In modern times, Ernst Mach has put great emphasis on this principle, pointing out the consonance between this principle and the principle of least action. With such a principle, there can be common ground for discourse in the assessment of the various metaphysical explanations beyond physical theories.

There are, however, several points in the essay that are not altogether clear, some are even rather puzzling. Queries may be raised concerning these points.

It is true that creation and providence are theological concepts, but what does it mean that "their experiential anchorage lies primarily in religious life" (p. 226)? In our attempt to explore the interface between science and theology, are we not trying to find experiential anchorage in the scientific exploration of the universe in addition to that in our religious life, so that scientific perception of the universe may have significant things to say about creation and providence? In the dialogue between science and theology, are we not moving between two experiential anchorages to see consonance between the two?

According to Polkinghorne, the basis in experience for the claim that "The universe is not God's puppet theatre ... neither is its history a tale told by an idiot" lies in "the deep-seated human intuition of hope" (*ibid.*). He does not explain, however, why he thinks that the basis is in hope nor has he explained the content of hope. Without explanation, such assertion can only give an impression of arbitrariness. Is it not possible that the basis is actually in faith — a deep-seated human intuition of assurance? Or, is it not possible that the basis is the overwhelming sense of wonder when people are confronted by the meticulous design in the natural order?

There are also queries concerning the way he deals with certain philosophical options regarding the quest for the understanding of the physical order. Polkinghorne can sound rather dogmatic to our colleagues in the field of philosophy. For example, "If we are not willing to regard the physical world as the expression of the divine creative will, then we must follow David Hume and treat it as a given brute fact" (p. 227). For Hume, the brute fact is not the brute fact of the natural order, rather it is the brute fact of sensory perception. According to Hume, one cannot even arrive at natural laws from the brute facts of experience. Scientists instinctively put aside the scepticism of Hume. If one chooses to follow Hume, there are still philosophical options. Kantians and modern constructionists may see the physical order as the creation of the human mind. Taoists or process philosophers may see the dynamic process of the universe as the ultimate horizon for explanation and understanding.

Likewise, one cannot simply say the refusal to ask a meta-question about why our universe is so finely tuned is due to "rational laziness" (p. 230). There are genuine problems concerning such metaquestions. It is one thing to ask the question, it is quite another to attempt an answer. Some people may have been so tough-minded as to have rejected quite a number of attempts, and out of despair or modesty, they have to acknowledge their ignorance.

The parable of the execution (*ibid.*) is helpful in bringing out the point that the asking of a metaquestion concerning origins is all too natural. There is no doubt that one should be struck by the incident with a deep amazement. And certainly one would want to know the origin of the remarkable escape. Further, it seems more rational to conjecture that "the marksmen are on your side" than to insist that all the marksmen happened to miss by chance. Yet the parable has its limitations when applied to conjecturing about the origin of the fine-tuning of the universe. In the parable, we are confronted with marksmen who are known to have not only great precision in shooting, but also human intentions. Suppose we know only that the marksmen have great shooting precision, but do not know that they are capable of having intentions. The scenario would then be that we are greatly puzzled by the escape from shooting with great precision. In this case, conjecture about the origin of the miss is a little more complicated, and the possibility of shooting with the intention to miss does not naturally come up as a likely option. Now that we know something more about the marksmen who are involved in the puzzling incident, that they are capable of shooting with the intention to miss, then the situation is quite different. In our conjecture, we have to take their intention into consideration. Yet for the fine-tuning of the universe, we do not have more information other than the fact that great precision is involved. The conjecture then is much less uncertain, and the attempt to answer that meta-question is much more difficult.

Polkinghorne points out with insight that the "interplay of chance and necessity is a *creatio continua*" (p. 232). It would help his readers if he expounded on this. Almost immediately, he asserts that "A universe able to explore its own God-given potentiality in this way will *inevitably* be a universe with ragged edges and painful malfunctions" (p. 233, my emphasis). But again the explanation is far from clear. Why does it have to be the case that "A world allowed to make itself cannot be a world free from pain and suffering" (*ibid.*)? Why is not possible that God creates a world of chance and necessity with a touch of his perfect goodness, that the self-exploration of the universe precludes any pain and suffering, and that pain and suffering are not possibilities allotted to humans while he endows them with possibilities of all kinds to make it genuinely free? If God has not allowed the possibility of pain and suffering, would it then make a person less free? So long as we accept that, being human, we have not been endowed with infinite possibilities, then we would also accept that there are certain possibilities which are not available to human beings Then why is it the case that the possibility of suffering has to be there to make our freedom more sound? Perhaps Polkinghorne needs to explain a little more the inner relation between free process and the possibilities of painful malfunction.

The essay is rich with stimulating thoughts. It spurs my mind to explore in various directions for possible developments. I have read the paper with great interest and gratitude. My queries about a few points here and there do not lessen my appreciation of a very fruitful attempt at a dialogue between science and theology.

Biographical notes

Professor Jack Dodd, Emeritus Professor of Physics, University of Otago, New Zealand; President, Royal Society of New Zealand.

Dr Norma Emerton, Wolfson College, University of Cambridge, United Kingdom, teacher of medieval philosophy and science.

Professor Lloyd Geering, Emeritus Professor, Department of World Religions, Victoria University, New Zealand.

Dr Grant Gillett, Departments of Philosophy, Bioethics and Neurosurgery, University of Otago, New Zealand.

Professor Owen Gingerich, Professor of Astronomy and the History of Science, Harvard-Smithsonian Center for Astrophysics, Cambridge, Massachusetts, United States of America.

Revd Dr John Honner, Jesuit Theological College, Melbourne, Australia.

Dr Stephen May, St John's Theological College, Auckland, New Zealand.

Revd Dr Nancey Murphy, Associate Professor of Christian Philosophy, Fuller Theological Seminary, California, United States of America.

Revd Dr John Polkinghorne FRS, President, Queens' College, Cambridge, United Kingdom; physicist and theologian.

Revd John Puddefoot, Head of Mathematics, Eton College, Windsor, United Kingdom.

Dr John Stenhouse, Department of History, University of Otago, New Zealand.

Revd Dr Carver T. Yu, Head of Department of Religion and Philosophy, Hong Kong Baptist College, Hong Kong.

Index of Persons

Tipler, F., 230n.
Titus, Letter to, 206
Torrance, Thomas, 7, 26, 51,
        203n., 207n., 220-1
Trefil, J., 53n.
Turner, Harold, 7
Tyndall, John, 93
van Huyssteen, Wentzel, 139
Weber, Max, 132
Webster, John, 77f.
Weinberg, Steven, 52-3
Weizsäcker, Carl, von, 213
Welles, Orson, 54-5
Wells, H. G., 14, 54-8
Wheeler, John, 189n.
Whiston, William, 16, 80
Whitman, Walt, 41
Wigner, Eugene, 228
Wilczyk, Frank, 53n.
Wiles, Maurice, 200, 226n.
Wilson, E., 88
Wittgenstein, Ludwig, 49n.,
        60, 115, 127, 132
Yu, Carver, 7, 9, 12-13, 25

Index of Subjects

Absolutism, 217
Agnosticism, 9, 25, 92, 174
Anthropic principle, 9, 12,
    13f., 15, 24, 42, 58, 65,
    66, 69, 86, 98-99,
    155, 230-31
Apologetics, 17, 73f., 86, 96,
    114, 149
Atheism, 27, 39, 40, 41, 68,
    81
Auxiliary hypothesis, 105,
    106-7, 129
Big Bang, 35, 47
Book of Nature, 15, 48, 69,
    76, 95, 114
Book of Scripture, 15, 48, 69,
    95
Boyle's law, 110-112
Cartesian scepticism, 158
Charity, 114, 116, 117, 121
Christian theism, 95, 150, 167
Christian theory of
    discernment, 120-121,
    124, 125
Christian worldview, 14, 44,
    68, 70
Christology, 14, 27, 46, 48,
    91, 97, 203f., 223
    and creation, 24
    and human suffering,
    124, 233
    and reconciliation, 24,
    106, 154, 174, 233
    and revelation, 135,
    171, 201f.

Coherence theory of, 14, 52,
    58, 59, 68, 123,
    231
Complexity theory, 52, 65
Core theories, 106, 129
Cosmological argument, 73,
    79, 81, 83-4, 86
    229, 230-31
Covariance, 187, 189-190
Creation,
    and natural theology,
    6
    and providence, 226,
    236, 242, 249
    and science, 6, 84,
    229, 239, 242, 244
    and the the anthropic
    principle, 24
    creatio ex nihilo, 23,
    171, 172, 188
    creatio continua, 24, 53,
    199, 200, 216
    doctrine of, 3, 24, 83f.,
    200f.
Critical thought, 89,
    148, 159-60,
    175-76
Darwinism, 85, 92f.
Deconstruction, 175
Design, argument from, 14,
    30, 72, 79, 85
    and biology, 30-33,
    39f., 77
    and cosmic teleology,
    33, 42, 48

Sponsors

We are indebted to the following people and organisations for their donations and support.

Otago-Southland Synod of the Presbyterian Church, New Zealand
Templeton Foundation, United States of America
University of Otago, Faculty of Theology, Dunedin, New Zealand
Selwyn College, Dunedin, New Zealand
Catholic Diocese of Dunedin, New Zealand
General Committee of the University of Otago, Dunedin, New Zealand
University of Otago, Division of Humanities, Dunedin, New Zealand
University of Otago, Division of Sciences, Dunedin, New Zealand
Cabra Dominican Sisters, Adelaide, Australia
Sisters of Mercy, Adelaide, Australia
Little Company of Mary, Wellington, New Zealand
Benedictine Monastery of the Holy Spirit, Melbourne, Australia
St Joseph's Convent, Lochinvar
Presentation Sisters, New Zealand
Catholic Diocese of Wollongong, Australia
Sisters of Mercy, New Zealand
St Francis Xavier Seminary, Adelaide, Australia
Catholic Diocese of Palmerston North, New Zealand
Trustbank Otago, New Zealand
Dominican Fathers, Melbourne, Australia
Holy Faith Sisters, New Zealand
Forsyth Barr, Dunedin, New Zealand
Revd J. Stack, New Zealand
T. K. S. Sidey, Dunedin, New Zealand
J. P. S. Orr, Dunedin, New Zealand
Winston Darling Travel, Dunedin, New Zealand
Vincent George House of Travel, Dunedin, New Zealand
J. & D. McGinn, Adelaide, Australia
M. M. Regan, Adelaide, Australia
The Royal Society of New Zealand
Revd Gordon Watson, Melbourne, Australia
Revd W. Creevey, United States of America
AMP Perpetual Trustee Co., New Zealand
Pacifica, Melbourne, Australia
New Blackfriars, Oxford, United Kingdom